# Stephanie's
# Feasts
## and
# Stories

Dedicated to the memory of a fine
cook and a dear friend
Josephine Pignolet
1956–1987

# Stephanie's
# Feasts
## and
# Stories

STEPHANIE ALEXANDER

ALLEN & UNWIN

Illustrations by Julie Patey
Designed by Blue Boat Design
Cover design by Kim Roberts

Hardback edition first published 1988
First paperback edition published 1992
Second paperback edition published 1996
Reprinted 2000

Allen & Unwin
9 Atchison St
St Leonards NSW 1590
Australia
Phone:    (61 2) 8425 0100
Fax:      (61 2) 9906 2218
E-mail:   frontdesk@allen-unwin.com.au
Web:      http://www.allen-unwin.com.au

National Library of Australia
Cataloguing-in-publication

Alexander, Stephanie, 1940
   Stephanie's feasts and stories.
   Bibliography.

   Includes index.
   ISBN 1 86448 254 0

   1. Cookery. I. Title. II. Title: Feasts and stories.

641.5

Set by J & M Typesetting
Printed by Southwood Press, Australia

# CONTENTS

FEASTS & STORIES

ACKNOWLEDGEMENTS

I would like to thank Julie Patey for her evocative drawings.

I would also like to thank Valerie Lawson and Susan Wyndham, past editors of *Good Weekend* for their encouragement.

Once again it was a pleasure to work with my publisher, Susan Haynes. Her enthusiasm and positive thinking were wonderfully helpful during my frequent lapses into gloom.

The book could never have been written without the support of Dur-é and the entire staff of Stephanie's restaurant, who made it possible for me to take big chunks of time out, and who helped in the testing (both cooking and eating) of the dishes.

My thanks are due to authors and publishers for permission to quote recipes from the following books: Jo Bettoja and Anna Maria Cornetto, *Italian Cooking in the Grand Tradition*, Dial Press, New York; Genevieve Dormann, *Colette—a passion for Life*, Thames & Hudson, London; Mogens Bay Esbensen, *Thai Cuisine*, Nelson, Melbourne; Jane Grigson, *The Observer Guide to British Cookery*, Michael Joseph, London; Marcella Hazan, *The Classic Italian Cookbook*, Macmillan, London; *Madeleine Kamman, In Madeleine's Kitchen*, Atheneum, New York; Diana Kennedy, *Mexican Regional Cookery*, Harper & Row, New York; Irene Kuo, *The Key to Chinese Cooking*, Knopf, New York; Charmaine Solomon, *The Complete Asian Cookbook*, Weldons Pty Ltd, North Sydney; Michael Symons, *One Continuous Picnic*, Duck Press, Adelaide.

*Special note.* In my first book, *Stephanie's Menus for Food Lovers*, I included detailed notes outlining mise-en-place skills and kitchen organisation. I refer readers to those notes. This book gives both metric and imperial measurements. They are approximate conversions. It is very important to use one set of measures or the other—do not mix them.

For several years I wrote a fortnightly column for the colour supplement *Good Weekend*, distributed by Melbourne's and Sydney's biggest daily newspapers. Many friends and readers suggested that I should collect these pieces in book form. It was with this in mind that I began to write *Feasts and Stories*. However, stories change in the re-telling, as dishes do in the recooking: every time I include a 'golden oldie' on a new menu, I find that I want to change it, either a little or a lot. Similarly each story has been changed from its original form. Many have been expanded, some have been rearranged, new incidents and adventures have to be included. Life has been lived in the intervening years, and I have learnt new things and feasted on new dishes. It has been hard to know when to stop writing. Long after the time when I was able to make changes to the text, I discovered that extra-virgin olive oil does keep much of its flavour past 140°C (290°F), despite having said in the text that it does not, and I certainly sauté food in it whenever I want the fruity, peppery flavour in a dish. Reluctantly I accept the inevitable. The printed word fixes for ever what in reality is a constantly moving landscape. What is not understood or ever dreamed of today will probably be part of another story—sometime.

I admit to a respectful voyeurism towards the flavours and dishes used and enjoyed by every culture. I am interested in everything edible. My friend Jean's stories of eating rancid yak's milk in Mongolia and Penny's story of the quivering, freshly slaughtered liver in Africa are fascinating insights into other ways, other lives. I don't want to eat rancid yak's milk or raw, warm liver, but what interests me is that a whole population does want to. Prejudices and preferences in eating customs are most revealing.

I have learnt never to say 'this is the only way' or 'this is the best way'. The more one travels to eat, the more one reads, the more one listens, the less definite the ethnic boundaries become. One is continually humbled by a glimpse of other connections. A bread-based salad, panzanella, eaten in Florence echoes the pan bagnat of Nice, and then one reads of fattoush, the Syrian bread salad described by Claudia Roden, and the whole concept gains an extra dimension.

A feast is a shared occasion, one is regaled, one feasts on sumptuous dishes, and it is a joyous affair. A feast offers gratification to the senses. Feasting to me implies richly coloured, laden platters. It means generosity, hospitality and friendship. Many feasts are made of absolutely delicious, homely dishes.

Stories are very important in order to understand who we are and where we have come from. Through stories we can learn of old skills, old traditions and, of course, old dishes. We can glimpse the continuity of human life and learn of places we shall probably never visit. Many stories and even certain words can make us nostalgic for the food of our childhood or for some other happy time.

Australian Aboriginal elders pass on the dreamtime stories of the land, the hunting, the myths and the history through oral traditions and through dance. The storytelling is considered to be the most serious part of a young person's education, and it is the only way the social and cultural heritage of the Aboriginal people has endured through 40,000 years of continuous existence.

Tragically, few young cooks in Australian society have access to someone who can tell them stories and pass on the culinary experience of a lifetime. Our European, Asian and Middle Eastern migrant mothers and grandmothers are the keepers of these culinary traditions. Their knowledge is our national treasure, and anyone with a close friend whose background traditionally places more value on eating than our Anglo-Saxon culture does should eagerly beg for stories.

This book reflects my life and the experiences that I have had. In no way have I tried to compile a comprehensive catalogue of my favourite foods. It would be impossible. My favourite food is the delicious, mouth-watering, aromatic triumph that I last tasted, whatever and wherever it was.

The stories are my responses to people, places and flavours. The individual dishes and feasts are my attempts to remember and recreate some of the experience in my own restaurant for my guests. This book will have succeeded if this enthusiasm spills over and inspires the reader to create his or her own feast, hopefully altered by his or her personal style. As well, it attempts to be a practical and reliable cookbook: its dishes drawn from a multitude of cultures, their ingredients part of the astonishingly wide range of excellent produce this vast country produces.

I am learning every day. If I were to cook many of the dishes tomorrow, I'm sure I would add something—and sometimes take something out. I'm sure many readers will do the same thing. This is how it should be.

# OYSTERS & OTHER SHELLFISH

## ➤ FEASTS & STORIES ➤

$M$y first ever *plateau de fruits de mer* was in the raffish little town of Biscarosse on the French Atlantic coast. The beaches stretched long, white and empty. It was May and still very cold. A strong gusty wind whipped at our legs and blew at the raggy flaps of the awning over the outside terrace of the lone beach café. It seemed an unlikely spot for a great gastronomic experience, but the seafood was memorable. A big, heavy, freshly cooked crab, cut in quarters, oysters that squirmed at the first drop of lemon, raw mussels glisteningly pink, some pale-apricot langoustines, a heap of bigorneaux, small as the smallest garden snail with pins to extract them, and all accompanied by a generous bowl of yellow mayonnaise, some rye bread and a sauce-boat of mignonette sauce—fine-quality red wine vinegar with finely chopped shallots and coarse ground white pepper—and a bottle of the local Tursan white wine.

A few days later we happened to lunch at Soubise near La Rochelle, where the chef, Liliane Benoit, offered a special Wednesday treat of as many oysters as we wanted before one of her lovely fish dishes. We were really loving these oysters. A few *plateaux de fruits de mer* later and I was convinced that I would never eat oysters any other way again.

Australia produces several varieties of oysters. Sydneysiders are convinced that nothing can touch the Sydney rock oyster (*Crassotrea commercialis*) for flavour, Tasmanians are delighted with the larger Pacific oyster (*Crassotrea gigas*), both varieties with craggy shells and both basically oval in shape. The native flat oyster (*Ostrea angasi*) closely resembles the Belon (*Ostrea edulis*) and is now being cultivated in Tasmania and experimentally in Victoria. My preference is for the Tasmanian Pacific oyster, and we serve them freshly opened, brimming with their natural juices, and of course still firmly attached to the shell. I present them on a platter of gathered seaweed. The best time to gather seaweed is just before the low tide turns.

The seaweed needs to be soaked well to rid it of sand, little chips of rock and any living creatures. At my beach I find lots of kelp, some sea-lettuce and another pretty plant, which is darker brown and has clusters of 'grapes' on it. In my search to identify this plant I came across the fascinating book *The Sea Vegetable Cookbook*, by Judith Cooper Madlena.

The author points out that in the English language the suffix 'weed' has described marine algae, defining their value in a pejorative manner. Edible seaweeds are appreciated for what they are—sea vegetables—in many parts of the world. This book contains an absolutely astonishing and fascinating wealth of detail regarding the identification and nutritional characteristics of more than a hundred species of sea vegetable and a collection of extraordinary recipes.

I have used sea-lettuce as a vegetable steamed very lightly with oysters or with steamed fish. I find it crisp and pleasant with a subtle sea-like flavour. One of Judith Madlena's recipes is a salad from the Philippines combining this fresh sea-lettuce with sliced tomato, onions, vinegar, salt and hot peppers.

Those who enjoy Japanese food will be familiar with the black wrappers on their sushi rolls. This sea vegetable, sold dried and pressed into thin sheets, is known as nori to the Japanese and laver to the Welsh. Nori is usually passed briefly over a flame to crisp before being filled with its vinegared rice or before crumbling it over squares of fresh bean curd and saucing it with light soy as a snack.

The Welsh, on the other hand, gather their laver at low tide in the spring and autumn or buy it ready-cooked at the market. The laver is traditionally formed into little cakes, is coated with oatmeal and eaten at breakfast with bacon rashers and cockles. Dried laver sheets have to be soaked back to normal weight. Then the laver is washed and boiled to a soft mass before being mixed with the fine oatmeal and fried in bacon fat.

In a small booklet I own, called *Welsh Recipes: a collection of the traditional dishes of Wales*, I have read some other things to do with laver. One can mix it with a squeeze of lemon juice and a few drops of olive oil, pepper and salt and spread it on toast as a savoury, or serve piping-hot laver bread mixed with a squeeze or two of Seville orange juice as an accompaniment to Welsh mutton.

For most of us, it is more practical to purchase dried seaweed, certainly if we intend to eat it rather than use it as the bed for our oysters. Two other Madlena recipes I have tried use the thin shreds of hijiki. Try a salad of soaked hijiki sauced with bean curd, rice vinegar and sesame paste mixed into a creamy dressing with a little mild-flavoured oil (grapeseed, for instance) and served scattered with spring onion; or use the Oriental dressing on page 188; or sauté the hijiki in a little butter and then toss it with unsalted butter, cream and Parmesan cheese.

At La Rochelle I enjoyed a bowl of mouclade, the simple dish of mussels opened with white wine, parsley stalks and a chopped onion, the strained fumet simmered with curry and cream, poured over the mussels and bubbled under the grill. At La Rochelle we ate our mouclades out of doors and appreciated the whiff of the sea and its traffic in this busy little port. That evening we sat on a Brittany beach at 10 p.m. summertime, watching the sunset fading from silvery pink to amethyst shadows on the sea: an enchanting and tranquil part of France.

For several years I have been lucky in having very close friends resident in Paris. Their apartment is large and their hospitality genuine. We have been friends for well over twenty-five years and feel very comfortable together. Jean doesn't really like to cook, but she loves to eat. Each visit of mine has been the excuse for several memorable parties. I once catered for fifty at a buffet, but the more pleasurable evenings have been when I shopped for and cooked a meal for about ten people. During one of my stays I prepared this mussel dish, and it has been enjoyed by hundreds of my customers since. In Paris and on the French Atlantic coast the baskets of shellfish are bursting with very small, very sweet *bouchot* mussels. The word describes both the variety of mussels (cultivated) and the ropes they grow on. The shells are intensely blue-black, and I find the flavour and texture irresistibly sweet and tender. I always admire the shiny cream and red shells of the vernis and the amandes, but it is the mussels I buy. I call my mussel dish 'Jean's mussels', a play on words as Jean is as slender as a wand!

## JEAN'S MUSSELS

This recipe may sound complicated, but as will be apparent over and over again in this book, many processes are long in the description, but pass in a flash in the doing. It is essential to have everything measured and as pre-prepared as possible. A brunoise is a mixture of vegetables cut into 1 mm dice. It is frequently used to garnish a consommé or, as here, a sauce.

- 6 dozen small mussels, thoroughly scrubbed
- 1 bulb fennel, diced into brunoise dice
- 2 medium carrots, peeled and diced into brunoise dice
- 2 sticks celery, destrung and diced into brunoise dice
- 60 g (2 oz) unsalted butter
- 2 cloves of garlic, chopped fine
- 200 g (7 oz) walnuts, blanched and peeled of their inner skin

- 1 bunch well-washed parsley, chopped fine
- 3 or 4 parsley stalks, chopped roughly
- 2 onions, chopped roughly
- 1 bottle of dry white wine
- good pinch saffron threads
- 100 ml (3 fl oz) cream
- 300 g (10 oz) unsalted butter

Place all the dice of vegetable with the 60 g (2 oz) of butter in a wide pan and barely cover with water. Bring slowly to simmering point and then strain through a colander.

Film a non-stick pan with oil and briefly colour the garlic. Add the peeled walnut halves and sauté 2–3 minutes. Run the walnut/garlic mixture through a food-processor until quite finely ground. Stir in the parsley. Place in a bowl.

Have 6 wide soup plates ready and waiting and hot.

Place mussels in a large baking dish, preferably in a single layer (or do this in two batches), scatter over parsley stalks, onion slices and white wine. Cover the dish and place over high heat for a few minutes until all the mussels have opened.

Strain the juice into a large enamelled cast-iron saucepan, add the saffron and cream and start to boil hard to reduce by two-thirds. Do not choose a small pan, as a reduction needs to boil really hard and will rise up quite high as it reduces.

While the sauce is reducing, remove the top shell from each mussel and place the halved, steamed mussels in a wide sauté pan which has a lid.

Pour in about 1 cm (½ in) of water, which will provide the gush of steam needed to re-heat the mussels, and scatter over the vegetable dice.

Place the lid on the pan with the mussels and place over high heat. At the same time, whisk the chunks of cold unsalted butter into the now simmering reduction. Taste for seasoning. The sauce should be a warm golden colour and be pleasantly briny from the mussel fumet. Stir into it the walnut/parsley mixture. It should now be quite green.

Ladle the mussels and vegetables into the serving bowls and pour over the sauce.

My favourite accompaniment is a slice or two of toasted fennel-seed bread, which we make from a recipe found in Madeleine Kamman's excellent book, In Madeleine's Kitchen.

It is an interesting recipe, as it necessitates using a leaven, prepared two days beforehand. The bread also tastes good with a rich fish soup, such as the recipe on page 28, or to accompany a stew of Mediterranean vegetables.

I have included Madeleine's recipe for this bread in the chapter on breads.


Reduction is the basic principle on which much French sauce-making is based. A beurre blanc is well known. Large amounts of butter are whisked directly onto a reduction of white wine and shallots cooked together until moist, but no longer obviously liquid, and a bearnaise sauce commences with a reduction of tarragon, white wine or wine vinegar before the egg yolks are added to foam into a sabayon. One heavily reduces red wine with shallots, a bay leaf and thyme and then adds well-reduced veal stock to make a mellow sauce bordelaise in the modern manner. This is later softened and shone with butter, or a combination of butter and bone marrow, or a vegetable purée.

The degree of reduction, the amount of butter or purée added, and the ingredients chosen for the reduction determine the character and consistency of your sauce. The variations possible are endless, and the next recipe illustrates all these points. It is for a mousse of crayfish (as known in Victoria), or rock lobster or lobster (as the same species is called in New South Wales), which is subtly seasoned with garlic, herbs and vegetables. The sauce uses a fumet made from the crayfish shells reduced with a separate sauce of fresh tomatoes cooked in butter and finally mounted with butter. The result is a lovely blush-coloured sauce with the unmistakable sweetness from the shells balanced by the acidity of the tomatoes. It is the seasoning that lifts the mousse from the totally predictable. We have used it to shape quenelles to garnish a crab consommé, we have filled heart-shaped pieces of chervil-flavoured pasta dough with it to create a romantic dish for one of our special St Valentine's Day dinners. The hearts puff up like little pillows. We have given the mousse even more panache by stuffing it in a long, lime-green spicy pepper and baking it like a soufflé.

## CRAYFISH (or PRAWN) MOUSSE

- 500 g (1 lb) raw meat, cleaned of any intestinal thread
- 1 tablespoon carrot, cut into brunoise dice
- 1 tablespoon celery, cut into brunoise dice
- 2 teaspoons butter
- 150 ml (5 fl oz) egg white
- salt, pepper
- 1 clove garlic, very finely chopped
- 300 ml (10 fl oz) cream

Chill food-processor canister for at least 1 hour. Chill cream. Make the carrot and celery dice as small as possible.

Sweat vegetables in butter for 3–4 minutes. Drain. Purée flesh in food-processor, combine very well with egg whites in processor. Remove and press purée through tamis sieve. Chill purée for 30 minutes. Return to food-processor. Blend in some salt and pepper and the garlic. Add cream in steady stream with motor running. Remove mousse, fold in vegetables and check for seasoning either by eating a little of the uncooked mousse or by poaching a ball of mixture in salted water, allowing it to cool and then tasting.

Chill mousse before either forming it into quenelles with two spoons dipped in hot water or piping it onto a sheet of pasta.

If you wish to make ravioli, I find it best to brush one sheet of pasta lightly with egg wash, place half the length of dough into the indentations of the ravioli form, press lightly, pipe on the filling, and then fold the sheet of dough over the filling and press the edges firmly together between each little bump.

If you prefer to cut out individual shapes, such as hearts, lay out one long strip of dough on a lightly floured table, brush with egg wash, pipe the filling the size you wish and fold over the other half of the pasta to cover and press well before using your heart cutter.

Filled pasta shapes, each with about 2 teaspoons of filling, will steam-cook in about 6 minutes. If they are to be dropped into water, it is preferable to snap-freeze the shapes, as they are very delicate if the filling and pasta are both soft.

## BASIC PASTA DOUGH

Recipes abound, and by all means use your favourite.

- 300 g (10 oz) plain flour
- a pinch of salt (optional)
- 3 eggs (we use 55 g–2 oz–eggs)
- 1 tablespoon olive oil

Run flour and salt (and chopped herbs if you wish) in the food-processor. Add eggs and oil and process until the mixture forms a ball of dough. It should feel firm, but not crumbly. Adjust with an extra egg yolk if too dry or a little extra flour if soft and sticky. Adding purées of vegetable to colour pasta, such as carrot, beetroot, etc., will frequently require the use of a little extra flour.

Wrap the dough in plastic wrap and rest it for an hour before rolling it through a pasta machine. As everyone knows, it is necessary to cook pasta in LOTS of water, say 1 litre (32 fl oz) to each 100 g (3 oz) of pasta. If the pasta is freshly made, it will be cooked after only 2–3 minutes rapid boiling. If it has thoroughly dried, it will need at least twice as long.

Although the recipe for the crayfish and tomato sauce is included, it would be much simpler and equally delicious if, instead of filling your pasta with the mousse, you poach spoonfuls of the mousse in lightly salted water and toss your pasta in one of the following fast pasta sauces.

## PINK PASTA SAUCE

- 5 really ripe tomatoes
- 1 cup basil leaves
- 5 tablespoons best olive oil
- 3 tablespoons cream
- salt, pepper

Blend all together in food-processor or blender for 3 minutes. The mixture will be pink and frothy. Pour the sauce into a saucepan and cook over low heat for 4–5 minutes while your quenelles are poaching. Drain pasta from boiling water, serve into heated bowls, pour pink sauce over and top with poached crayfish quenelles.

## PASTA with CAPERS, OLIVES, ANCHOVIES

- 2 cloves garlic
- 2 tablespoons olive oil
- 30 g (1 oz) capers
- 60 g (2 oz) pitted, sliced black olives
- 2 tablespoons water
- 3 tablespoons parsley
- pepper
- 3 anchovy fillets in oil, chopped

Lightly sauté garlic in the oil. Add capers, olives, water, parsley and pepper. Cook 4–5 minutes. Add anchovies and stir until they are mashed. Pour sauce over hot, drained pasta and top with poached quenelles.

## CRAYFISH and TOMATO BUTTER SAUCE

### — CRAYFISH FUMET —

- carcass of 1 × 1 kg (2 lb) crayfish, head sac removed
- 2 tablespoons oil
- 1 onion, finely chopped
- 1 stalk celery, chopped
- 1 carrot, chopped
- 1 bay leaf
- 1 sprig fresh thyme
- 6 mushrooms, sliced
- 2 tablespoons brandy
- 1 glass white wine
- 1 litre (32 fl oz) fish stock

### — TOMATO SAUCE —

- 2 tablespoons butter
- 1 onion, sliced
- 2 cloves garlic, chopped
- 500 g (1 lb) ripe tomatoes, peeled and seeded

## To make crayfish fumet

Heat oil in flat baking tray on top of stove. Add all vegetables and herbs and cook over moderate heat until well softened and golden. Chop the crayfish carcass with a cleaver into several pieces. Add the carcass to the pan, stir and lift until all pieces of carcass have turned a bright red colour. Warm the brandy in a ladle and tip onto the crayfish. Flame the contents of the pan with a match. Shake until flames die out. Tip on the white wine, scrape the bottom of the pan well to ensure that no little piece of vegetable is burning and then tip on the fish stock. Bring to simmering point, transfer the contents to a conventional saucepan and simmer for 25 minutes, skimming the surface of debris once or twice. Strain into a bowl, pressing well on the solids. Discard the solids. Return to the rinsed-out pan and reduce by half.

## To prepare tomatoes

Melt butter in a large enamelled cast-iron pan, add onion and garlic and soften for a few minutes. Add tomatoes and cook for 5 minutes or so, until the tomatoes have collapsed.

Pour on the reduced crayfish fumet and simmer together gently for 15 minutes. Purée sauce in the processor or blender and then press it through the tamis sieve. Taste reduction. It should be strongly flavoured with both tomato and shellfish flavour.

## To finish

You will need about 150 ml (5 fl oz) of strained reduction to 400 g (13 oz) of butter for sufficient sauce for six. If you have excess sauce base, freeze it for a future occasion. It makes a good sauce for steamed fish fillets or a grilled fish cutlet.

Bring the reduction to the boil and whisk in your cold butter a piece at a time over moderate heat. You should add the next piece of butter just as the last chunk is melted. The sauce keeps very well over hot water without change of either colour or flavour. Taste it for seasoning.

Once I decided it would be amusing to flatten out some prawns between sheets of plastic and then to use these prawn pancakes to encase the mousse. We served the prawn balls in consommé with squares of pasta. Each square had a coriander leaf rolled into the dough, so that it was barely visible, like a fossil in an ancient rock. Clever, but the dish was very fiddly.

## CRAB CONSOMMÉ

- 4 green (uncooked) blue swimmer crabs
- olive oil
- 1 × 5 cm (2 in) piece ginger, peeled and sliced
- 4 cloves garlic, peeled and chopped
- 1 large onion, chopped
- 2 sticks celery, sliced
- 1 large carrot, peeled and chopped
- 2 leeks, washed well and sliced
- 2 tablespoons pernod
- 1 pinch saffron threads
- 1 tablespoon tomato paste
- 300 ml (10 fl oz) dry white wine
- 2 litres (64 fl oz) fish stock
- tabasco sauce

### — FOR CLARIFICATION —

- ½ onion, chopped very small
- ½ carrot, chopped very small
- 1 × 5 cm (2 in) piece ginger, peeled and chopped small
- 1 cup egg white, whisked well

Crack open crabs, remove bony stomach sac section and throw away. Pull off and discard the dead men's fingers (the gills) and chop the crab into pieces.

In a heavy-bottomed pan, sear the ginger and garlic in a film of hot oil. Add the onion, celery, carrot and leek. Stir and allow to cook until the vegetables are soft and have started to colour. Scrape from the pan, heat a little more oil to smoking, add the pieces of crab. Turn until all are a bright red. Return the vegetables to the pan. Heat through and add the pernod and the saffron. Add the tomato paste and the white wine. Boil hard for 3–4 minutes. Add the fish stock. Allow to come to the boil over a moderate heat and then reduce the flame to a bare simmer. Simmer for 30 minutes and then strain through a sieve into a bucket, pressing hard on all the debris. Allow to cool completely before clarifying.

Combine the egg white and the chopped vegetables in the food-processor. Stir into the cold crab stock. Whisking slowly and continuously bring the stock to the boil. As soon as it starts to simmer, turn the heat low and leave it undisturbed for 1 hour. It should just be moving in one spot. Turn off heat. Allow to settle for 10 minutes. Push the thick scum (the 'raft') to one side very gently and ladle the sparkling consommé into a very clean container through a sieve lined with damp muslin. Adjust seasoning with drops of tabasco and salt if necessary.

## CRAYFISH or PRAWN QUENELLES in CRAB CONSOMMÉ

- 1 quantity of mousse (see pages 6–7)
- crab consommé (preceding recipe)

Form quenelles using spoons dipped in hot water. Place on a sheet of kitchen parchment until needed. Bring a pan of lightly salted water to the simmering point. Slide the quenelles into the water by immersing the sheet of paper. Poach until firm, 5–7 minutes, depending on size. Turn once. Drain well on a cloth before sliding into the hot consommé.

Garnish each bowl with a blanched julienne of ginger, coriander leaves or anything else you fancy.

The best food we ate in northern Italy was the shellfish. A friend of a friend who lived in Verona gave us the vital local information that enabled us to ignore the many ordinary trattorie and to eat some delicious dishes. At the Veneziano we had a mouth-watering risotto di frutte di mare, bursting with tiny clams, thumbnail-sized scallops and cuttlefish. Around us platters of dramatic grilled scampi were carried triumphantly to the exuberant diners.

The scampi looked marvellous with their fiery shells scorched around the edges. Hot on the heels of the shellfish came the oil for the anointing and the deep bowl of lemons. And again in Venice, when we lunched at La Furantola, we shared an exciting antipasto di frutte di miste, which included squid, school prawns, fried baby scampi and soft-shelled crabs to be munched entire.

The next day, still in Venice, we followed another local recommendation. After nearly an hour of searching through the maze of tiny calle we found Da Fiore. It is a magic city, and it is eerie but thrilling to feel quite alone and quite safe in the misty light and the silence. One's senses seem to sharpen, and a footfall on the flagstones rings loud and clear. We had to rap several times on a dark door before gaining admittance to a brilliantly lit restaurant full of chattering Venetians.

We had lovely, lovely food. Another mixed antipasto with shrimps boiled with lemon and other shrimp in light mayonnaise. We also had sea snails and squid 'eggs'. This was a revelation. These tender, vaguely oval, milky coloured, egg-flavoured shapes were the gelatinous 'milk' from inside the pouch of the squid that I have always discarded along with the beak and intestines of the squid. Here they were gently simmered and sliced and marinated with oil among the other antipasti. We had fragoline di mare (strawberries of the sea), the poetic name given to these baby octopus because of their round shape and rosy colour. We had large, grilled razor-shell clams and then the best of all—the grilled scampi. They were flattened and sauced with nothing but the loveliest virgin oil and a twist of the pepper grinder.

The Da Fiore recipe is more a technique than a recipe, therefore you will decide how many shellfish to prepare depending on numbers, appetite and available variety.

Prawns vary enormously in size. Scampi also vary enormously in size. These marine crustaceans are trawled in nets in deep water off the coast of Western Australia. The vast majority of the catch is frozen on board the boats. I don't use frozen shellfish except in a dire emergency, so until I can try fresh scampi, I have been more than pleased to use our large tiger prawns. At certain times of the year we have leader prawns, which weigh up to 400 g (13 oz). One of these would be a portion.

Here is the recipe, if indeed it can be thought of as a recipe, for the grilled scampi.

For each crustacean, pull off the head and with it the intestine, if possible. Using scissors, and working from head to tail, cut the shell open along the top, that is the outer curve of the prawn shell. With a small sharp knife, slice into the flesh so as to butterfly the meat. Do not slice too deeply. The thickness of the flesh where it is opened out should be the same as the thickness at the two edges. Repeat. Place a sheet of plastic film over the exposed meat and, using a small rolling pin or a bottle, roll the flesh to fully open the meat. You should now have a flattish surface held as if in a boat by the shell.

Ensure that the barbecue or grill is very hot. Brush the shell with olive oil and place shell down on the heat source, pressing lightly to flatten out the prawn. When you can see that the exposed flesh is just starting to look opaque and cooked around the edges, turn the prawn or scampi for a brief few seconds to sear the meat.

To make it easier, use bamboo skewers. Thread the number of prawns per portion crosswise on the one skewer pushed through the thickest part of each prawn, and then run a second skewer through the tail of each prawn. The prawns will lie crosswise, like the rungs of a ladder, and the turning is greatly simplified.

Rush the prawns or scampi to a very hot platter, drizzle over some extra-virgin olive oil, either top with some superfine slivers of hot chilli (which I like) or grind over some pepper, and eat at once with a little lemon juice and a flake of sea salt.

I like to nibble at the shells, but most people find this aberrant!

The 1986 Hong Kong Food Festival was one of the highlights of my year. I was very apprehensive at being asked to judge Chinese food. I need not have worried. The Western judges were assisted by local experts, who gave us the very necessary briefings. Some might feel that good taste needs no explanation. Perhaps, but certainly elements of the dishes held special significance that I as a Westerner was unable to appreciate or comprehend without help. Even visual appeal can be discussed in its own right. Certain colours have symbolic meaning to the Chinese. Some colour combinations may appear garish and crude to Western eyes and rich and imposing to Chinese eyes.

Many aspects of Chinese food are dictated by the basic philosophies of Confucius and of Taoism, which stress harmony between different elements (Confucius) and the quality of nourishment of the body and happiness of life (Taoism).

In the display class the chefs worked for hours to create landscapes depicting peasants toiling in the fields and pushing carts, or scenes of quiet gardens, or bowls of exquisitely formed chrysanthemums—all made from vegetables, nuts, fruits and coloured pastry. The predominant colours of the dishes were those of decorated porcelain rice bowls or Chinese scroll paintings—rose-pink, green, gold, orange and red. A hollowed carrot and melon were illuminated with tiny lights and set in a magic garden where birds trilled and where the shadowy foliage was made from ginger knobs.

At the end of the competition the winners were presented with their awards, and the judges were given sheets of rudimentary 'recipes' for the dishes. For the first time we had explanations of the Chinese title of each dish. I wished I could look at all the dishes again with this extra insight.

'Crispy meat and seafood roll' was translated more correctly as 'South of the Yangtze River crispy leg'. The translation says that to a Chinese the geographic description has many happy associations—scenic beauty, ancient traditions, a land where poets find peace. Nothing in fact to connect it to its ingredients of pork caul, prawns, chicken, water chestnut, sea-cucumber, bamboo shoots and mushroom. Another winning dish was entered on the original form quite simply as 'Shark's fin with bamboo fungus, asparagus and crab claws'. Its Chinese title is 'Gossamer curtains veiling exquisite feminine shadows'. The bamboo fungus is envisaged as a curtain of delicate fibres, through which the beguilingly beautiful forms of the shark's fin can be glimpsed.

So it is with a certain humility that I include here a version of a dish that I much admired at the festival. Its English title was 'Stuffed lobster tails'. Its Chinese title was 'Healthy and spirited dragon and horse. The literal translation cannot convey the symbolic values of the poetically rhyming Chinese characters. In the Cantonese dialect (I was told), a lobster is a 'dragon shrimp', and the sound for the 'horse' character is similar to the characters for water chestnut. Both creatures summon up images of power, stamina, elegance and other desired virtues, which a diner feels will be acquired by eating the dish.

All of the above is meant to suggest that the indiscriminate use of an Asian ingredient here and there is fine, just fine. But the dishes one creates are certainly not Chinese, and will probably be quite misunderstood by the Chinese.

My version of stuffed lobster tails was most definitely inspired by the award-winning dish, by Chef Ip Wah of the Regent Hotel, but this version is my recipe, and I am responsible for its success or lack of it.

Before proceeding to the recipe I must add the note that Hong Kong's unofficial ambassador Willie Mark, who visited London to devise a menu to celebrate the wedding of Prince Andrew and Sarah Ferguson, designed a dish where a deep-fried prawn was wrapped in bacon and accompanied by stir-fried scallops. The descriptive title given the dish was 'The prince riding the dragon'.

## STEPHANIE'S STUFFED BUG TAILS

This species of crustacea is found in both northern and southern waters of Australia. Its flesh is very sweet, and similar to that of the rock lobster (French *langouste*). It is known by various names, many of which relate to local habitat: Moreton Bay bugs, Spencer Gulf bugs, Balmain bugs, or, more descriptively, long-tailed reef bugs, shovel-nosed lobster or slipper lobster. Small lobsters or rock lobsters (called crayfish in the southern part of Australia) could be used for this dish. Ideal weight would be 800 g (25 oz). Half would be one serve. As the bug tails are much smaller, I have allowed two per serve. Fish sauce is made from fermented fish, and is a basic requirement in much South-East Asian cookery. It is sold under various names, for example, nam pla, and is widely available in Asian stores.

- 12 large green bugs (each weighing
250–300 g–8–10 oz–before shelling)

## — FOR STUFFING —

- 10 dried Chinese mushrooms, soaked for 30 minutes in hot water
- 30 g (1 oz) long rice noodles (sold wrapped in packets, looking like shredded cellophane)
- 1 teaspoon hot red chilli, slit, seeded, chopped fine
- 2 spring onions, washed and finely chopped, including some green
- ½ cup finely grated or shredded carrot
- 6 water chestnuts, rinsed and finely chopped
- 1 cup finely shredded lettuce leaves, loosely packed
- 2 teaspoons fish sauce, or to taste

## — FOR CRUMBING —

- 1 beaten egg, mixed with a little milk
- 1 cup fine, dry breadcrumbs

## — COCONUT CURRY SAUCE —

- ⅔ cup coconut milk
- ¼ cup chicken stock
- 60 g (2 oz) butter
- 2 teaspoons curry powder
- 2 teaspoons fish sauce
- ¼ cup cream
- 2 teaspoons cornflour, slaked with 1 tablespoon chicken stock

## — SAUCE FOR STEAMED BUG TAIL MEAT —

- 1 cup fresh tomato sauce, sieved (prepared as in the recipe for crayfish tomato butter sauce on pages 8–9)
- ¼ cup light soy
- ¼ cup dry sherry
- 1 cup chicken stock
- 2 teaspoons sugar
- 2 teaspoons cornflour, slaked with 25 ml (1 fl oz) water
- 2 teaspoons sesame oil

### TO PREPARE BUGS

Slit membrane where head joins tail and pull tail section from head. Discard the head. Using scissors, cut the thin membrane on each side of the tail and remove the tail meat in one piece. Usually the intestinal thread will remain behind, attached to the hard shell. Check that no dark thread remains in the meat. Discard the thin membrane. Place clean bug meat on a plate, cover with plastic and refrigerate until needed. Rinse the empty shell. This is the container for the stuffing. The portion will be two stuffed shells and the steamed tail meat of two bugs.

### If using small rock lobsters

Dip tail of rock lobster into boiling water for 1 minute so that the tail meat is easily detached from the shell. Split the rock lobster in half. Remove the head sac and the intestinal thread from the tail meat. Remove the tail meat and place it, like the bug meat, on a plate covered with plastic until needed. The tail cavity of the rock lobster will be the container for the stuffing. The portion will be one stuffed shell and one steamed half tail.

### To make coconut curry sauce

Combine coconut milk and chicken stock in a jug. Melt butter, stir in curry powder. Cook together for 1–2 minutes, stirring. Gradually add the coconut milk–chicken stock mixture, stir till smooth. Add the fish sauce and the cream. Mix the cornflour with the 1 tablespoon chicken stock. When sauce is simmering, add a ladleful to the cornflour mixture, stir to combine and then add cornflour mix to the sauce. Stir till it thickens and is simmering. Allow to get quite cold.

### To prepare stuffing

Squeeze soaked mushrooms, discard hard stems and slice finely. Put slices in a bowl. In another bowl pour boiling water over the rice noodles. Let stand for 3–4 minutes, then drain and with scissors cut the noodle strands into 2 cm (1 in) pieces. Add noodle pieces to bowl with mushrooms. Add all other ingredients, including the cold coconut curry sauce, mix well and taste for salt. Add extra fish sauce if needed.

### To stuff bugs

Pack stuffing firmly into the shells, forcing in as much as possible. Refrigerate until needed.

### To make bug sauce

In a pan, simmer together your fresh tomato sauce with the soy, the sherry, the stock and the sugar. Simmer 3–5 minutes. Slake the cornflour with the water and add the sesame oil. Add a little of the hot sauce to the cornflour mix, and then add the cornflour mix to the simmering sauce, stir till smoothly thickened. The sauce will not be very thick. Keep warm in a bain-marie or refrigerate until needed.

The stuffing and the sauce can be made a day ahead. The coconut curry sauce can be made two days ahead.

### To cook

Have a steamer ready with a flat plate that will comfortably hold the bug meat in a single layer and still allow steam to circulate freely.

Spoon egg wash generously over the stuffed tails, and then press the crumbs onto the egg wash.

Have a heavy cast-iron pan (or two) ready with clean hot oil. You may have to shallow fry the stuffed tails in two batches. In this case, have the oven on a low setting and a plate in it to hold the first batch while you are frying the second batch.

Fry the bug tails for 6 minutes, shell side down (rock lobsters will need an extra minute or two to be properly hot). Turn extremely carefully with a spatula and fry the stuffed side for 2–3 minutes, just until it is golden brown.

Steam the tail meat for about 4–5 minutes. It should still be translucent in the centre. Transfer the meat to a small non-stick pan and ladle on some of the sauce. Allow to bubble and blend and then serve the bug tail meat with the sauce and the stuffed tails alongside.

### Garnishes and accompaniments

At Stephanie's we also serve with this dish stir-fried lettuce leaves, tossed in smoking oil, with a slice of ginger and a shake of salt.

## AH FOON'S TURNIP CAKE

One of the yum cha dishes I really enjoy is turnip cake. My recipe is from Hong Kong, and a slice of this sautéed with the bugs is quite delicious. The dish will still be lovely without it, but I wanted to include the recipe. It makes a great snack sprinkled with sesame seeds and fresh coriander.

- 100 g (3 oz) lup yook (dried pork)
- 100 g (3 oz) lap cheung (Chinese sausage)
- 1 tablespoon dried shrimp, soaked for 30 minutes in 2 tablespoons rice wine or dry sherry (optional)
- 1 kg (2 lb) daikon or Chinese radish, also known as turnip by the Chinese
- 300 g (10 oz) rice flour
- 1 teaspoon salt
- 1 teaspoon sugar

Slice pork and sausage very thinly. Finely chop soaked dried shrimp, if using. Sauté the pork and sausage in a non-stick pan until fragrant. Tip into a large mixing bowl. Grate the peeled Chinese radish or turnip fairly coarsely. The shredding device on a food-processor is excellent for this.

Mix all ingredients together and pack into an oiled tin (square or round depending on the variety of steamer you have). Steam for 1 hour. Allow to cool.

When cold, cut in 1 cm (½ in) slices and fry in oil. Serve with the stuffed bugs or with any other dish. Sprinkle with sesame seeds, fresh coriander leaves and/or slivered spring onions.

Two of the award-winning chefs from the Hong Kong Festival later visited me in Australia. They were to cook some of their special dishes at a series of banquets, and one was to take place at Stephanie's. We were all very excited and looked forward to learning lots. Neither Chef Hui nor Chef Li spoke any English, but with the help of the official translator and my friend Tony Tan, not only an excellent Asian and European cook, but fluent in both Cantonese and Mandarin, we managed and had lots of fun. Chef Hui shook his head in disbelief that with such a big restaurant I open only five days a week. He clearly found my explanation of children, writing, thinking, resting quite frivolous.

I frequently 'velvet' prawns by mixing them with some cornflour and egg white, which prevents the prawns being hard and 'woody'. Chef Hui's treatment was different and resulted in pearly-white prawns with a lovely texture when cooked. He added several handfuls of cornflour and about 3 tablespoons of bicarbonate of soda to about 4 kg (8 lb) of shelled prawn meat, mixed it really well, turned on the cold tap for a minute or so and massaged the prawns really hard for 5 full minutes. A great deal of the reddish matter from the intestinal canal was forced from the prawn. I was astonished that they did not break but they did not. He next left them in a colander under running water for a full 30 minutes before de-veining them. Interestingly, in over half of the prawns, the vein had already been forced from them, leaving them perfectly clean.

## PICKLED GINGER PRAWNS

- 1 kg (2 lb) prawns, shelled
- ½ cup cornflour
- 1 tablespoon carbonate of soda
- 1 red onion, sliced paper-thin
- ½ cup olive oil
- ½ cup white wine vinegar
- 1 teaspoon salt
- ½ teaspoon coarsely ground pepper

- ¼ teaspoon dry mustard
- tabasco
- 2 onions, chopped fine
- 3 cloves garlic, chopped fine
- 2 cm (1 in) piece ginger, sliced into fine julienne
- lettuce cups or small red peppers with top one-third sliced off

Velvet the prawns using the cornflour and carbonate of soda in the manner described above.

Mix together the sliced onion, ¼ cup of the oil, vinegar, salt, pepper, mustard and tabasco. Place dressing in a large bowl.

Heat remaining ¼ cup oil in a large frying-pan. Sauté the chopped onion and garlic and cook over a low gas flame for 5 minutes, until the onion is soft and yellow. Raise the heat and add the ginger. Sauté 1 minute, stirring all the time, add the prawns, cook 3–4 minutes, just until the prawns change colour. Remove and tip contents of pan into the bowl with the dressing. Marinate for several hours, but do not refrigerate.

Lift the prawns and dressing into lettuce cups or into red pepper cups to serve.

Australian distances are formidable. For years my brothers have lived in Darwin, the Top End as it is affectionately known by its residents, yet until recently I had never travelled the 2000 kilometres to visit them. They urged me to come in 'the Wet' and were insistent that the Territory is best appreciated in its lush season—humidity, rain and wind notwithstanding.

Cyclone Hector was off the coast. The sea was grey and turbulent and infested with the deadly blue-ringed octopus. Banana trees flapped their sodden leaves, rain came in furious sheets, and the wind bent and beat at the palm trees. Sound and fury was everywhere! As a southerner it didn't seem right to me that this angry, violent rain should be so warm. And then the storm eased and the sun shone. The trees were lustrous, the hibiscus glorious, the frangipani fragrant, the poinsettia lush and the grass was astonishingly green. It was very humid.

One could sniff that familiar tropical smell of imminent decay. Fallen leaves were dragged off by nameless insects, and it was a relief when the steaming vegetation was once again damped by rain.

Knowing how I adore crabs, one of my brothers and family had spent four hours crabbing in the pouring rain to provide the feast that evening of wok-tossed chilli mud crabs.

Darwin has a large Asian community: Chinese, Indonesian, Timorese and, the most recent arrivals, many Vietnamese. The best and freshest food I saw was being sold either in Asian food shops or in outdoor markets, such as Rapid Creek flea market. I saw bunches of pawpaw flowers (blanch three times before frying), lime leaves and cassava root. Years ago in the West Indies I had delicious fried bami cakes, which were made from grated cassava.

There were heaps of brilliantly green vegetables, as well as freshly gathered lemongrass, coriander and newly dug ginger.

I also saw banana flower for sale. Dur-é, our Malaysian manageress, once gave me a banana flower, assuring me it was edible. Neither of us knew how to prepare it. I tried to eat a slice, only to find it overwhelmingly bitter and horrible. My brother had a copy of an excellent little book produced by the Darwin Garden Club in 1978, *The Darwin Gardener's Gourmet Guide*, and it gave clear instructions on how to deal with a banana flower.

Pick a banana flower and slice through like an onion. Rub well with fine salt and leave to stand in a covered container for 2–3 hours, then wash thoroughly under running water. Place in a pan, cover well with cold water, bring to the boil and simmer for ten minutes. Drain and put in a sealed container in the refrigerator, where it will keep for a week before being fried with other things.

I bought some delicious green pawpaw salad prepared by a Timorese woman who pounded the ingredients in a very deep, stoneware mortar with a huge pestle. First garlic, chilli and a little ginger. Then in went a heap of finely shredded, pale yellow-green pawpaw, a pin of sugar, a slurp of fish sauce, some sliced tomato, a few more vigorous poundings, a scatter of raw peanuts, and the salad was made.

The pawpaw used for this salad was quite unripe. The shreds resembled the cabbage we might use for coleslaw both in colour and crispness. Back home in the south I wanted to make this salad to serve with freshly cooked yabbies (Australia's freshwater crayfish, as in *écrevisses*) and I was confronted by a ridiculous situation. Pawpaws are picked unripe to facilitate transport to the southern states and are then ripened before sale. One cannot purchase either a properly tree-ripened fruit or a completely green pawpaw.

After a visit to one of our Thai restaurants, where I was served a similar salad with the addition of lemongrass, I decided to follow their lead and to use grated carrot as the base of my dish. This then is our salad, but I would urge anyone with access to green pawpaw to substitute it.

## YABBY SALAD with THAI SEASONING and a COCONUT SAUCE

### — CARROT SALAD —

- 2 cups finely grated carrot (if done in the food-processor, return any juice to the carrot)
- 2 cloves garlic, very finely chopped
- 1 red hot chilli, slit and seeded and chopped fine (or more if you want)
- 3 cm (1¼ in) piece of ginger, peeled, sliced and finely chopped
- 1 teaspoon brown sugar

- 1 stalk lemongrass, very finely sliced (use the tender bulb part only)
- 3 limes, juice only
- 2 teaspoons fish sauce (see page 15)
- 2 tablespoons torn coriander leaves and finely chopped stems
- 2 tablespoons raw peanuts, roughly chopped

Mix together and leave to marinate for several hours.

### — COCONUT SAUCE —

- 2 teaspoons tomato paste
- 2 teaspoons sambal oelek or other minced chilli paste
- 2 limes, juice only
- ½ cup coconut milk (make sure that the brand you buy is unsweetened and has no added thickener)

- 2 tablespoons coriander leaves and stems, finely chopped
- 1 cup light oil (such as grapeseed or peanut, if you like it)
- salt to taste

In a blender, whizz the first four ingredients until smooth. With the motor running, slowly add the oil, as if making a mayonnaise. Taste for salt and stir in coriander stems and leaves. The sauce should be like a thin mayonnaise.

Allow 4 yabbies per serve, if they are of good size—i.e. about 90 g (3 oz) each

- 24 yabbies
- juice of 2 limes and grated zest of 1
- 1 tablespoon fish sauce
- 1 stalk lemongrass, very finely sliced

Mix the lime juice, lime zest, fish sauce and lemongrass in a bowl. Have ready a really large pan of boiling water. Immerse the yabbies, stir around with a large spoon and leave for 3–4 minutes until the shells are bright pink. Lift out and, as soon as you can, pull off and discard the head, shell the tail meat and drop the tails into the lime juice marinade. Stir with your fingers to coat the shellfish. Do not refrigerate. Serve as soon as possible.

### TO ASSEMBLE SALAD

Choose plates about 20 cm (8 in) in diameter. Place a heap of seasoned carrot in the centre. Pour a ribbon of sauce on the plate around the carrot. Place the yabby tails around and drop on a few tender sprigs of coriander. Serve with a wedge of lime.

If you dislike coriander or would like a change, substitute mint. Should you not have yabbies in your creek or dam, use prawns or bug tails (see page 15). If using bug tails, extract the meat from the shell before cooking, and then cook in exactly the same way as for the yabbies. Slice the tails lengthwise before arranging them, if they are very large.

OYSTERS & OTHER SHELLFISH

23

# FISH

Australia's oceans, rivers, inlets and harbours teem with fish and shellfish. The variety is extraordinary, although many varieties remain local in their availability.

Our biggest and best fish markets are a revelation to many food-loving visitors. I once had a conversation in Sydney with Jeremiah Tower, chef of the highly regarded San Francisco restaurant Stars. He had accompanied Serge Dansereau, the chef of the Regent Hotel in Sydney, while Serge was doing his marketing. Jeremiah said that the fish market in Sydney made the San Francisco markets look like a desert. The next day I visited the market myself with friends who were intending to prepare a Sydney bouillabaise. They considered that the market was not at its best that day, but none the less were able to select baby red mullet, or barbounia as it is called by our Greek fish merchants, tiny sparkling leather jacket, rock cod (*rascasse*), gurnard (*rouget-grondin*), live blue rock lobsters of every size imaginable, rock flathead, huge, muscular, silver-pink snapper, like the French *daurade*, prawns of three different varieties, from very small school prawns like the *crevettes roses* of the Mediterranean and the Atlantic coast to our huge and sweet tiger prawns.

Elsewhere in the market one could buy sea urchins, cockles, pipis (the same as the *praires* in France), cuttlefish, two varieties of squid, octopus, and live bugs. There were also fish from warmer northern waters. Fresh tuna and a 50 kg (100 lb) swordfish shared a marble slab. There were turquoise and pink parrot fish, live 'muddies' (mud crabs) and the pride of the north, the mighty barramundi. At yet another stall one could buy superb sea-run trout and Australian farmed salmon, sold here as Atlantic salmon. Yet many Australians are still anxious about preparing and eating fish.

When I visited Billingsgate market in England, I was interested to note that although many of the fish varieties are quite different, there were plenty that were instantly recognisable. We too have excellent John Dory, and Mirror Dory and Silver Dory. We don't have sole or plaice, although we have flounder. We have exquisite King George whiting, not the same fish as the English whiting, but it can be cooked the same way. I was envious of the huge turbot: I always wanted to own a copper turbot-poaching kettle. But we have many large sweet fish that can be similarly poached: the butterfish or the pearl perch or the red emperor.

In my part of the country the most commonly caught fish are the rock flathead, the garfish, like a miniature swordfish, the snapper and a variety of breams, sand whiting and the humble couta. Flathead is the fish of my youth. Around the bay where I grew up, my dad would frequently return from a morning's fishing with several dozen flathead. They are a delicate and delicious fish but are often scorned as they are quite bony. With a 1 kg (2 lb) fish there is no problem, but it is far more common to catch smaller fish. We developed a family favourite for these small fry. After gutting and scaling them, Mum would purée the fillets in a powerful blender (it was before the days of food-processors), season them with some herbs, salt and pepper and, using a little egg and cornflour, form them into small balls. She then fried them in oil until they were golden and crisp. Magically all the bones had vanished.

These little fish balls make a pleasant appetiser if served with a saucer of light soy diluted with a little rice wine and perhaps a sliver of pink pickled ginger or a pea-sized pellet of green wasabi horseradish paste.

Garfish have even more bones. If the fish are slit down the belly and then rolled firmly with a small rolling pin, one can pull out the backbone with most of the bones attached. They are one of the most delicate and sweet fish, and there is no better way to cook them than to dust them with flour and pan fry them in enough frothing butter so that they are golden and cooked through in no more than one or two minutes each side. A squeeze of lemon, lime or orange juice and a spoonful of parsley can be swirled in the pan with a fresh nut of butter. Allow the butter to turn toasty in the pan and then pour it onto the tender fillets in classic meunière fashion.

The snapper is a very different kettle of fish. Snapper range in size from 300 g (10 oz) up to 10 kg (20 lb). Plate-sized fish are everyone's favourite to grill, either on a solid plate or even better over a wood-fired barbecue. The flesh is firm and sweet. It is equally good hot or cold. The skin crisps nicely when it is grilled. The fish is quite thick through behind the head and it is usual to make one or two cuts on each side of the fish before grilling it to help it cook evenly.

After cleaning and scoring, rub the skin with any herbs or spices and a liberal amount of olive oil. Rub the oil well into the skin. If you are using a hinged wire fish-grill, oil the bars of this lightly. Fish with wet skin (that is wet with water or wine) will stick to the grill, and unless you oil them it will be impossible to turn or remove the fish without leaving most of the delicious crispy skin on the grill bars.

Your finished dish can change its character completely, depending on the content of the mix you use to massage into the flesh. Three flavour combinations loosely borrowed from three different traditions follow.

Any one of these combinations could be used with a very large fish (i.e. one too large to grill). After massaging and allowing sufficient time for the fish to marinate (at least 2 hours, preferably 3 or 4 for a large fish), oil a suitable-size baking dish, place a wide, doubled band of foil in the bottom of the dish, cut long enough so that the ends overlap the dish, oil the foil and place the fish on the foil. Pour in 1 cupful of white wine mixed with 1/2 cup of oil.

Cover the dish loosely with more foil and bake in a moderate oven for approximately 10 minutes per 100 g (3 oz). The timing can only be approximate as it depends on the thickness of the fish rather than its length. Check the fish after 15 minutes, and baste it with the juices, which will have collected in the baking pan. If it is in danger of drying up, add a few more spoonfuls of water or wine. For the last 10 minutes of the cooking, remove the top sheet of foil and increase the oven heat so that the skin may crisp. Lift the fish into a very hot platter with the help of the foil strip. Remove the foil.

## CARIBBEAN JERKED
## FISH MARINADE

Enough for 6 snapper of approximately 350–400 g (11–13 oz) each. Sea bass or bream are equally good if you do not have snapper.

- juice of 2 limes
- 1½ tablespoons ground allspice
- 6 spring onions, chopped, including the green part
- 1 whole hot chilli, slit and seeded, cut very fine
- 1 teaspoon salt
- 3 tablespoons olive oil

Mix all ingredients well in a mortar and rub over the sides and inside the fish. Allow to marinate for at least an hour. Place in a hinged wire grill after oiling the bars. Barbecue approximately 6 minutes per side, turning once. Garnishes to consider include: white rice, slices of lime, pickled hot chillis.

## NORTH AFRICAN
## FISH MARINADE
### (Chermoula)

- 6 tablespoons oil
- 1 onion, finely chopped
- 2 cloves garlic, finely chopped
- 2 envelopes powdered saffron, diluted in ¼ cup hot water
- 4 tablespoons parsley, finely chopped
- 4 tablespoons coriander leaves, finely chopped
- 1 teaspoon ground pepper
- ½ teaspoon powdered ginger
- ½ teaspoon ground cumin
- ½ teaspon powdered paprika
- 1 teaspoon salt
- 2 bay leaves, crumbled

Heat the oil and slowly cook the onion and garlic until quite soft. Add the saffron and water and increase heat until the water has evaporated. Stir in the rest of the spices and herbs. Rub mixture all over and inside the fish. Marinate for at least an hour, and then grill as above. Garnishes to consider include couscous, fresh coriander leaves, limes or lemons.

## INDIAN-STYLE MARINADE

- 1 teaspoon coriander seeds
- ½ teaspoon black cumin seeds
- ½ teaspoon fenugreek seeds
- 6 cloves garlic, chopped finely
- 2.5 cm (1 in) piece green ginger, chopped finely
- 2 teaspoons paprika
- 1 teaspoon salt
- 2 teaspoons white vinegar
- 1 tablespoon lime juice
- 2 tablespoons oil

Place the coriander, black cumin and fenugreek seeds in a heavy black pan and dry-roast for 1–2 minutes until they are fragrant. Grind in a spice grinder. Place the ground spices in a mortar with the garlic and ginger, the paprika and the salt and work together until you have a paste. Stir in the vinegar, lime juice and the oil.

Rub the mixture all over the fish and marinate for at least an hour. Grill as in the other recipes. Garnishes to consider include chopped mint mixed with lime juice, or a salad of paper-thin onion rings.

## WINTER FISH SOUP

When I want to make a 'big affair' fish soup, as the Chinese would say, I buy a kilo or two of flathead and, if I can, a snapper head. This soup is ideal for cold days, as it is rich and thick. The fish chunks and shellfish can easily be increased, so that the soup and fish can be served in big bowls as a one-pot meal.

### — FOR SOUP —

- 3 large carrots, washed and peeled
- 1 large bulb of fennel, washed
- 3 large onions, peeled
- 2 leeks, well washed
- ½ head of garlic, each clove lightly crushed
- ½ cup olive oil
- 2 kg (4 lb) cleaned, scaled fish, cut into chunks
- 1 fish head, well washed, gills removed
- 1.5 kg (3 lb) can of peeled tomatoes, with juice
- 250 ml (8 fl oz) dry white wine
- 1 teaspoon saffron threads dissolved in ¼ cup hot water
- 2 envelopes powdered saffron
- ½ cup pernod

## — GARNISH —

- garlic croutons
- 1 kg (2 lb) mussels
- 500 g (1 lb) scallops, cleaned of intestinal thread and any wisps
- 6 fillets of fish, each approximately 100 g (3 oz)
- chopped parsley

Chop all vegetables into even-shaped pieces. Brown in the olive oil. Add the fish chunks and the chopped fish head and seal and stir for 3–4 minutes. Add the tomatoes and juice, the wine, the saffron and the pernod. Add cold water to cover all vegetables and fish and bring slowly to simmering point, stirring once or twice. Skim well and allow to simmer undisturbed for 30 minutes.

Press the soup (vegetables, fish debris and all) through the coarse disc of a mouli-mill. You should be trying to capture as much of the vegetable and fish fragments as possible. When you have nothing but fibre and bones in the top section of the mouli, you can stop! Taste the soup and adjust with salt and pepper. Leave the soup a touch undersalted, as you will be adding a little mussel fumet. Either leave the texture of the soup as it is for a rustic feeling or blend it.

### To make garlic croutons

Cut thin rounds from a breadstick. Paint lightly with olive oil on each side and bake the bread rounds in a moderate oven till a pale gold. While the croutons are still warm, rub each one gently with a cut clove of garlic. Store in an air-tight container until needed.

### To serve soup

Wash the mussels well. Place them in a single layer in a pan with 2 cm (1 in) of water or white wine. Cover and cook over high heat for 3–4 minutes until all the mussels have opened. Remove them and discard the top shell. Strain the fumet very well and add to the fish soup carefully, tasting as you go.

Either poach the scallops and the fillets of fish separately in a small pan with some of the soup or steam them. I prefer the former. Place the fish and shellfish in each heated bowl and ladle over the soup. Strew lavishly with chopped parsley and serve the garlic croutons in a separate basket.

In the weeks before Easter in Melbourne the Italian and Greek delicatessens display salted fish, traditional Lenten food in both cultures. There are two types sold: fat fillets, which are usually layered in wooden crates and which exude a powerful smell, and the more expensive variety of salted codfish, stacked like grey cardboard cutouts of fish. You need to know the difference before you embark on any recipe using salted codfish, as the soaking times are quite different. In my experience, the fat fillets are sufficiently soaked after 8 hours, whereas the completely desiccated variety needs at least 24 hours with at least one or two changes of water. In Italy I have seen this type of fish in a deep enamelled basin carefully positioned under a gently trickling tap so that the water is being constantly renewed. The fillets of codfish are usually the most convenient to buy, as a whole dried fish is probably more than you will need to use.

My first introduction to salted cod was many years ago, when I worked as an assistante in a French school in the town of Tours. A favourite start to a meal was a bowl of brandade, a creamy purée of the saltfish whipped with lots of garlic, olive oil, pepper and cream. It was always served piled in a bowl decorated with black olives and with triangles of fried bread. I still love brandade, but in far more modest quantities. One of our most popular entrées is a puff pastry case that we split, fill with brandade, top with a lightly poached egg, and finish with a spoonful of hollandaise. On the side is a small salad of crisp salad hearts, which has a dusting of bonito flakes. They dissolve on the tongue like a grown-up's fishy fairy floss.

My next contact was a few years later. Harry Belafonte sang that 'ackee, rice, saltfish are nice . . .' I certainly didn't know what an ackee was. Soon after, I married a West Indian and visited his home island of Jamaica and discovered not only the curious ackee, but saltfish, alias salted cod. The ackee is the fruit of a large tree (Blighia satida). The fruits are scarlet-skinned, poisonous until ripe, when they crack open, exposing the creamy edible parts. Ackee and saltfish was revealed as a traditional Jamaican breakfast cooked with onions and tomatoes. The ackee always reminded me of an avocado. They have the same smooth, waxy texture and a very similar colour, but the ackee has a rather sappy taste and is small and shaped like an acorn. I have given the recipe here, as I believe that avocado can be substituted for the ackee and the dish is too good to ignore!

I am also including another dish of salted codfish cooked with vegetables.

Both the Jamaican and the Mediterranean recipe produce dishes that are ideal to serve for a light meal with a salad or, as in the Jamaican model, for breakfast or brunch.

## SALTFISH and ACKEE

- 500 g (1 lb) salt cod fillets
- 150 g (5 oz) skinned pickled belly pork
- 6 strips streaky bacon
- 2 onions, peeled and chopped finely
- 1 hot chilli, slit, seeded and chopped finely
- 4 spring onions
- 4 large tomatoes, peeled, seeded, diced
- 2 medium avocados or 1 can ackee, drained and rinsed

Soak the fish fillets in plenty of cold water for 8 hours. Rinse and place in an enamelled pan. Cover with cold water and bring very slowly to simmering point. Simmer very gently for 10–15 minutes until the fish is tender. Lift from the water with a fish slice and carefully flake into a warm bowl, discarding all skin and bones. Cover with some plastic film to stop the fish drying out.

Cut the salt pork into 1 cm (½ in) dice. Place in a pan of cold water and bring to the boil. Drain. Place the pork in a heavy frying-pan and fry slowly till the fat is rendered. Remove the crisped pork to a plate. Fry the bacon strips in the remaining fat until crisp. Remove from pan. Fry the onion, chilli, chopped spring onion in the fat until soft. Add the diced tomatoes and cook a further two minutes. Return the flaked fish to the pan and warm through, turning over and over with a fork so as not to break it up. Add the peeled and chunked avocado. Turn the dish into a very hot serving dish and scatter over the crisp bacon, the crisp pork dice and a little finely chopped spring onion.

## BRAISED CODFISH with POTATOES and PINENUTS

- 500 g (1 lb) salt cod fillets
- ½ cup virgin olive oil
- 2 sliced onions
- 1 clove garlic, chopped
- 1 bay leaf
- ½ cup dry white wine
- 3 even-shaped large waxy potatoes, peeled and quartered lengthwise
- ⅔ cup reduced veal stock
- 3 tomatoes, peeled, seeded, puréed
- 1 tablespoon black olives, pitted
- pepper
- 1 tablespoon parsley, chopped
- 2 tablespoons fried pinenuts

Soak fish in plenty of cold water for 8 hours. Rinse and drain it. In a cast-iron enamelled pan, heat the oil and slowly soften the onions and the garlic with the bay leaf. This will take about 15 minutes, stirring from time to time. Add the wine, simmer uncovered for a further 10 minutes. Add the fish cut into chunks, the potatoes and the stock. Cover the pan and simmer on the lowest heat possible for approximately 30–40 minutes until the potatoes are tender. Push the pan off the heat. Lift out the pieces of fish, flake to remove all skin and bones. Stir tomato, olives, pepper and parsley into the pot and return the fish flakes to the pot also. Taste for seasoning. If too liquid, give a fast boil for 2–3 minutes.

### TO SERVE

Divide the potatoes and the fish between 6 small oven-proof dishes. Spoon over the juices, dividing the olives equally, and place the little bowls in a hot oven or under the grill to bubble the top. Scatter over the pinenuts.

Still on the subject of salt cod, I have collected two other recipes. Once again one is from the West Indies, codfish fritters known as Jamaica 'Stamp and Go', and the other a quite different recipe for fritters from I don't know where.

## JAMAICA 'STAMP and GO'

- 125 g (4 oz) raw salted codfish (i.e. unsoaked)
- juice of 1 lime
- 1 medium onion, chopped finely
- 1 clove garlic, chopped finely
- ½ hot chilli, slit, seeded and chopped finely
- 2 spring onions, chopped finely
- 2 medium tomatoes, peeled, seeded and chopped finely
- oil for frying
- 2 tablespoons plain flour
- pinch of paprika

Wipe the fish free of loose salt, then chop very finely. Pour over the lime juice. Set aside. Combine the chopped onion, garlic, chilli, spring onion and tomato.

Heat a film of oil in a small pan and fry this mixture until softened.

Place the fish and lime juice in a bowl. Stir in the flour and sufficient cold water to make a pancake batter with the consistency of cream. Stir well until smooth. Add the fried mixture and the paprika.

Fry spoonfuls of the mixture in very hot oil until golden brown and crisp on both sides. Drain on kitchen paper and keep warm in a low oven. Serve at once as a snack or as part of a hot buffet.

## ACCRAS DE MORUE
### (Deep-fried Codfish Fritters)

#### — BATTER —

- 200 g (7 oz) plain flour
- ½ teaspoon salt
- 2 eggs
- 3 tablespoons cooled, melted butter
- 1 cup milk

#### — FISH MIXTURE —

- 250 g (8 oz) salt cod fillets, soaked
- 1 hot chilli, slit, seeded and chopped
- 2 spring onions, chopped
- 1 clove garlic, chopped
- 1 tablespoon chopped parsley
- 2 teaspoons chopped chives
- black pepper
- oil for frying

Sift together the flour and the salt. Lightly whisk together the eggs and the butter. In a food-processor combine the flour and the egg mixture. Gradually add the milk. Allow the batter to stand for 2 hours.

Remove the codfish from the soaking water, flake it and remove any bones. Process with all other ingredients. Stir into the batter and taste for pepper. Let the batter and fish mixture stand for 30 minutes. Drop the mix by spoonfuls into very hot oil. Turn the fritters once. When golden brown, drain on paper and serve at once.

In December 1986 Tasmania released its well-kept secret onto the Australian market: the first farmed Atlantic salmon. In their natural habitat in the Northern Hemisphere, the Atlantic salmon are born in freshwater rivers, swim to the sea in spring where they live for two, four or up to six years before returning to the same breeding-ground to spawn. Our salmon are farmed in Dover, 1 ½ hours drive south of Hobart. I drove there in the springtime via the pretty Huon Valley, famous in Tasmania as an apple-producing area. We drove past fields of black-faced sheep and past acres of apple orchards, with here and there a few red and gold balls still clinging to the bare, pruned boughs. Journey's end was the shining expanse at the mouth of the Esperance, glassy and poetic under the low afternoon sun.

The salmon start their life in a freshwater hatchery, which approximates to the river in the natural cycle. The baby Atlantic salmon are then progressively acclimatised to seawater by increasing the levels of salinity, approximating the natural stage of the fish descending the river into the sea. The young fish are then transferred into large floating sea enclosures in the salt water at the mouth of the Esperance. Dover is quite remote, far from any township, and therefore has no pollution. The water is deep and close to shore and continually has a flush of fresh water from the river estuary, which acts like cleansing salts. An ideal habitat, and the fish are thriving on it. I was told by the enthusiastic manager that the Tasmanian fish were 30 per cent ahead on condition when compared to their Norwegian brothers and sisters hatched at the same time.

A similar procedure has been used to farm the ocean trout, also released for the first time in 1986. The super trout spend up to 12 months of their life in seawater where they gain condition and are marketed at between 1 and 2 kilograms (2–4 lb). Several people are already producing magnificent cold-smoked and hot-smoked ocean trout and salmon, some with specialised cures and marinades. One hopes that Australia will soon be able to produce enough smoked salmon to supply a large proportion of its domestic requirements and possibly create an export market.

The availability of these two glamour fish has been most exciting for cooks. Every restaurant in the country has been experimenting, and the public has been offered an astonishing range of specialities. Here are the three dishes I have served using both the salmon and the ocean trout. The two fish have their own special flavour, but the similarity of texture and the ability to cut each into the same sort of pieces has meant that the recipe that works well for one fish works well for the other. Cooking times may need to be adjusted as the salmon is a much larger fish.

---

## SEARED ESCALOPE of ATLANTIC SALMON with GREEN TOMATOES and ROASTED FISH SKIN

---

- 1.5 kg (3 lb) fillet of salmon or 1.5 kg (3 lb) centre-cut of salmon

### — GREEN TOMATO SAUCE —

- 6 green tomatoes
- 1 large onion
- 1 clove garlic, chopped
- 1/4 cup olive oil

- 1 bay leaf
- 1/2 teaspoon sugar
- 1 teaspoon salt
- pepper

### — HOLLANDAISE SAUCE —

- 3 egg yolks
- 2 teaspoons cold water
- 2 teaspoons lemon juice
- 250 g (8 oz) butter
- salt, pepper

- 1 tablespoon of selected herb (optional)
- 200 g (6 oz) freshly made fettuccine, plain or flavoured with 2 tablespoons of a single herb (see page 7)

## To prepare fish

Using a pair of tweezers, remove all of the bones that run down the centre of the fillet. After 'plucking' the fish in this manner, with a sharp, flexible knife separate the skin from the tail. Grasp the tail flesh firmly with your left hand and hold it taut while you slip the fish knife against the skin, removing it in one piece. Keep the skin.

Weigh the skinned fillet and divide it into 6 equal portions. You may wish to discard the very skinny tail-end. Either cure it as in the recipe on page 47 or slice it paper-thin and eat it raw with some virgin oil and pepper for lunch.

Cut each fish chunk horizontally to make 6 thin escalopes. Place a piece of plastic film over each one and pound lightly to flatten the fish. Brush both sides with a trace of the very best oil and place the fish on a tray lined with aluminium foil.

If you have purchased a centre-cut piece of fish, the procedure is the same, except that you will need to lift the two fillets from the backbone before proceeding with the plucking, skinning and slicing. You will have less waste and may have to have something else for lunch.

## To make green tomato sauce

Roughly chop the green tomatoes. Purée them in a food-processor. Cook the onion and garlic in the olive oil for 4–5 minutes until softened and yellow. Add the tomato, the bay leaf, sugar, salt and pepper, and simmer for 10–15 minutes. Discard the bay leaf.

The sauce can be reheated over a gentle heat or steamed hot.

## To make hollandaise sauce

It is quite possible to make hollandaise over direct heat, but most home cooks will be using only a few yolks, and it is difficult to properly whisk 2 or 3 yolks in the bottom of a pan. I would recommend a basin over simmering water as a better way to achieve a proper mousse-like sabayon of the yolks.

Place egg yolks, water and half the lemon juice in a basin and whisk well over simmering water until the yolks are thick and creamy. Whisk in a large lump of the butter, about 30 g (1 oz), and continue whisking over a low flame until all the butter is absorbed and the sauce is well emulsified. Whisk in a further 30 g (1 oz) of butter in the same manner. The sauce can now be completed either by continuing to add small pieces of the butter and whisking well after each addition, still keeping the pan and basin over a low heat, or the balance of the butter can be melted and slowly added to the emulsified sauce off the heat, whisking all the time. Taste the sauce and adjust with drops of lemon juice, salt and pepper. I like to stir in a heaped tablespoon or two of the herb used in the fettuccine just before serving the sauce.

Hollandaise sauce will stay warm in its basin over very hot water for 30 minutes or so. Or place in a jug with the jug resting on a folded towel inside a saucepan (to insulate the sauce) in a warm corner of the stove away from any direct flame.

### To roast fish skin

With the back of a knife scrape off any scraps of fish still clinging to the skin. Place the piece of fish skin in a very heavy cast-iron pan with a film of oil. Heat slowly. The skin will take about 30 minutes to properly crisp and will render quite a bit of oil. Drain the skin once it is quite brittle and then crumble or cut into small pieces. The skin provides a crisp note in what is otherwise a dish of mainly soft texture.

Make and cook the fettuccine according to the method on page 7. To reheat, have a large pan of boiling, salted water ready with a conical sieve resting in the water. The pasta is dropped into the sieve for a minute, the sieve is then lifted to drain, and the hot pasta is ready for a quick toss with butter and cheese, sautéed mushrooms or chicken liver, or, as here, with the reheated green tomato sauce. Fresh herbs should be added at the very last instant to keep their full flavour and fresh colour.

### To cook fish and serve

Have heated dinner plates ready.

Place a suitable size non-stick frying-pan on the stove. Have two or three frying-pans, if necessary, so that the 6 pieces of fish can be cooked and served simultaneously. When the pans are really hot, slap in the fish escalopes, best side down. Wait 2 minutes and then turn the fish, using a fish slice. Cook the second side a further 2 minutes and then turn the slices onto the centre of the serving plates.

Quickly pile the pasta/green tomato sauce onto one end of the plate, spoon some sauce partly over the fish and scatter a few flakes of the fish skin over the pasta. A second crunchy vegetable could be added, or alternatively a small salad, garnished with the fish skin.

The salmon should still be deep pink and moist in the middle. This is essential when cooking this fish or it will seem dry and characterless.

```
┌─────────────────────────────────────────────┐
│ ╔═══════════════════════════════════════════╗ │
│ ║   OCEAN TROUT (or SALMON)                 ║ │
│ ║   HOT-SMOKED over VINE CUTTINGS           ║ │
│ ╚═══════════════════════════════════════════╝ │
└─────────────────────────────────────────────┘
```

First find your vine cuttings. As we increasingly become a nation of wine producers, more and more people have a friend who makes wine. If not, there are plenty of suburban grapevines that need a prune in the late autumn. Cut the prunings into short lengths with strong secateurs and bundle them loosely into something where air can still circulate. I use string onion bags donated by the greengrocer. As is often the case, my problems of supply are quite different from those of someone who may wish to make this dish a few times only. I had to locate enough prunings to prepare the dish up to twenty times a night for twelve weeks. We are very grateful to the friendly vigneron who donated the trailer loads of prunings and to Gail Thomas, who collected them, and to Victor and Lorrie, our gardeners, who obligingly fed these prunings through a clean mulching machine so that we had bags and bags of vine chips, absolutely ideal for hot-smoking or for fuelling a wood barbecue.

In the recipe on page 84, I have included veal stock as one of the ingredients for the rosemary and garlic butter. The garlic skins are simmered in the stock, which is then reduced down to a glaze. The veal stock can be replaced with light fish stock or shellfish stock, which would make a very special butter. If you have neither, make the butter without any reduced liquid.

- 1 × 2 kg (4 lb) ocean trout or 2 × 1 kg (2 lb) ocean trout or similar weight of salmon
- ¼ cupful vine prunings
- 1 baked-enamel oven roasting tin with lid (sold as an oven roaster)
- 1 roasting rack that fits inside the roasting tin
- 6 × 5 mm (¼ in) slices of garlic and rosemary butter (see page 84)

## — POTATOES —

- 12 best quality waxy potatoes
- 4 unpeeled cloves garlic
- 1 large sprig rosemary
- ¼ cup best olive oil

## — STUFFED PEPPERS —

- 1 cup virgin olive oil
- 1 cup fresh breadcrumbs
- 30 g (1 oz) pinenuts, toasted till golden
- 2 tablespoons sultanas
- 20 black olives, pitted
- 2 anchovy fillets, chopped
- 2 tablespoons capers, chopped
- 2 tablespoons chopped parsley
- salt, pepper
- 6 medium red peppers

### To prepare fish

Lift fillets from the backbone of the fish. Pluck the small bones with tweezers as in the previous recipe. Do not remove the skin. With the larger ocean trout, each fillet should be cut into 3 portions. The smaller trout fillets will probably yield 1½ portions each. Set the fish aside until you are ready for dinner.

### To make stuffing

Using two-thirds of the olive oil, toast the breadcrumbs, spooning them over and over until they are quite golden. Tip the crumbs into a bowl with the toasted pinenuts, sultanas, olives, anchovies, capers, parsley, salt and pepper. Mix well, adding a few extra drops of olive oil if the stuffing does not cling together well. Stuff and cook according to the recipe.

### To make pepper rolls

Roast peppers over a gas flame, turning until quite charred. Rub off the black skin, using as little water as possible. Slice the end off each pepper, discard all seeds and cut the pepper lengthwise in half. Place a spoonful of stuffing in each half and roll up. Place the filled pepper rolls in a lightly oiled baking dish and brush them with the rest of the oil. Bake in a moderate oven for about 20 minutes.

These pepper rolls make a delicious dish for a cold buffet.

### To cook potatoes

Roll the peeled potatoes, the garlic and the rosemary in the olive oil. Add a little salt and pepper and bake in a moderate to hot oven for at least 45 minutes, shaking a few times to ensure that the potatoes are not sticking. When cooked, they should be golden and crusty and exude an irresistible aroma.

### To hot-smoke fish

We use our smoker on top of the charcoal grill. This method is recommended if you are cooking outside on a barbecue. Inside, the smoker does need some efficient means of ventilation. It may be easier in a domestic situation to cook the fish in the oven. In that case, time the cooking of the potatoes and pepper rolls so that they can be placed at the bottom of the oven before you need the middle shelf for your covered baking dish.

Lightly dampen the vine cuttings. Sprinkle them on the bottom of the roasting dish. Place the rack in position and place the lid on the roasting dish quite firmly. Place the tin in the oven without any fish for at least 10 minutes to become really hot. Check by lifting the lid that there is a gentle haze of smoke rising. If so, place the fish fillets, skin side down to the smoke, on the rack. Close the lid and the oven and cook for about 5 minutes for trout fillets and 8 minutes for thicker pieces of salmon. Check at the end of this time. Remember that the fish should still be moist.

When cooked, turn the fish fillets carefully onto heated serving plates, crispy skin uppermost. Rub lightly with the slice of rosemary and garlic butter and allow to rest to melt around the fish. Serve the pepper rolls and the roasted potatoes and a wedge of lemon if you wish.

---

ROASTED SALMON, larded with
ANCHOVIES and SAGE,
with ANCHOVY BUTTER

---

This is a dish for when you have a very large salmon. One can roast the thickest part of the fish and sugar-cure the rest of it. The skin is removed and the fish is wrapped in a veiling of caul fat, which nourishes it during its relatively long cooking. Although I have specified salmon, this dish is quite wonderful with a chunk of swordfish or a thick fillet of blue-eye trevalla, a splendid fish caught in southern waters.

- 1 x 1–1.5 kg (2–3 lb) piece of salmon or swordfish or blue-eye trevalla
- 3 anchovy fillets
- 6 fresh sage leaves or oregano or rosemary
- 1 large piece of caul fat, soaked overnight in lightly salted water until quite white, then squeezed dry in a clean cloth
- ¼ cup olive oil
- 3 whole cloves garlic, lightly smashed

## — ANCHOVY BUTTER —

- 6 fillets anchovies
- 1 tablespoon chopped parsley
- 200 g (7 oz) unsalted butter
- tabasco (optional)

Combine all ingredients in the food-processor. When smooth, scrape into aluminium foil and store in a roll, or else spoon it into individual pots.

### To prepare fish

Remove the skin with a sharp filleting knife. Make 6 incisions in the fish at equal intervals and insert half an anchovy fillet wrapped in a sage leaf.

Spread out the piece of caul and pat it dry with a clean cloth. Wrap the fish, using as little caul as possible. Tie the parcel lightly to secure the caul and rub it with olive oil. Set the fish in a small baking dish with the smashed garlic cloves alongside, and drizzle over the rest of the oil.

Cook in a very hot oven 240°C (460°F) for 20 minutes. At the end of this time inspect the fish. It should feel firm but not hard, the juices should look like white pearls, and the caul itself should be golden.

Unwrap the fish and slice. Each portion should be accompanied by a generous portion of anchovy butter, some plain steamed potatoes rolled thickly in parsley and, when in season, some oval red tomatoes, peeled and gently softened in butter with salt and pepper in a covered pan. This is a very gentle dish and relies on superb fish and sensitive timing. The cooking time will vary depending on the thickness of the fish rather than its weight. The cooked fish can rest, covered, in a hot dish for 10 minutes if it is ready before you are.

Anchovy butter is one of my favourite things, and I frequently use it with fish. Traditionally, in France, it is served with red mullet or other whole baked fish. It is often incorporated into red wine butter sauces, which I enjoy more than the more usual beurre blanc. Whenever I serve anchovy butter with fish and steamed potatoes, I find that I spread the butter thickly on the potatoes as well as the fish!

Red wine sauces with fish sounds bizarre to many people. My former husband disliked them very much and I love them. So be warned: this is controversial stuff!

One of the most startlingly dramatic and delicious dishes I have eaten was a ragôut of red mullet and sea bass with spinach and beet stems at Alain Chapel's in Mionnay. The dish was sauced with a crimson stain on the plate in which a few slicks of melting butter trailed. It was a daring composition: the sauce more a strong 'note' than an accompaniment. I imagine it was made by reducing red wine with shallots and some red wine vinegar until the reduction was quite syrupy before the small amount of butter was swirled into the pan. No attempt was made to complete the liaison.

## FILLETS of RED MULLET or CORAL PERCH with RED WINE BUTTER SAUCE

- 6 × 250 g (8 oz) whole fish or 6 × 180 g (6 oz) fillets
- 500 ml (16 fl oz) red wine
- 250 ml (8 fl oz) red wine vinegar
- 1 tablespoon sugar
- 2 shallots, chopped very finely or ½ small onion, chopped finely
- ½ bay leaf, parsley stalks
- 300 g (10 oz) unsalted butter or 250 g (8 oz) unsalted butter and 60 g (2 oz) anchovy butter

- 12 cloves garlic, peeled
- 12 small, peeled pickling onions, cooked till just tender in lightly salted water
- 24 small mushrooms
- oil

Fillet the fish and place the fillets in the refrigerator until needed.

Place the fish bones (skeleton only, not head) in an enamelled pan with the wine, the vinegar, the sugar, the shallots and the bay leaf and the parsley. Simmer until it has reduced by three-quarters.

Strain the sauce reduction and transfer it to a clean, small pan. Bring to the boil and mount with the butter, adding it one piece at a time, and whisking all the time. Do not let the sauce get too hot. (Re-read the comments on page 42.) Check for seasoning.

Place the garlic, onions and the mushrooms in a small, oiled baking dish. Shake to coat with the oil and roast in a moderate oven for 10 minutes until they are tender, and the onion and garlic are golden. Set aside.

## To COOK THE FISH

Place a non-stick pan on the flame to get really hot. Slap in the fillets of fish, skin side down. The skin should hiss as it sears. Cook for 1 minute and then turn the fillets and cook the other side for 1 minute.

The red wine sauce will be keeping warm in a jug standing in a pot of hot, but not boiling, water. Drop the garlic, mushrooms and onions into the hot sauce.

Serve the fish fillets onto very hot plates, skin side uppermost, as it is so pretty, and spoon the sauce, garlic, onions and mushrooms around. If you wish to serve steamed potatoes with this dish, offer them from a heated bowl as they look a bit strange mixed with the reddish-brown sauce.

The French prize the liver of the red mullet, and would either sear it for a second or two in the non-stick pan and serve alongside the fish as a special garnish, or sear, purée and incorporate the liver into the sauce.

Alain Dutournier is one of my favourite French chefs. For many years I have eaten his interesting and aromatic dishes at Au Trou Gascon. He has now also established his more formal restaurant Le Carré des Feuillants near to the Place Vendôme in Paris. Alain's food has always been special in that he has managed to design dishes and whole menus that celebrate the fine products traditional to the Gascons, but he has also shown a sensitive understanding of the spices and flavours of North Africa, India and even farther afield. In the midst of that period of excess when chefs seemed to be determined to display dishes with unfortunate flavour-combinations, I always found that although Alain's dishes were out of the ordinary, they tasted wonderful. His *escabèche* of red mullet with eggplant is a successful and personal version of a method used to marinate cold fish in many cultures. The word is originally Spanish, but is known as a *scabèche* in North Africa, *escavèche* in Belgium, and *escoveitch* in Jamaica.

He prepares tiny onions with sultanas, lemon, tomato and chilli and spices, such as cumin and coriander. This mixture is used to marinate the rapidly seared fillets of fish, which are then served with a purée made from roasted eggplants mixed with torn mint.

Red mullet seems to be more readily available in Sydney than in Melbourne, but don't let the non-availability of red mullet put you off trying the dish. It is equally good with small tail fillets of flathead. The method for escoveitched fish from Jamaica is a little different and is much sharper. It could be served with avocado pear, but in Jamaica would probably be served with johnny cakes (a scone mixture that is deep-fried) or bami cakes (a flat unleavened bread made from cassava flour). I have given a recipe for parsnip chips on page 59. The chips are just as delicious if made from sweet potato, and a basket of these would be an appropriate side dish for the pickled fish.

## MONTY'S ESCOVEITCHED FISH

In Jamaica the fish selected for this dish was more often whole small fish, such as small snapper, parrot fish or mackerel. The initial frying time in the hot oil would obviously be much longer for these than for tiny fillets.

- 1 kg (2 lb) boneless fish fillets, skin on, such as red mullet, coral perch, flathead
- salt, pepper

- olive oil
- juice of 2 limes
- zest of 1 lime, removed in thin strips with a zester

- 2 onions, sliced into paper-thin rounds (red onions are best)
- 2 hot chillis, slit, seeded and cut into julienne shreds
- 2 tablespoons whole allspice, cracked with a meat mallet
- I cup cider vinegar
- I teaspoon salt
- coarsely cracked white pepper
- I choko or chocho or christophene, sliced, and cut into strips (the pale seed can be sliced also) or I cucumber, peeled, sliced lengthwise, seeds removed and cut into thick strips
- I sweet red pepper

Lightly season the fish fillets.

Heat oil in a non-stick pan and sear the fish, skin side down. The fish should be turned after I minute. Cook the other side for I minute and then remove the fish to a deep platter. Sprinkle over the lime juice and the lime zest.

To make the pickle, place the onions, chilli, allspice, vinegar, salt and pepper in an enamelled pan. Bring to the boil, drop in the strips of choko, the sliced choko seed or the cucumber, and the strips of red pepper and simmer for 2 minutes. Pour this hot pickle over the fried fish. Allow to marinate for several hours. I prefer to serve this at room temperature rather than refrigerate it overnight. There is no need to peel chokoes unless they are no longer young.

## JAMAICAN JOHNNY CAKES

These johnny cakes are real 'soul food'. They are undeniably heavy and a bit indigestible, but a much-loved way of sopping up gravy and juices.

- 375 g (12 oz) plain flour
- I teaspoon baking powder
- ¼ teaspoon salt
- I teaspoon lard
- I teaspoon butter
- cold water to mix
- oil for frying

Sift flour, baking powder and salt. Cut in the lard and the butter with a pastry-cutter or with fingertips and add sufficient cold water to make a soft scone-type dough.

Roll out 1 cm (½ in) thick. Cut in rounds and fry in deep, hot oil until golden.

The last two dishes present cold, cooked fish. Increasingly, the public is showing a great liking for raw fish and for cured fish. Raw salmon is almost universally offered these days in French starred restaurants. It is delicious, and is a splendid start to a meal, leaving the mouth clean and stimulated. If you have a spanking fresh fillet of salmon or ocean trout, or blue-eye trevalla, or tuna, serve it raw. Remember that the fish must be, beyond question, very fresh. The fillet should be plucked of all tiny bones. It should be deep-chilled to facilitate cutting, and the knife used should be a proper long-bladed salmon knife and very sharp.

Accompaniments range from the very simple (a cut lemon or lime, a jug of virgin olive oil, a scattering of chives or chervil, some coarsely cracked white pepper, a flake or two of sea salt) to the more adventurous.

A Japanese influence will bring pickled pink ginger slivers, a dipping sauce of light soy with rice wine, a tiny pyramid of green wasabi horse-radish and a tangle of fine daikon or white radish shreds. Often the fish will be cut thickly into precise strips, rather than paper-thin. Other seasonings that I have used have included crushed coriander seeds, a paste of green peppercorns spread very lightly over the fish, or a fine grating of raw unsoaked salt cod instead of salt. One can roll the raw fish at the last minute around little pieces of Japanese vegetable pickle or make sushi rolls with the raw tuna. Soaked, sautéed hijiki seaweed can be combined with bean curd and sesame paste, as I have mentioned on page 3, to make an interesting side-salad, and so on and so on. I have described our dish Petals of Raw Fish in my first book, Stephanie's Menus for Food Lovers, and I gave the recipe for pickled ginger.

In that recipe I mentioned that the bright pink colour of much of the com-mercially available pickled ginger is the result of being dyed. I still believe that this is so, but since the publication of my first book Gail Thomas, who is responsible for many of the interesting vegetable plants that grow in our garden, has successfully grown perilla (Perilla frutescens crispa) also known as beefsteak plant. As she says in her book A Gourmet Harvest:

Both the leaves and the seeds of the red/purple perilla are used for culinary purposes. The leaves can be used fresh or pickled—the Japanese use them in making tempura. The addition of both seeds and leaves to pickled root ginger gives it the rich red colour, making it a spectacular garnish.

Sugar-cured fish is also very popular. Known as gravlaks in Scandinavia, the word means 'buried salmon'. Originally the fish was salted, spiced, wrapped and buried in the earth. Today we use a variety of fish, although salmon is still my favourite, and after salting and spicing the fish is weighted and kept under refrigeration for 1–3 days, depending on the size of the fish. Tuna is also very good cured by this method. Recipes vary in the proportions of salt and sugar.

---

## SUGAR-CURED SALMON or TUNA or TREVALLA or other FIRM-TEXTURED LARGE FISH

---

Traditionally, in Scandinavia, this dish is accompanied by a mustard sauce.

- 1 large fillet of fish, at least 1 kg (2 lb)
- 400 g (14 oz) sugar
- 500 g (1 lb) rock salt

- 4 cloves garlic, lightly smashed
- ¼ bunch dill, chopped roughly
- ¼ cup Noilly Prat vermouth

Ensure that all small bones have been removed from the fish, using tweezers. Mix sugar, salt, garlic, dill and vermouth together. Rub the fish fillet well with this mixture. Bury the fish in the mixture, cover it with a sheet of plastic and press weights on the fish. Place in the refrigerator. Turn the fish after 12 hours and every 12 hours after: 24 hours' curing will be long enough if the fillet is less than 1 kg (2 lb). If larger, allow an extra 24 hours.

Remove excess salt and herbs and pat the fish dry before slicing it thinly. Serve with rye bread, fresh horseradish stirred into some cream, or with hot toast, or any other way you fancy.

### — SCANDINAVIAN MUSTARD SAUCE — FOR GRAVLAKS

2 tablespoons Dijon mustard, stirred together with 3 teaspoons red wine vinegar and 1 teaspoon sugar. Add 4–6 tablespoons good olive oil and stir vigorously to emulsify. Season with salt and pepper and add chopped dill if you wish.

## SALADE TAHITIENNE

All over the Pacific region fish is cured using lemons or limes. In Tahiti and in New Caledonia I have eaten raw fish salads that were delicious, flavoured with rich coconut milk. Usually the fish is served cut into small pieces, but there is no reason why it could not be cut into thin slices before being marinated.

- 500 g (I lb) skin-free, firm, white fish fillets (choose any favourite sweet variety of fish)
- juice of 2 limes or I lemon
- ½ cup coconut milk (see below)
- ½ red pepper, cut into small dice
- ½ green pepper, cut into small dice
- I ripe tomato, skinned, seeded and cut into dice
- ½ small red onion, cut into paper-thin rings

Cut fish into cubes or into thin slices. Put into a glass bowl and pour over the citrus juice. Cover and chill for a minimum of 3 hours, no more than 8. Turn the fish after an hour.

When the fish is quite opaque, drain it through a stainless steel strainer or colander. Press gently to extract as much of the liquid as possible. Discard this liquid. Spoon the coconut milk over the fish. Arrange on a flat plate or in an empty coconut shell with the peppers and tomatoes as a base for the white fish. Strew over the onion rings.

For a more South-east Asian salad, you could omit the sweet peppers and tomatoes and substitute a little finely chopped lemongrass, some shredded mint and perhaps a drop or two of fish sauce. Tinned cocount milk is adequate for this dish, but fresh is better.

### — COCONUT MILK —

Place 400 ml (13 fl oz) of desiccated coconut and 500 ml (16 fl oz) boiling water in a blender and blend for a minute. Strain through a double piece of muslin, squeezing well. This is the first milk and is richer in flavour. Use it for the salad. Repeat the process, using another 500 ml (16 fl oz) of hot water. This milk will have a good flavour, but will be thinner. Use for a curry. Don't discard the squeezed coconut. Use it to make a cake or biscuits.

I haven't mentioned poached fish or wrapped fish or deep-fried fish or steamed fish. I have favourite fish dishes using each of these methods. Some are so simple that it is pointless to give a recipe.

When poaching fish, remember to drain it well. Use a fish kettle with a rack, if you have one, as a large fish is quite difficult to lift from a conventional baking dish. If you do not have one, use bands of foil under the fish with ends dangling over the side of the dish to facilitate removal. You will probably need help.

At lunch with some very dear friends we feasted on poached salmon, steamed yellow potatoes and a generous bowl of mayonnaise into which had been stirred an equally generous amount of chopped parsley, tarragon and chervil. I find it hard to do better than this for poached fish.

Fish can be wrapped in all manner of things: foil, parchment, lettuce leaves or banana leaves, to name a few. In Australia's far north there is an abundance of banana leaves, coconuts and barramundi. Those three combine to produce a wonderful parcel for baking in the oven or over a barbecue. This dish was a speciality of the Catalina Restaurant, at Port Douglas, a paradise on earth found in Far North Queensland. Banana leaves are not just protective and very decorative, they impart a definite sappy, 'green' flavour to the fish. Unwrapped, the fish is moist and surrounded by its juices, which have mingled beautifully with the coconut. A successful variation is to stew softly sweet peppers, celery and tomato and to add fresh chillis to taste.

---

## STEAMED BARRAMUNDI with
## GENTLE SPICES
### (from Catalina Restaurant, Port Douglas)

- fresh fillets of barramundi (or similar fish)
- 2 large onions
- oil
- 1 lemon
- 2 cloves garlic
- 2 large green peppers
- 1 teaspoon fresh chopped ginger
- ½ cup fresh coriander leaves
- 1 teaspoon ground cumin
- ½ teaspoon ground fenugreek
- ½ cup grated fresh coconut
- 1 teaspoon garam masala
- salt
- foil
- banana leaves

Chop one of the onions finely and sauté in a little oil. Peel and segment the lemon, removing the pips. Peel the garlic. De-seed the peppers. Put the lemon segments, the second onion, ginger, garlic and peppers, coriander leaves, cumin, fenugreek into the blender. Process until fine, then add the grated coconut. Blend a little longer. Combine with the softened onion, stir in the garam masala and season with salt. Cook the mixture gently for 15 minutes.

Cut pieces of foil and banana leaf in large enough pieces to wrap single serves. Blanch the banana leaves in boiling water to soften.

Put the foil pieces on the bench, lay a piece of banana leaf on top, then a piece of fish fillet and top with some prepared vegetable purée. Wrap the banana leaf around the fish, then the foil around the lot, so that if the leaf breaks in cooking, no juice will be lost. Steam for 15 minutes.

The whole world seems to love deep-fried fish. Whenever it is on the menu it is amazingly popular. We use either King George whiting or one of our mighty deep-sea fish, hapuka. If neither of these is available, occasionally we are lucky and can obtain whitebait. I use the beer batter, for which I have given the recipe on page 57. Whitebait are tossed very lightly in flour only. Sometimes we have superb sardines, lovely with a spicy tomato sauce. I have taken the Chinese speciality, mermaids' tresses, and used it as a garnish with fried fish as a change from fried parsley.

Mermaids' tresses are finely cut shreds of white cabbage, which are deep-fried for a few seconds only, until they darken. As soon as they are lifted from the oil and drained on kitchen paper they are very lightly salted and a pin of castor sugar is tossed through them. They are wispy and crunchy. Celery leaves are a lovely garnish. They are actually so good that we often serve them as a vegetable among a platter of vegetable fritters. Use only the inner pale yellow leaves. They are best dipped in a more lacy batter than the beer batter.

In 1987 we combined with two chefs from Hong Kong to devise and cook a dinner to celebrate the year of the rabbit. Chef Hui Ping-wing left me this excellent recipe that is suitable when one wants a crisp veiled coating rather than a batter to hold food together or to protect the food from oil.

## CHEF HUI PING-WING'S BATTER

- 250 g (8 oz) cornflour
- 250 ml (8 fl oz) cold water
- ¼ cup egg white

Mix the ingredients together with your hand. You are better able to judge the correct consistency. The batter should drip from your fingers and appear translucent.

I have long been a champion of steam-cooking. The method is shown to its best advantage with fish. It is possible to steam a fillet of fish and eat it quite unadorned, but who would want to? Its appeal is that the method permits of infinite versatility in saucing.

The fish kettle can be used as a steamer by reducing the amount of water one has under the rack. As with all steaming, it is imperative to judge correctly the volume of water needed for the length of time you need steam. Fish will need no more than 3–5 minutes of full steam, depending on the thickness of the fillet. One can buy utensils specifically designed as steamers, and they usually permit the rack to be positioned at different levels so that quite large amounts of water can be included. This is, of course, necessary when steaming a pudding.

## VARIATIONS on a STEAMED FILLET of FISH

1. Season fish with salt and pepper, sauce with Sauce Vierge (tomatoes, oil, lemons, herbs: see page 187–8).
2. Season fish with salt and pepper; sauce with the mussel, parsley and walnut sauce on page 4. Perhaps steam some mussels as well.
3. Season fish with salt and pepper; sauce with the crayfish tomato sauce on page 8–9. Perhaps steam some crayfish legs for a colourful garnish.
4. Season fish with salt and pepper; sauce with a slice of anchovy butter and a lot of chopped parsley (page 41).
5. Season fish with salt and pepper; sauce with a classic beurre blanc, or a beurre blanc into which you stir a large spoonful of hot spinach purée, or a spoonful of butter-sautéed cucumber chunks, etc.

6. Season fish with slivers of ginger, shredded spring onion and pour over a mixture of light soy, rice wine. Steam on a plate to catch all the juices.

## — CLASSIC BEURRE BLANC —

- 3 shallots, chopped very fine or ½ mild onion
- small pinch of white pepper
- 1 glass dry white wine
- 1 tablespoon cream
- 250 g (8 oz) unsalted butter, cut into 6 pieces
- salt, if necessary

Make a reduction by gently simmering the shallots or onion and pepper with the wine in a small enamelled or cast-iron pan until the liquid is practically evaporated and the shallots look moist. Add the cream and boil vigorously for 1 minute. Whisk in the butter one piece at a time, adding the second piece just as the first is absorbed. The butter should be added quickly enough so that the sauce does not overheat and turn into oil. Do this over a moderate flame. Once all the butter is incorporated, taste for salt.

In my experience more people fail with beurre blanc because they are tentative rather than brave. The balance has to be maintained between the sauce getting too hot and oiling (therefore add the cold bits of butter at quite a speed to cool the rest of the sauce) and the other extreme of proceeding so slowly that the sauce is barely tepid.

Keep the sauce warm by standing it in a bain-marie, but insulate the bottom of the jug by placing a folded tea-towel under it.

The final word is—experiment. Fish varieties are different everywhere. Thank goodness! If you like the idea of a recipe, try it with a fish you enjoy.

Although I would strongly deny that I am a vegetarian, I salivate readily at meatless and fishless meals. Vegetables are so versatile, and besides the colours are fantastic! I have found it difficult in this chapter to single out my very favourite recipes.

Some of the best vegetable experiences I have had have been in Italy. On a visit to Piazza del' Erbe in Verona, the oldest market in northern Europe, the bunches of zucchini flowers glowed brilliantly orange. They were stored in ancient wooden buckets under the village pump and kept damp to delay the inevitable closing of the petals. Crimson cherries were displayed strung over wire as we might tuck cherry pairs over a child's ears. The sheen on the golden, red and green peppers and the purple eggplants made one gasp. The skins were taut and healthy: they were very sexy vegetables. On another Italian market excursion, I rose early to view the famous Rialto fish market in Venice. I was too late for the fish, but enjoyed another display of vegetable texture, form and colour.

We ate many dishes using squash blossoms. The most unusual dish was in the Emiliano restaurant at Stresa near Lake Maggiore. It was our farewell dinner after a holiday spent reading, walking and generally marvelling at the empty, faded villas, their stucco colours evoking memories of a long-forgotten paintbox: burnt sienna, rose madder, ochre, umber . . . The chopped flowers had been infused in chicken stock, and the stock was then used to make a glorious, apricot-coloured risotto. At the same meal we had an outstanding dish of wide hand-cut pasta cooked in cream with a generous portion of sliced porcini mushrooms.

Another Italian treat was our first taste of the speciality of Modena, the tortelli or tortellini di zucca, a stuffed pasta with a wonderful medieval mix of sweet and savoury flavours: pumpkin and mustard fruits. Many North African dishes have this same intriguing blend of sweet and savoury. I have included the recipe for a dish of sweetened pumpkin cooked with cinnamon and perfumed with orange-flower water, to be served as a vegetable. I ladle it over some spicy couscous for vegetarians, and it goes beautifully with braised lamb shanks cooked with ginger, saffron and preserved lemons (recipe page 89).

The French do not understand pumpkin. In fact they mostly scorn it, although Paul Bocuse received much acclaim for his pumpkin soup. He serves a whole pumpkin, hollowed and filled with seasoned cream. One scoops the soft flesh into the hot cream. Very rich! I sometimes halve and bake a small pumpkin with a filling of seasoned ricotta cheese. The small butternut or golden nugget variety can be stuffed with almost any filling you might use in a filled pasta. Wrap the filled halves in oiled foil and bake until tender—probably around 30–40 minutes. Slice the filled pumpkin in wedges to serve.

If the French scorn pumpkin, they are incredulous at the idea of using parsnip! Food for the pigs, they think. One of the great tastes is baked parsnips, particularly skinny ones so that the ends are quite brown and chewy. Our parsnip chips are delicious, and the staff pounce on any that are left over at the end of service.

Almost every antipasto in Italy included eggplant. Frequently they were cut on the bias with the skin left on, good olive oil poured over (and they are greedy for oil), and then the slices were grilled over a wood fire. I was surprised to see so much cooking done over open fires, both in northern Italy and in Burgundy. It produced excellent results, and in both cases the equipment was extremely basic. A series of hinged wire grills (such as we take on a picnic) was used, suitable for either fish, meat or vegetables, with a simple arrangement of layered racks permitting a particular item to be closer to or farther away from the coals.

We spent a few days in the hill towns of Umbria. At the Ristorante il Molino at Spello I was introduced to my first bruschetta rustica as part of a procession of lovely dishes that made up the lavish antipasto for our Sunday lunch. A large slice of the local beige-coloured bread was grilled, rubbed with a cut clove of garlic, and three cooked artichoke bottoms were mashed onto it with a film of green extra virgin oil. The other 'flavours' served were minced white truffles, a purée of fat, white butter beans, and a purée of fresh, uncooked tomatoes.

Perhaps the very finest antipasto was experienced at Urbino. We arrived on a perfect early summer's afternoon and walked around the walls of the famous ducal palace to feel the atmosphere of this lovely town. One looks down onto a landscape of cypresses, rolling gold-green hills with, in the foreground, great elder trees with their spreading panicles of creamy flowers. It looked so classically perfect that I could almost imagine a Madonna and child in the foreground, so much did it evoke a Giovanni Bellini painting.

The palace itself is justly famous for its elegance and beautiful proportions. The spacious rooms with their vaulted ceilings and glowing tiled terracotta floors were magnificent, and the decorative stonework was reminiscent of the designs we see on Florentine notepaper. The antipasto at the local trattoria was outstanding. A few strips of lonza ham, made from a fillet of pork, and then an arrangement of vegetables, all with shining, strong colours.

We ate grilled, sliced zucchini with a rich smoky flavour from the grill. Roasted skinned peppers, grilled eggplant slices, mealy, fat white beans, artichoke hearts cooked, quartered and deep-fried with a coating of eggs, Parmesan and parsley, small, wrinkled garlicky black olives, and the dressing was a bowl of green olive oil, thick with fresh chopped parsley and a few roughly chopped garlic cloves.

Each ingredient impressively simple, ordinary one might say, but each ingredient accorded just the right amount of tender loving care.

## COOKED ZUCCHINI FLOWERS

Remove most of the stalk, leaving just enough to hold in order to dip the flower in either a batter or egg and breadcrumbs. Snip off the green sepals.

The flowers close up a short time after being picked, so have the stuffing ready if you intend to stuff them. The flower that has the baby fruit attached is the female. The larger flower on a simple stalk is the male. Both can be stuffed. In Italy it is more usual to stuff the male flower.

There are many possible fillings, and remember that there is no need to stuff them at all. Sautéed in butter, they have a delicate flavour, not surprisingly rather like garden-grown, very small zucchini!

## — ZUCCHINI SOUFFLÉ FILLING —

- 250 g (8 oz) zucchini
- 1 egg
- 1 extra egg white
- 3 tablespoons Parmigiano-Reggiano
- pepper, salt

## — BÉCHAMEL —

- 1 tablespoon butter
- 1 tablespoon flour
- 1/3 cup warm milk

## — SUGGESTED FILLINGS —

1. Cooked rice, mixed with a little cooked onion, toasted pinenuts, chopped parsley and some best quality Parmigiano-Reggiano.
2. Mozzarella cheese and a small amount of chopped anchovy.
3. Leftovers of a risotto made with mushrooms, peas, fish or anything else.
4. Salsa verde (recipe page 101).
5. Make a soufflé base by combining some lightly cooked, very well-drained chopped zucchini with a thick béchamel sauce. Beat in some Parmesan and egg yolk, lighten with egg whites, spoon into the flowers, fold over the petals and dip quickly in a light batter and deep-fry for at least 8 minutes to cook and puff the mixture. You will need only a heaped teaspoonful of the mixture for each flower, and you will need to serve the flowers at once.

## TWO FRYING BATTERS

Everyone has his or her own favourite recipe for a batter. I have included two that I use all the time. Please use your own if you prefer it. There is a third batter recipe on page 51.

## — BEER BATTER —

This batter has the advantage of not needing to rest before using it, so that if you run out you can simply add more flour and adjust with beer and water to the correct consistency.

- 500 g (1 lb) self-raising flour
- salt
- 250 ml (8 fl oz) beer
- 600 ml (20 fl oz) water

Mix flour with salt. Make a well and gradually stir in first the beer and then the water until you have a smooth batter the consistency of thick cream. Reserve a little of the water, as all flours are different and will absorb more or less liquid.

## — WHITE WINE BATTER —

- 300 g (10 oz) plain flour
- pinch of salt
- 2 tablespoons olive oil
- 4 tablespoons dry white wine
- 350 ml (12 fl oz) water
- 6 egg whites

Sift flour with salt. Make a well and add the oil and the wine. Start to mix to incorporate some of the flour. Add the water gradually, mixing vigorously to avoid lumps. Let the batter rest for 1 hour. Just before using, fold in the firmly whisked egg whites. Use without delay. This batter gives a thicker coating than the beer batter.

There is a lot of vigorous beating called for in both of these batter recipes. I am not one to strain my muscles unless I am quite convinced it is necessary. I make these preparations in my food-processor. It is important to stop the machine and carefully scrape the bottom as it is easy to allow a layer of flour and liquid to become caked on the bottom of the food-processor bowl.

## TORTELLINI DI ZUCCA
### (as enjoyed at the Ristorante Greppia in Verona)

• 300 g (10 oz) pasta, using recipe and method on page 7

• 2 envelopes powdered saffron (add to pasta with the eggs)

— FILLING —

• 1 kg (2 lb) butternut pumpkin, or other variety that cooks dry (weighed with skin and seeds removed)
• 100 g (3 oz) mustard fruits, sold as mostarda di Cremona, puréed till smooth in a food-processor

• 100 g (3 oz) fresh breadcrumbs
• 1 tablespoon Amaretto di Saronno liqueur
• salt, pepper, nutmeg

Cut skinned pumpkin into even-shaped pieces and steam until tender. Dry off in a low oven for 5 minutes. Purée the pumpkin and add the puréed mustard fruits, breadcrumbs and Amaretto. Season with salt, pepper and nutmeg. Chill thoroughly.

Follow instructions on page 6 for filling ravioli shapes, or shape pasta in any way you prefer. Snap-freeze on flat tray, dusted with flour.

— TO SERVE AND SAUCE —

• 3 fresh sage leaves, per serve

• 1 tablespoon best quality unsalted butter, per serve

Have a pot with 5 litres (8 pints) of water at a rolling boil. Add salt and a spoonful of oil to the water. Make sure the pasta bowls are very hot. Drop in the tortellini. Boil for 5–7 minutes, depending on the thickness of the pasta. Test one for tenderness. Drain at once. Transfer to heated bowl and at the same time place sage leaves in a heavy-bottomed pan already heating over moderate heat until the leaves start to crisp at the edges. Drop in the butter, which should hiss, melt and sizzle instantly. Splash the sage leaves and foaming butter over the dish and rush to the table with it. The best possible Parmigiano-Reggiano cheese should already be at the table so that there is no delay before tucking into this delicious dish.

# PERFUMED PUMPKIN

This recipe is taken from a book called *North African Cookery* by Arto der Haroutunian, a splendid and exciting collection of dishes from Morocco, Algeria, Tunisia and Libya. The original version uses dried jujube (*Ziziphus jujuba/ Ziziphus sativa*), apparently a fruit of Indian origin that grows in warm climates. Haroutunian describes them as being olive-sized and covered with a smooth, leathery red skin. The recipe in the book is called Maslouq and is for gourd. We have substituted pumpkin and call our modified version of the dish Perfumed Pumpkin. The only jujube I have found is a pickle sold in the Asian supermarket, so I have omitted it from our version.

- 1 kg (2 lb) pumpkin cut into 5 cm (2 in) cubes (weighed after skinning and seeding)
- 450 ml (15 fl oz) water
- 30 g (1 oz) butter
- 1 onion, very finely chopped
- 1/4 teaspoon black pepper
- 1/4 teaspoon ground ginger
- 1/2 teaspoon ground cinnamon
- 1/2 teaspoon salt
- 1 envelope powdered saffron
- 1 tablespoon icing sugar
- 1 tablespoon orange-blossom water

Place water, butter, onion and all spices in a pan and bring to the boil. Simmer together for 5 minutes. Add pumpkin and cook gently until just tender (about 10 minutes, depending on variety). Stir in the sugar and orange-blossom water. Simmer a further 5 minutes.

Serve as a vegetable to accompany a North African tagine, a spicy, rather liquid, stew, or with a sweet chutney or relish over a plateful of couscous, barley or brown rice. The liquid will have reduced to provide a fragrant sauce.

# OUR PARSNIP CHIPS

If possible, choose parsnips that are fat in shape rather than very thin. There are no quantities for this dish; my experience is that they will all be eaten no matter how many you make.

Peel parsnips and slice lengthwise very thinly, using a mandoline for preference. The slices should be 2 mm thick.

If you have an electric deep-fryer, heat oil to 160°C (320°F) and fry the slices for 2–3 minutes until golden brown. Do not crowd the fryer.

Lift the slices from the oil and drain on layers of kitchen paper. Shake over a little salt or poppyseeds. The chips are delicious hot or cold.

If you do not have a thermostatically controlled electric fryer, you can still fry the chips in a heavy pan in oil to a depth of 5 cm (2 in). It is advisable to check the temperature of the oil with a thermometer. If the chips are intended to be eaten cold with drinks or as the 'biscuit' for a dip, it is probably a good idea to complete the frying well before your guests arrive, as deep-frying needs your full attention.

While on the subject of deep-frying, I am instantly reminded of all manner of delicious, crispy titbits, namely vegetable fritters.

Providing the cook has taken care that the oil is of good quality and is scrupulously clean, that the thermostat or thermometer is reliable, and that there is lots of clean kitchen paper to drain them on, fritters are never greasy or indigestible.

## JERUSALEM ARTICHOKE FRITTERS
### with GARLIC MAYONNAISE

- 500 g (1 lb) large, firm Jerusalem artichokes
- ¼ cup vinaigrette, with chopped parsley or chives

- batter for dipping (see recipes on page 57, or use your favourite one)
- garlic or herb mayonnaise

Peel the artichokes, smoothing off any knobs. Cut into thick slices, about 1.5 cm (½ in), and steam-cook until just tender. Marinate in the vinaigrette for an hour.

Heat the oil in the deep-fryer or heavy frying-pan to 190°C (375°F). Drain the artichoke slices, dip in the batter and deep-fry. Drain on kitchen paper and serve piping hot with the mayonnaise. An alternative sauce would be any of the butter sauces, hollandaise or bearnaise.

```
╔══════════════════════════════════╗
║      WESTERN-STYLE               ║
║      CARROT FRITTERS             ║
╚══════════════════════════════════╝
```

- 3 cups grated carrot
- 220 g (7 oz) plain flour
- 3 tablespoons finely chopped shallots
- 1 tablespoon chopped parsley
- 1 tablespoon baking powder
- 1 teaspoon salt
- ½ teaspoon ground pepper
- 1 teaspoon fresh thyme or oregano leaves
- ¾ cup milk
- oil for deep-fryer

Mix all measured ingredients together gently. Cover and allow flavours to blend for a couple of hours. Heat oil to 180°C (350°F) and drop spoonfuls of the batter into the oil. Fry until golden brown, about 10 minutes, turning once. Drain the fritters on kitchen paper and serve as a first course with a sauce bearnaise. If you make much smaller fritters, they can be eaten quite plain as a pre-dinner offering.

```
╔══════════════════════════════════╗
║      INDIAN-STYLE                ║
║      CARROT FRITTERS             ║
╚══════════════════════════════════╝
```

- 150 g (5 oz) plain flour
- 1½ teaspoons ground cumin
- 1½ teaspoons ground coriander
- ½ teaspoon turmeric
- ¼ teaspoon cayenne
- 1½ teaspoons salt
- ½ cup beer
- 1 large egg, beaten to mix
- 6 spring onions, chopped (include most of the green tops)
- 150 g (5 oz) grated carrot

Sift the salt and spices with the flour and place in a bowl. Add the beer and the beaten egg, mixing well. Stir in the chopped spring onions and the carrots.

Heat oil to 180°C (350°F) and deep-fry by the spoonful until golden brown. You will need to turn the fritters once. Drain well on paper. I serve these as pre-dinner snacks on a flat plate covered with well-washed, tender sprigs of coriander.

## ZUCCHINI FRITTERS

- 3 zucchini, grated
- 2 eggs
- 3 spring onions, finely chopped
- 1/4 cup chopped parsley
- 1/4 cup chopped mint or basil
- 1/2 cup grated Gruyère cheese
- 1/4 cup plain flour, approximately
- salt, pepper

In a large bowl mix together the grated zucchini, eggs, spring onions, herbs and cheese. Gradually add enough flour to add cohesion, but not to make the mixture thick or pasty. Season to taste. Deep-fry at 190°C (375°F) until golden brown. This will take only a few minutes. Do not fry any longer, as the cheese will ooze. Drain and serve as they are or with a sour-cream dip, or a sauce bearnaise, or a mayonnaise, or a fresh tomato sauce, or yoghurt and so on.

## CHEESE FRITTERS

These should not really be in a chapter about vegetables, but I have made an exception as they are excellent served with a green salad or as part of a platter of mixed vegetable fritters.

Frequently one sees platters of cold vegetable fritters as part of an antipasto table in Italy. I don't find cold fried food very appetising, and would prefer to eat my fritters piping hot, probably with a dipping sauce of tomatoes, chillis and roasted red peppers. For a change, serve a small bowl of freshly roasted spices in which to roll each fritter.

- 250 g (8 oz) best-quality Gruyère cheese
- 3 egg whites
- salt

Grate the cheese, keeping it as loosely packed as possible. Beat the egg whites firmly, sprinkle over one-third of the grated cheese. Fold in gently. Add the rest of the cheese and fold in gently. The mixture will be lumpy.

Fry in small spoonfuls at 190°C (375°F) until golden brown, about 4–5 minutes. Drain well and serve as a special garnish with a bitter-leaf salad— such as curly endive or torn radicchio.

There are hundreds of fancier recipes for vegetable fritters, but I'm sure you get the idea. Vegetables can be sliced thin and sandwiched with thin slices of onion (beetroot, for example), or cheese (eggplant), before being dipped in a batter and deep-fried. Vegetables that actually require some cooking in the oil rather than just browning should be fried at a lower temperature: 160°C (320°F) or 180°C (350°F), not 190°C (375°F).

## SPINACH and COCONUT CREAM SOUP with COCONUT WAFERS

Here is a recipe for a spinach soup I found in an Australian cookery magazine. It is extremely easy, but its relevance here is that it has as one ingredient a mix of roasted spices. I have given quantities of spices far in excess of that needed for the soup so that you can enjoy them with some crispy mouthfuls.

- 1 bunch spinach, stemmed and washed
- 1 large onion, finely chopped
- 2 tablespoons butter
- 3 cups good chicken stock
- 180 ml (6 fl oz) coconut cream
- 2 teaspoons roasted spices
- shredded spinach to garnish

### — ROASTED SPICE MIXTURE —

- 2 tablespoons coriander seeds
- 1 tablespoon cumin seeds
- 2 tablespoons black peppercorns
- 1 teaspoon cardamom pods
- 2 cinnamon sticks, crumbled
- 1/2 teaspoon whole cloves
- 1/2 nutmeg

Roast the spices (except the nutmeg) one at a time in a heavy iron pan until they start to smell fragrant. Put all roasted spices into a spice-grinder (coffee-grinder) and grind to a powder. Grate in half a fresh nutmeg.

Store the mixture in a screw-top jar until needed. The spice mixture is great sprinkled on vegetable fritters or many other dishes. In households where salt is not used, the spice mixture can enliven dishes that might otherwise taste flat. ▸

Chop the spinach roughly, reserving a few leaves for garnish. Sweat the onion for 3–5 minutes in the butter. Add the spinach and stir until it has wilted. Add the stock and simmer 5 minutes. Purée the soup in a blender, return to the pan and add the coconut cream and the spices. Cut reserved spinach leaves into julienne and scatter over the soup.

## — COCONUT WAFERS —
### (from Charmaine Solomon's *Complete Asian Cookbook*)

- ½ cup rice flour
- 2 tablespoons ground rice
- 1½ teaspoons roasted spice mixture
- ¼ teaspoon ground turmeric
- ½ teaspoon salt
- 1 cup coconut milk, canned or fresh (see page 48)

- 1 clove garlic, crushed
- 1 small onion, very finely chopped
- ¾ cup freshly grated or desiccated coconut
- oil for frying

Sift all dry ingredients and the coconut into a bowl. Add the coconut milk, garlic and onion. Heat oil to very hot. Test one wafer. It should be thin enough to spread into a lacy wafer. If too thick, add a little water. Fry until golden on each side. Drain on paper.

---

## ROASTED EGGPLANT with PARSLEY and ANCHOVY

---

Anglo-Saxons seem to be wary of this superbly versatile vegetable. Do try to select examples that are of medium size. The very big ones are more likely to have pronounced seeds, and frequently have been tunnelled by little worms. The skin should be trim, taut and terrific, as in Italy.

Slice as many eggplants as you wish lengthwise into 1 cm (½ in) slices. Heat a layer of olive oil in a baking pan until hot, and then place the eggplant slices in the oil, side by side. They should sizzle as they touch the oil. Return the pan to the oven and check after 5 minutes. If the underside is golden, turn the slices with a spatula and bake for a further 5–7 minutes. Lift out the slices, drain them on paper, then arrange the slices on a flat plate and scatter over a mixture of chopped parsley with a finely chopped fillet or two of anchovy and a finely chopped clove of garlic. Grind over some pepper. Like most oily dishes this is at its best warm or hot and should not be served chilled.

If your eggplants are not as wonderful as you would like, you will need to salt them lightly for 1 hour to draw out the bitter juices, rinse, dry well and then proceed to oven bake the slices.

Slices prepared the same way could be dipped in any of the frying batters and deep-fried. They are delicious served like this with a wedge of lemon and a spicy home-made tomato sauce.

During the early eighties, vegetable custards were very much in vogue. There were terrines constructed of layers of separately baked vegetable custards, individual custards served as an accompaniment to a meat dish, and dishes that combined a vegetable custard with a non-vegetable. One of the nicest of these was the green pea and foie gras terrine with a hazelnut oil dressing at Girardet in Crissier, Switzerland. I have included recipes for three vegetable custards: a mushroom terrine that is an accompaniment to a dish of sautéed sweetbreads (recipe, page 155), a spinach and ricotta terrine and a garlic custard. The recipe for the garlic custard, or flan, is quite delicious, but very, very strong. I make it in porcelain snail pots and serve it with pot-roasted white rabbit. It is intended more as a seasoning.

## MUSHROOM TERRINE

This is an autumn dish, and any sort of mushrooms can be used. We particularly like to use the golden pine forest mushrooms, which are plentiful in the autumn. They have a glorious colour and a 'meaty' texture. I also include dried mushrooms, but they do add to the expense of the dish and can be omitted. Usually we are lucky enough to be able to buy real mushrooms in the autumn; that is, mushrooms with black gills, which smell of damp leaves and run with shiny, black juices when cooked. The small cultivated button mushrooms slice neatly and are more delicate in raw mushroom salads, but it is the glory of the field mushroom that provides the lush flavour in this dish.

- 30 g (1 oz) dried morel or porcini mushrooms
- 2 tablespoons butter
- 250 g (8 oz) button mushrooms
- 250 g (8 oz) field mushrooms
- 150 g (5 oz) golden pine forest mushrooms
- juice of ½ a lemon
- ½ onion, chopped finely
- salt, pepper, nutmeg
- 500 ml (16 fl oz) cream
- 2 egg yolks
- 4 eggs
- chopped parsley

Soak dried mushrooms in plenty of warm water for at least 1 hour. Change the water at least once by lifting the mushrooms out of the water and into a fresh bowl of water. Don't tip the mushrooms through a strainer, as the sand and grit will lodge again in the mushrooms. Cook the soaked mushrooms in fresh water to barely cover until they have absorbed the water or until they taste tender. Drain through a colander and then lightly sauté in the butter for 3–4 minutes. Set aside.

Wipe fresh mushrooms with a damp cloth, trim off any battered edges, peel only if the skins are really tough. Remove stems (keep for the stockpot), and leave the mushrooms whole. Combine cooked dried mushrooms, whole fresh mushrooms, lemon juice, onion and seasonings, and cook in cream for 10 minutes. Drain mushrooms in a colander set over a bowl. Reduce the mushroom cooking cream for 20 minutes, until you have a scant 300 ml (10 fl oz). Strain the cream through a fine strainer, pressing hard on any fragments of onion to extract the maximum flavour. Cool.

Whisk eggs and yolks to combine and add parsley. Mix eggs into cream and then stir in the mushrooms. Taste for seasoning. The nutmeg should be very subtle. Pour the mix into an oiled Le Creuset terrine mould. Check that the mix of mushrooms looks interesting in the mould: not all the orange mushrooms in one spot, a good mix of large and small, buttons and flats. Cook in a baking pan half-filled with boiling water for approximately 50 minutes. Test with a fine skewer to ensure that the custard is quite set in the centre. Allow to cool completely in the bain-marie.

When cold, unmould and slice with a sharp knife. Either serve the terrine cold with a crisp salad as an entrée, or place slices on flat plate and steam hot for 2–3 minutes if the terrine is to accompany sautéed liver or anything you fancy. As its texture is soft, have something crisp somewhere.

# SPINACH RICOTTA TERRINE

- 1 large bunch spinach, washed, stemmed and drained of excess water
- 1 tablespoon olive oil
- 3 spring onions, finely chopped
- 2 cloves garlic, finely chopped
- 350 g (11 oz) very fresh ricotta
- 8 eggs
- 1½ cups pure cream
- ¼ cup grated Parmesan
- seasoning
- light oil for terrine (e.g. grapeseed)

Grease a Le Creuset cast-iron pâté mould. Line with cooking parchment. Oil the sides of the terrine again and the paper. Sprinkle base and sides with the Parmesan.

Heat olive oil in a wok. Add the spring onions and garlic, sauté 1 minute. Add torn spinach. Turn and tumble until spinach is wilted and bright green. Place in food-processor and run until smooth. Add ricotta. Process until smooth. Add eggs, cream and seasoning to taste. Blend well.

Pour into the mould and cover with buttered foil or paper. Bake in a bain-marie at 180°C (350°F) for approximately 1 hour. Test to see if the middle is firm. Allow to cool in the bain-marie.

# FRESH PEAR DRESSING

In a blender (NOT the food-processor) purée 2 ripe, juicy pears. Slowly combine with 1 cup walnut oil and 1 cup olive oil. Add salt and pepper and a little good-quality red wine vinegar.

Serve slices of terrine with the sauce around and a salad of watercress leaves, fresh pear slices, a scattering of small olives and some lightly toasted walnuts.

# GARLIC CUSTARD

- 150 g (5 oz) peeled cloves garlic, firm, crisp and white
- 1 cup chicken stock
- 1 tablespoon butter
- ½ teaspoon sugar
- a few drops of white wine vinegar
- salt, pepper
- 1 cup cream
- 60 ml (2 fl oz) milk
- 3 eggs
- 1 egg yolk

Drop garlic into cold water, bring to boil, drain. Repeat process. Chop garlic cloves roughly and place in a small enamelled pan with the stock, butter, sugar, vinegar, salt and pepper. Simmer steadily until the garlic is quite soft and the liquid is reduced to a syrup on the bottom of the pan.

Pour on the cream and the milk and bring to the boil, stirring with a wooden spoon to ensure that no fragment of garlic is sticking. Blend, pass through a fine sieve and cool completely. Mix eggs well. Stir into the garlic reduction. Strain again. Pour into very small, well-buttered moulds. Steam gently or bake in a bain-marie until they are quite set. The length of time will depend on the size of the chosen mould.

The reason we steam these custards is that they are moulded in porcelain snail pots. It is impossible to cook such tiny containers safely in a water bath. If you wished to cook the garlic custards in 60 ml (2 fl oz) moulds, it would be preferable to bake them in the oven with boiling water half-way up, exactly as described for the mushroom terrine.

A bavarois is a special sort of custard, or rather, a custard set with gelatine and lightened with whipped cream. But some dishes described as bavarois are more correctly mousse; that is, they are purées that have quantities of whipped cream folded in and frequently are also set with gelatine. I have included here a trio of favourites, all of which at one time or another have been offered as the complimentary appetiser as customers relax and read the evening's menu.

# RED PEPPER MOUSSE

- 500 g (1 lb) very red peppers
- 2 tablespoons cold water
- pinch of salt
- pinch of sugar
- 175 ml (6 fl oz) cream (approximately)

- 3 leaves or 1½ teaspoons powdered gelatine
- 2 tablespoons boiling water
- 2 teaspoons cognac
- salt, tabasco

Remove seeds and stems of the peppers. Slice roughly. Place in a pan with 2 tablespoons cold water, salt and sugar. Cover and cook gently until the peppers are quite soft, about 30 minutes. Purée the contents of the pan and measure. You will need half the volume of cream.

Whip the cream until it is sludgy. Not an attractive image, perhaps, but quite descriptive. The cream will not fold in properly if it has been over-whipped.

Soak the gelatine leaves for a few minutes in cold water. Squeeze and drop into 2 tablespoons of boiling water. Swish to completely dissolve. Stir the gelatine mixture into the pepper purée. Allow to cool. Season with salt, cognac and a few drops of tabasco. Gently fold in the softly whipped cream. Pour into oiled moulds and leave to set.

If using powdered gelatine, place the 2 tablespoons of water in a cup and stand it in a pan of simmering water. Sprinkle on the powdered gelatine and allow it to dissolve gently. There is no comparison in my mind between the neutral flavour of leaf gelatine and the often gummy taste left after using powdered gelatine. You may not agree.

Unmould the mousse and surround with a pool of fresh tomato vinaigrette (recipe page 187). We serve a slice of toasted olive bread with this summer appetiser.

## AVOCADO MOUSSE

Despite earlier remarks, this mousse has no cream.

- 2 ripe avocados
- 2 leaves gelatine or 1 teaspoon powdered gelatine
- 1 tablespoon water
- salt, pepper
- sherry vinegar
- tabasco
- 1 tablespoon finely chopped parsley
- 1 bunch of young watercress

Soak the gelatine and dissolve it in the water in exactly the same manner as for the red pepper mousse. Purée the avocados in the food-processor and, with the motor running, add the dissolved gelatine mixture. Season the mixture to your own taste, using drops of sherry vinegar and tabasco. Add the parsley.

Sometimes I brush the empty shells of the avocados with lemon juice and spoon the mousse back in and serve it with a green salad. For an appetiser I use the versatile porcelain snail pots, oiled with hazelnut oil, and spoon in the mixture. When they are turned out, we add some sprigs of watercress and either some parsnip chips or Melba toast.

## PARMESAN and PARSLEY BAVAROIS

Parmesan is the English name given to the unique and magnificent Italian cheese Parmigiano-Reggiano. Each cheese has this name incised into the crust and a Parmigiano-Reggiano may, by government decree, be produced only around Parma, Reggio Emilia and Modena. The maturing of the cheese takes between 2 and 3 years: the older the cheese the better and the more expensive.

- $2/3$ cup milk
- 3 egg yolks
- 2 leaves gelatine or 1 teaspoon powdered gelatine
- $1/3$ cup grated Parmigiano-Reggiano
- 1 tablespoon finely chopped parsley
- $1/2$ cup cream

Scald milk. Pour onto beaten egg yolks. Strain into a clean pan and cook until the custard coats the back of a spoon, about 83°C (178°F) on a standard thermometer. Strain into a bowl. Dissolve the gelatine in the same manner as for the two preceding recipes. Add it to the cooling custard. Stir to combine. Add the cheese and the parsley. Allow to cool completely before folding in the softly whipped cream. Pour or spoon into lightly oiled moulds.

These little bavarois are lovely served with hot cheese straws. Sauce them with either the fresh tomato vinaigrette or a vegetable purée, such as asparagus or red pepper thinned to a sauce consistency with a little of their cooking water or a mild chicken stock.

Fashion in food is infuriating! If I found vegetable custards at every turn in Europe in the mid-eighties at least there were fewer plates of baby purées. A well-made purée of an interesting flavour is often the perfect balance to the main dish, but pointless little saucers of tri-coloured pap have dampened the enthusiasm of many, I suspect. Combinations that work very well are parsnip purée with boeuf à la mode, a purée of potato and celeriac with oxtails braised with red wine and olives, a sweet purée of potato and Jerusalem artichoke to accompany a poached loin of lamb, and so on. Apart from flavour, these purées absorb the rich juices and can be enjoyed with a spoon, an alternative to bread for sopping the sauce.

Some of the loveliest and best-loved soups are based on a single vegetable or a combination of vegetables being cooked in stock or water and then puréed. The same principle can be used to make original sauces and dishes. Quickly blanched parsley, cooked in cream and then puréed, makes a luxuriant sauce for poached lamb, or if there is some blanched garlic in the cream, the finished sauce is good with oysters and mussels.

Cook some springtime green peas in chicken stock, purée and season with a few drops of sherry vinegar, and you have an unusual, light sauce to accompany fritters of brains or tripe. I have described this sauce and the dish as it is served at Stephanie's on pages 157–9.

In the heyday of nouvelle cuisine, chefs everywhere abandoned flour-based sauces and substituted clear stocks, which they thickened with large amounts of butter. The stocks were heavily reduced in order to concentrate flavour and to achieve a coating consistency. In many, many cases what also happened was that the natural salts present in the vegetable matter used to make the initial stock became so concentrated that the sauces tasted very salty, even though no extra salt had been added. I find that this reliance on reduction destroys the fresh taste in a sauce. If I have carefully made a stock from the carcasses of some rabbits, I can taste at what point the reduction should cease. At this stage it will still be sweet and delicate, not tarry in flavour. It will also be thin. What I have been doing is adding some separately made puréed vegetable, which adds character and body to my sauce without destroying the delicacy of the stock and without using unhealthy amounts of butter.

Here are some combinations that have been most successful:

Rabbit stock + purée of celeriac

Rabbit stock + purée of apples and Calvados

Duck stock + purée of fresh tomatoes

Red wine beef stock + purée of glazed turnips

Lamb stock + purée of garlic

Chicken stock + purée of parsley.

If you have combined your vegetable purée and your stock in an electric blender, you may be dismayed at the colour of your sauce. Don't be! The blender has whipped a considerable amount of air into your sauce. Simply bring the sauce back to simmering point on the stove, stirring to prevent any solids sticking, and magically the colour will return to your sauce.

You will have to work out your own proportions of purée to stock, as it will depend on the quality and character of your stock and the degree of thickening you want to achieve. I find 500 ml (16 fl oz) of stock needs 200 ml (7 fl oz) of purée.

So much for purées and custards. At the other end of the spectrum is the humble, but favourite, potato. When I was about 10 years old, Dad burnt the summer firebreak around our country house. After the flames died away, there was left a one-metre-high pile of ash—white-hot in the centre. My sister and I spent most of the day poking potatoes into this heap. It was a most efficient oven. After 35 minutes the potatoes were retrieved almost clean of powdery ash, crispy of skin and fluffy inside. We consumed many of them with butter and, of course, burnt our tongues and the roofs of our mouths. I still prefer potatoes baked dry like this rather than roasted in fat. In our family we sometimes gazed in incredulous amazement at guests who delicately ate the centre of their potato and pushed the skin to the side. One of us would devour the skin later in the kitchen. Crisped potato skins are an excellent alternative to bread or biscuits to accompany a vegetable dip or one of the mousse appetisers I have already described.

## CARAWAY BAKED POTATOES

This is a fancier version of the bonfire-baked potatoes.

Wash, but do not peel, the required number of potatoes. Cut in two and dip the cut side first in melted butter then in caraway seeds tossed with a little salt.

Place directly on the rack in the oven and bake for 1 hour at 220°C (430°F).

Even when I decide to omit the caraway seeds, I still select potatoes that are as large as possible so that they can be cut in two. The cut side develops a puffed-up golden skin that is irresistible.

There are so many delightful vegetable dishes that I have not the room to describe them in detail. I shall have to content myself with a few final fleeting references.

Try grilling coarse lettuce leaves. Radicchio, in particular, is excellent brushed with oil and flattened on a cast-iron grill plate for a few seconds. The leaf should be turned, and it will develop a smoky flavour and be brittle (and fragile) at the edges.

A well-made stock can become a ruby consommé if a few raw chunks of beetroot are simmered in it. Serve it at once, as the consommé will change on re-heating from red to a russet colour. At a dinner in Melbourne last year, Jacques Maximim from the Negresco in Nice prepared a superb golden consommé, which was served from tureens at the table. The waiters ladled each serve of aromatic broth onto a pyramid of beetroot julienne. As one dipped the spoon, the beetroot flooded its glorious colour, so that the contents of the bowl were like shot silk.

# LAMB

FEASTS & STORIES

Everyone knows that Australia produces sensational lamb. It is available all year round, with the most delicious being available in springtime. It is also inexpensive, compared with prices in the United States and Europe, and it is everyone's favourite meal. If Mrs Smith cannot think of anything for dinner, she is most likely to grab some middle-loin lamp chops. Apparently Mme Dubois feels the same way. The French magazine *Cuisine et Vins de France* once published the results of a survey showing that most French men and women had nominated a leg of lamb as their all-time-favourite dish. And the overwhelming choice of our American visitors is lamb.

I often choose lamb myself, especially when a sensible cook has decided to leave well enough alone. Grilled lamb cutlets, browned on the outside and softly pink inside, with green beans from the garden, a few cloves of roasted garlic and perhaps some roasted red peppers appeals to me when I am tired, or needing uplifting, far more than pieces of something in a cream sauce with a mousse of something else.

I once ordered a trimmed saddle of lamb from a butcher in the south of France. It was cut from a very dainty beast, probably around 6 kg (12 lb) dressed weight. The piece of meat I collected that afternoon was a work of art. It was boned, trimmed of the breast flap, larded with a discreet amount of rosemary and garlic, and was encased in a thin layer of barding fat. The price was truly amazing! I can no longer remember the number of francs I paid, but I do remember that it was cooked with some reverence.

This year I bought myself a fancy gadget known as a *manche à gigot* in Paris at the beautiful store, Au Bain-marie. I had visions of my next leg of lamb with the shank bone left intact in the French manner. One screws on this elegant silver device and effortlessly carves thin slices from the joint.

The leg of lamb that was sent on my last two attempts was obviously bigger than one I would have received in France. The *manche à gigot* would simply not unscrew far enough to enable me to hold the shank bone at all securely. It is a pretty thing, and if I wait until we are serving suckling lamb again, I'm sure I shall be able to use it. I shared a tiny leg of lamb at Le Gavroche in London last June, and it was very elegantly carved at the table, the *manche à gigot* properly in place, so that the whole procedure was accomplished speedily and with great aplomb.

---

## BONED, STUFFED SADDLE of LAMB
### with GARLIC-SCENTED JUICES

My first lamb recipe requires a boned saddle of lamb. It is an excellent joint to use for a special dinner, as it carves beautifully and will serve 4–6 people. If your guests are accustomed to very large portions of meat, the saddle may serve only 4. All quantities can be doubled. I have given a very simple stuffing, based on my favourite tastes of cooked, puréed garlic and cooked parsley. As with many of the recipes in this book, your own imagination will suggest alternative fillings. I shall describe in detail the preparation of the meat, stuffing, sauce and the cooking and at the end of the recipe give a few tried and true variations.

Instead of asking for a saddle of lamb, my butcher suggests that a more accurate request would be for a pair of middle loins, boned but not split. Ask that the bones be included with the meat.

- I short saddle of lamb, boned
- I head of garlic, cloves peeled
- 2 bunches of young parsley, heads picked off and well washed (keep the stalks, or some of them, for the stock)
- I tablespoon olive oil
- I tablespoon butter
- 200 ml (7 fl oz) cream
- salt, pepper
- 2 bay leaves

## — FOR SAUCE —

- bones from the saddle
- 1 glass white wine
- 1 onion, sliced
- 1 carrot, sliced
- 1 leek, well washed and sliced
- 1 tomato, peeled and seeded
- mushroom trimmings or 100 g (3 oz) sliced mushrooms
- reserved parsley stems
- bay leaf, sprig of thyme
- water OR, better still, light veal or chicken stock
- 15 peeled cloves garlic

### TO PREPARE MEAT

The saddle consists of the two loins, the strips of lean choice meat running lengthwise each side of the backbone. Each loin strip is the equivalent of the porterhouse in beef. Underneath the loins lie two smaller strips of meat, known as lamb fillets or lamb tenderloin. They are the equivalent of the eye fillet in beef. The loin strips are attached to and protected by a covering flap of fat and meat, which extends well over the rib bones. This is called the flap or the apron. Depending on the age of the animal, its variety and the time of the year, the flap can be extremely fatty or very lean or somewhere in between.

The loin strips will still be attached to the covering of fat when you inspect your boned saddle of lamb. You will need to remove as much fat as possible from the apron ends. Leave the apron long enough to easily wrap over the stuffing. It can be trimmed away later. The most delicate part of the operation is taking off the excess outer fat over the loins without making a large hole.

I find the best method is to ease the whole loin strip away from the fat using a sharp boning knife and one's fingers. Roll it towards the other loin strip and carefully cut away the excess fat. Roll the loin back into position and repeat with the other side. You can feel with your fingers where the main fat deposits are. Cut them away ruthlessly, leaving the thinnest layer of fat and membrane to nourish the saddle as it roasts.

Slice away the thin layer of lean meat at each end of the apron. This can be minced and added to a stuffing, or seasoned and made into tiny meatballs to serve as an appetiser. The final cosmetic touch is to wrap the trimmed flap section around the loin and fillets, turn the roll over and delicately slice off any purple meat stamps: they are harmless, but not beautiful.

Season the meat and place it in a cool place while you prepare the sauce and the stuffing.

TO MAKE THE SAUCE

Place the bones from the saddle and the rib bones into a roasting pan with a few drops of oil and roast until they are a good brown colour. Pour off any fat, deglaze with the glass of wine and transfer to a large pan. Brown the sliced vegetables in a few drops of oil and when thoroughly browned add to the pot with the bones. Deglaze the pan again with some more wine or a little water. Add to the pan. Add the mushrooms, the tomato, the herbs and barely cover with stock or water. Bring to simmering point, skim and simmer for 4 hours.

Meanwhile drop all the cloves of garlic into cold water and bring to the boil. Drain, repeat twice more. Drain and keep garlic aside. Strain the lamb stock and press down hard on the vegetables. Add 15 of the blanched garlic cloves and simmer quite briskly for a further 30 minutes. Either press the garlic cloves through a fine strainer and return the purée to the sauce, or pass all through a blender. If the latter, you will then need to re-heat the sauce to simmering point for 5 minutes to restore the colour. As I mentioned on page 72, a blended sauce, while wonderfully smooth, will change colour due to the large amount of air you have whipped into it. Now taste the sauce for strength and seasoning. It should be fresh-tasting and aromatic. It will certainly not have a coating consistency, nor be syrupy. If it still tastes too weak, simmer for a further 15 minutes and taste again. Never adjust the seasoning until you are perfectly satisfied with the degree of reduction.

This basic garlic and lamb *jus* is the sauce I use for preference for all dishes based on the roasted saddle, the leg, the shoulder, or the rack of lamb, and for my exquisitely delicious poached loin of lamb. Grilled cutlets never have a stock-based sauce in my restaurant, although they will frequently be brushed with a nut of compound butter or be 'buttered' with a blob of pesto.

By changing the nature of the basic stock, the jus will change its character. It can have a few spoonfuls of peeled, seeded tomato, or beetroot cooked gently in butter, added to it. The *jus* can either be puréed after the vegetable has been added in the manner I described on page 72,

LAMB

77

or it can be strained so that the tomato or beet note is much more elusive. The other flavours I love with lamb are turnips, celery (either celeriac or common stick celery), Jerusalem artichokes, chestnut, garlic (of course), onion, leeks and so many more. Any of these, if sweated in butter gently to form a soft mush, could be used as the dominant note in your sauce, and by either incorporating more of the vegetable cooked lightly and separately to accompany the dish, you can achieve roast leg, or loin or saddle, or rack, with celery, artichokes, buttered leeks or celery.

### PARSLEY STUFFING

Have ready a pan of boiling, lightly salted water and a bowl of ice-cubes in cold water. Plunge the parsley heads into the boiling water for 2–3 minutes and then, using a lifter, submerge the blanched heads in the iced water to cool quickly and set the bright green colour. Drain well and squeeze dry in a cloth. Chop quite finely. Chop the rest of the reserved blanched garlic quite fine. Heat the olive oil and butter in a non-stick pan and cook the parsley and garlic together for 3–4 minutes, stirring. They should not fry, nor should the garlic even start to scorch. Add the cream and simmer together until the cream forms big, yellow bubbles and is very well reduced.

Taste for seasoning. If there was not much parsley, I have sometimes added some fine, white breadcrumbs to bulk the stuffing. For more interest you could use ground almonds or toasted, ground pinenuts. Allow the stuffing to cool before stuffing the saddle. The stuffing could be made the day before.

### TO ASSEMBLE AND COOK

Open out the saddle. Reshape, using the stuffing as glue. That is, place a thin layer of the stuffing between the flap and the loin strip. Add another layer along the top of the loin and place the fillets in position. Cover with a further layer of stuffing and pull the flaps firmly around. They do not need to overlap, so cut off any excess. Truss the roll of meat with kitchen twine and season it with salt and pepper. Tuck the two bayleaves under the twine at intervals. Heat some olive oil in a baking pan and seal the roll of meat well on all sides. Either leave it aside until you are ready to roast the meat or proceed at once to place the meat, in its pan, in the oven at 220°C (430°F) for 20 minutes. Test if it is done.

The professional way to test meat is to plunge a fine, cold skewer into the piece of meat. Count twenty and then lift out the skewer. Feel the temperature of the skewer on your lip. If it is warm in the centre of the plunged skewer the meat is cooked. If quite cold, replace in the oven and test after a further 5 minutes.

When cooked, wrap loosely in foil for 10 minutes to rest while you re-heat your sauce and drop your green beans into rapidly boiling water. Snip the twine and cut the saddle into twelve 1 cm (½ in) slices. Because the sauce is a non-thickened jus, I like to serve a creamy vegetable, usually one of my favourite purée combinations, which I have detailed in the chapter on vegetables. Another idea is a gratin of turnips or potatoes, and a specially delicious accompaniment is achieved by rubbing a gratin dish with garlic, layering it with sliced onions and potatoes, and pouring in enough jus to come half-way up the slices. The top slices become crispy and golden brown, and the underneath layers are soft and full of the flavour of the lamb. Be sparing with the jus: the finished gratin should be tender but not sloppy.

This sort of gratin works very well with stronger vegetables, such as thickly sliced fennel or kohlrabi. And finally, a well-made ratatouille is superb with a leg of lamb.

## VARIATIONS ON THE LAMB STUFFING

1. Try adding a few handfuls of washed and torn sorrel to the parsley, garlic and cream. Sauté strips of pancetta or dice of smoked bacon, and add pinenuts, basil and Parmesan cheese.
2. Add slivered olives and slivered sun-dried tomatoes with sautéed chunks of eggplant and crumbled rosemary needles, previously roasted until they were quite brittle.
3. Or add duxelles of mushroom sautéed and mixed with spinach, with or without a little ricotta. Garnished with slices of lamb kidneys seared quickly and served just as quickly with a grinding of black pepper.

And so on. A boned, stuffed leg of lamb of medium size (weighing 1.5 kg–3 lb—when boned) will need about 50 minutes in an oven at 220°C (430°F) and 20 minutes to rest. A stuffed shoulder is better braised gently in some of the stock at 180°C (350°F) for 1½–2 hours. Allow it also to settle before slicing.

To roast racks of lamb, seal the well-trimmed racks in a heavy iron skillet, season them liberally, and then scatter around some separated but unpeeled cloves of garlic and either a sprig of fresh rosemary or a bay leaf before placing the entire pan in the oven. The rack would take somewhere between 15–18 minutes in a 220°C (430°F) oven. For the last 5 minutes a persillade of white crumbs, parsley garlic and melted butter can be pressed into the skin. A little of the melted butter should also be drizzled over the coating so that it crisps.

All through springtime one year we served suckling lambs. Each lamb weighed around 6–7 kg (13–14 lb) dressed weight, and it was necessary to combine the various parts to create an interesting dish from such tiny animals. We combined several of the methods and ideas I have mentioned, and the plates looked very attractive. Each person received a slice from the leg stuffed with the garlic and parsley stuffing, a slice of stuffed, braised shoulder with a similar stuffing with the addition of the minced kidneys, a minuscule grilled lamb chop, a *soubise* purée made from slowly roasted onions and some freshly shelled peas. We ribboned on a little of the garlic jus as well. The meat was astonishingly tender.

So much for roasted lamb. But have you ever eaten poached lamb?

## POACHED LOIN of LAMB

- 1.5 litres (48 fl oz) lamb/garlic jus, as in previous recipe, or bones to make lamb jus
- ingredients for lamb jus/sauce as on page 76
- 2 boned loins of lamb or 6 × 4-rib racks of lamb

### — FOR PURÉE —

- 3 medium potatoes
- 500 g (1 lb) Jerusalem artichokes
- 6 peeled cloves of garlic, blanched 3 times in water and drained
- ½ cup (approximately) milk
- 1 tablespoon butter (optional)
- 1 cup shelled, peeled broad beans or snow peas or other vegetable

## — TABLE GARNISH —

- sea salt
- capers

- horseradish
- pepper

**This recipe** takes only 15 minutes to poach, rest and slice the meat, **therefore** the purée, the lamb stock and the vegetable preparation must all **be completed** before the cooking of the meat

### To prepare meat

**(a)** *If you have bought loins of lamb.* Trim off all membrane and fat from the loin **strips.** Cut each loin into 3 even-weight pieces. The skinny end of the **loin will** need to be cut as a longer piece as the meat will shrink in the **poaching** liquid. If you own a saucepan or oval casserole large enough **to hold** the uncut loins of lamb, poach them in one piece. There is less **shrinkage,** and you will not have to discard the first and last slice as you **may if** cooking smaller, individual portions.

**(b)** *If you have racks of lamb.* Using a very sharp knife, slice the meat away from **the bones.** Trim each piece of fat and membrane. Reserve the bones for **stock** either for this dish or freeze and label for another occasion.

### To make purée

**Peel and** boil the potatoes in lightly salted water until just cooked. Steam **the peeled** Jerusalem artichokes until tender. They become waterlogged if **cooked in** water. Simmer the garlic in the milk very gently until the garlic is **completely** soft. Crush the potatoes with a potato masher, transfer to a **food-processor,** process briefly with the Jerusalem artichokes, and blend **with the** garlicky milk. Taste for seasoning. The purée can be made the day **before and** can be quickly steamed hot when needed.

### To poach meat

*Prepare lamb stock if not already set aside.*

**Have the** lamb stock simmering in a pot of sufficient dimensions to hold **comfortably** the 6 pieces of meat without overlapping or the two uncut **lions.** The meat should be completely covered by the stock.

**Place the** meat in the simmering liquid and commence the timing from **the moment** the liquid returns to simmering point—8-minute simmering will be sufficient. Remove the meat to a heated and covered resting dish. It should feel quite springy to the fingertips.

Check that the stock is properly seasoned to serve as a sauce. Steam the purée hot, sauté the snow peas or drop the broad beans into the simmering stock for 3–4 minutes.

Serve the dish in deep bowls and serve a soup spoon so that your family of friends can enjoy the sauce. Spoon the reasonably liquid purée into the centre of the bowl, slice thin slices from each piece of lamb, ladle some sauce around and then scatter on the beans or snow peas. This dish should be accompanied at the table with flakes of sea salt, good pepper, maybe capers, and horseradish. I respond to this dish as I do to the very similar poached beef fillet, which I have lovingly described in my first book, Stephanie's Menus for Food Lovers. They are light in body, fragrant and point up the quality of good raw ingredients.

Richard Olney, editor of the Time-Life series The Good Cook, describes how to poach a leg of lamb, wrapped in muslin to keep its shape, in a very similar fashion to the way I have described. Because the leg poaches for 15 minutes per 500 g (1 lb), there is time for aromatic vegetables to flavour the water and create its own broth. His recipe is finished with a veloute sauce, made with this broth and enriched with egg yolks, lemon juice and cream. He also favours capers.

The picture of the finished dish looks wonderful, and I shall try this very soon. Anglo-Saxons beware! It is rather more than rosy pink.

I mentioned in the introduction to this section that my imaginary Mrs Smith frequently grabs lamb chops when short of inspiration. Of course, lamb chops and lamb cutlets provide a delicious aid to inspiration. Many of the famous London clubs have made their reputation on dressed-up lamb cutlets. I believe they must be grilled. Magnificent over a charcoal or wood-ember fire, held flat in a wire hinged grill for easy flipping, or still excellent over a gas-fired volcanic rock barbecue grill and very, very good if criss-crossed on a cast-iron grill plate or pan-heated over a gas flame. Trim chops or cutlets of excess fat, paint very lightly with olive oil to prevent the meat sticking to the grill, cook till pink inside and crispy outside, and season them with good pepper and salt after grilling.

I shall include here a recipe for our garlic and rosemary butter, which is quite wonderful with grilled lamb. Pesto is so well known it seems silly to give yet another recipe, but for ease of access I will do so. This recipe is taken from Marcella Hazan's *The Classic Italian Cookbook* and is designed to be made in the blender. As Marcella Hazan says, pesto made in a mortar and pestle is different. The texture is more like a mayonnaise, but it is more work, and besides, when basil is in season, one needs lots of pesto. I make quite large amounts in the blender, spoon it into screwtop jars and pour over a film of oil to exclude the air and enjoy it for months. We not only anoint the grilled chops with it, we also roll tiny, newly dug potatoes in it.

Grilled lamb chops and cutlets seem to me to be the perfect foil for one's homemade relishes, pickles and chutneys. Sometimes you can serve one of the main ingredients of the pickle as a vegetable and thus create a dish of your own with a true 'house' style. My friend Noel is very proud of his green tomato pickle. In fact he labels the jars a little like a wine vintage and uses them in a similarly considered manner. The '84 is especially good, I was told—it's even dried up so that it has developed the character of a South-east Asian sun-dried pickle.

I make a red-pepper-and-raisin relish, loosely based on a recipe of Escoffier's featured in Elizabeth David's volume *Spices, Salt and Aromatics in the English Kitchen*. If the pilaf of rice made to mound in the centre of the grilled lamb chops includes some raisins and some of the same spices, allspice, nutmeg and chopped ginger, and if one was to make hollows in the rice mound with the back of a spoon and fill them with the red-pepper-and-raisin relish and then surround the platter with halved, roasted and skinned red-pepper halves, the dish has been properly tied together. I would tear up a handful of mint leaves and scatter them over and perhaps leave a bowl of lemon halves nearby.

My last suggestion for embroidering your grilled lamb chops or cutlets was suggested to me when my restaurant celebrated its tenth birthday. I wanted to have a special celebration for all my staff, both past and present, and for all those who had offered me help, friendship and general support. It didn't seem fair to ask the staff to cook, so I invited a most talented couple, Danny and Honey Khoo of the Penang Coffee House, to prepare our feast. We created a Malaysian night street market in our garden and carpark, complete with brilliant banners listing the dishes available, wok burners, satay grill, Chinese lanterns and streamers. Fairy lights twinkled in the trees and a gentle breeze stirred the wind chimes. It was a fabulous night, but there was so much food left over! I froze Danny's superb satay sauce in plastic containers and remembered it one night when I needed to turn a bag of lamb chops into something special. Out came the satay sauce, I chopped up a quick mix of cucumber and fresh pineapple, and the chops were wolfed down with enthusiastic cries.

## GARLIC and ROSEMARY BUTTER

- 1 head of garlic, separated but unpeeled, rubbed lightly with olive oil, and pricked with a skewer
- 15 cm (6 in) sprig rosemary
- 500 ml (16 fl oz) lamb or veal stock
- 1 kg (2 lb) butter, softened
- 1 tablespoon parsley, chopped
- salt, pepper

Place the rosemary needles, stripped from the stalk, and the garlic cloves in a moderate oven for about 40 minutes until the garlic is quite soft. Squeeze out the pulp from the garlic and reserve with the fragments of rosemary needles.

Place the discarded garlic skins, together with any scraps of rosemary sticking to them, into a pan with the stock. The pan should be large enough to permit the stock to boil hard without boiling over. Reduce the liquid by at least three-quarters. It should be very concentrated.

In the food-processor, place the garlic purée, the softened butter, the parsley and the strained stock and process until smooth. Taste for salt and pepper. Cool and then store either rolled in aluminium foil rolls in the freezer until needed, or in plastic-lidded containers.

## MARCELLA HAZAN'S PESTO
### made in the blender

- 100 g (3 oz) fresh basil leaves
- ½ cup olive oil
- 30 g (1 oz) pinenuts
- 2 cloves garlic, crushed
- salt
- 60 g (2 oz) grated, best-quality Parmesan cheese

Put the basil, olive oil, pinenuts, garlic cloves and salt in the blender and mix. Stop once or twice to scrape the ingredients down. When evenly blended, pour into a bowl and stir in the cheese by hand (better texture this way).

Marcella Hazan adds 30 g (1 oz) of soft butter to her sauce and uses both

Parmesan and pecorino cheeses. I don't find the butter necessary, and I use all Parmesan, as we have an excellent and regular supply of it, but not of the other. She also notes that before spooning pesto over pasta, it is a good idea to thin it first with a tablespoon of the pasta water.

## POTATO SALAD with PESTO
### to serve with LAMB CUTLETS
#### topped with PESTO

- 1 kg (2 lb) small new potatoes, as fresh as possible
- ½ cup olive oil
- 2 tablespoons wine vinegar or cider vinegar

- 2 tablespoons dry white wine
- ¼ red onion, finely sliced or 3 tablespoons spring onions, chopped
- 2 tablespoons pesto
- salt and pepper to taste

Boil the washed potatoes until tender. Drain. Leave whole if very small or halve or slice if larger. Whisk together the oil, vinegar, wine in a bowl. Add the onion and the still-warm potatoes and toss gently. Leave for 30 minutes to blend the flavours. Dilute the pesto with a few drops of oil and toss gently through the potato salad. Add salt and pepper.

Serve grilled cutlets with the warm potato salad, and a platter of sliced, red tomatoes seasoned with virgin olive oil, torn basil leaves and a few drops of red wine vinegar, if needed. Top each cutlet with ½ teaspoon of pesto.

## DANNY'S PEANUT SAUCE

### __ SPICE MIXTURE OR REMPAH __

- 2 tablespoons finely chopped hot chillis
- 6 slices of root ginger or galangal, finely chopped
- 2 cloves garlic, finely chopped
- 5 candlenuts or macadamia nuts, finely chopped

- ¾ teaspoon ground turmeric
- 1 teaspoon ground fennel seeds
- 1 teaspoon ground cumin seeds
- 2 tablespoons ground coriander seeds
- 15 black peppercorns, crushed

## — SAUCE —

- 250 ml (8 fl oz) light oil
- 2 large onions, coarsely chopped
- spice mixture (rempah)
- 400 ml (13 fl oz) coconut milk, unsweetened
- 400 ml (13 fl oz) water
- 2 tablespoons sugar
- 1 teaspoon salt
- 2 tablespoons tamarind soaked in 4 tablespoons boiling water and squeezed through a coarse strainer
- 500 g (1 lb) roasted peanuts, coarsely chopped

Heat oil in a wok till smoking hot. Fry the onions until golden brown. Add the rempah or spice mixture and stir-fry over a low flame 2–3 minutes. Add the coconut milk and stir. Gradually add the water and stir until all the water has been absorbed, 8–10 minutes. Add the sugar, salt and tamarind liquid, stirring constantly.

Simmer until the oil floats to the surface. Add the roasted ground peanuts. Bring to the boil and turn off the heat.

Any sauce not used at once freezes perfectly.

## NOEL'S GREEN TOMATO PICKLE

This is a very piquant pickle.

### — FOR SALTED VEGETABLES —

- 2 kg (4 lb) green tomatoes
- 6 large brown onions
- 500 g (1 lb) green beans
- 300–500 g (10–16 oz) coarse sea salt

### — FOR SPICED VINEGAR —

- 1.2 litres (40 fl oz) brown vinegar
- 1 kg (2 lb) raw sugar
- 1 level teaspoon cayenne pepper
- 1 heaped teaspoon bird's eye chillis
- 1 heaped teaspoon whole cloves
- 1 heaped teaspoon black peppercorns

### — TO THICKEN —

- 3 teaspoons dry mustard
- 2 teaspoons turmeric
- 2 tablespoons cornflour

Using the food-processor slicing blade, slice tomatoes and onions. Top and tail the beans and slice coarsely. In a bucket, layer the vegetables, sprinkling each layer with salt. Leave overnight or at least 12 hours.

In a preserving pan, mix the ingredients for the spiced vinegar. Boil briefly and stand overnight or until quite cold. Strain. Drain vegetables from the salting bucket and combine with the pickling vinegar. Cook until vegetables are tender (approximately 30 minutes). Mix mustard, turmeric and cornflour in a small bowl. Add 1 cup of the simmering liquid to the small bowl. Stir till a smooth paste. Return the smooth paste to the simmering preserving pan and stir gently to thicken. Allow to simmer for a minute or two.

Bottle pickle while hot into sterilised jars. Cap jars with paper caps/lids to allow 'breathing'. Seal with a metal lid if you prefer to keep the pickle moist. Noel suggests paper seal only, as he prefers to encourage a slow dehydration of the pickle. The spiciness is enhanced by dehydration. It will take at least six months in a quiet cupboard, Noel tells me.

I have saved my last few lines regarding grilled lamb to extoll the praises of a lamb paillard. This way of serving lamb has become very popular. I have been serving it in the restaurant for at least ten years, on and off. It appeals to me as it is totally fat-free, it is juicy, and I like to think that the combinations we offer are exciting and original.

## LAMB PAILLARD

### — TO PREPARE A PAILLARD OF —
### LAMB FOR GRILLING

- 2 fat-free loins of lamb, sold often as lamb strap if already boned; if not, you will need to slice the strip of meat from the backbone, as you did for the meat from the rack for the poached loin of lamb (see page 81)

- heavy-duty plastic bag
- flat-sided meat mallet
- olive oil

Ensure that the strip of meat is totally free of fat and membrane. Cut each strip into three pieces. Using a sharp knife, slice into the meat longitudinally, but not quite through. Open out the piece of meat. Pound it a little with the flat of your hand to even the thickness, place it in the plastic bag, or place the plastic over it and gently and evenly pound it until you have a slice of meat of even thickness a little less than 1 cm (½ in) thick.

Paint the meat with a thin film of oil and refrigerate until needed.

### To cook paillard of lamb

Heat a ridged cast-iron grill plate to very hot. Salt and pepper the meat. Have serving plates at the ready, for this procedure takes 4 minutes in all. Slap the meat on the grill, turn it 45 degrees after 1 minute. After a further minute, turn it over and repeat. Remove the lamb to its serving plate, add any garnishes and serve at once.

Have a bunch of crisp watercress at the ready, and some garlic and rosemary butter, and we usually heap on a small pile of something crispy, such as deep-fried zucchini chips, or parsnip chips (see page 59) or eggplant slices.

Another favourite accompaniment for this dish is to sizzle small individual vegetable frittate using a mixture of seasoned egg and lightly sautéed vegetables in a cast-iron blini pan.

To complete this section on lamb cookery I have included two braised dishes, both using lamb shanks. The meat from the shank is so sweet, so gelatinous and so melting that, providing they are thoroughly cooked, shanks are delicious quite plainly cooked. A popular household dish when I was at school was shanks simmered in water with lots of onions, served with a fairly dreary parsley sauce made from the broth. Had the simmering liquid had a few more aromatic vegetables and herbs, and had the finished sauce been enriched with an egg yolk or two and a little cream as well as lots of parsley, we would have had a dish far more like the poached leg of lamb described by Richard Olney and mentioned on page 82.

- 12 lamb shanks, skinny end cut off, otherwise left whole
- 2 tablespoons ground ginger
- 3 tablespoons olive oil
- 2 good pinches of saffron threads
- 2 envelopes powdered saffron
- ½ cup hot water
- ½ cinnamon stick
- 4 cloves garlic, lightly crushed
- 2 large onions, peeled
- 1.5 litres (48 fl oz) lamb stock
- salt
- 3 tablespoons pitted black olives
- 1 pickled lemon, sliced (see page 218)

Rub shanks well with the ginger. Brown well in oil and transfer to a cast-iron casserole as each batch is done. Soak the saffron threads and saffron powder in the hot water. When all shanks are browned, tip off any fat and deglaze the pan with the saffron water. Tip the de-glazing liquid over the shanks in the cast-iron casserole and add the cinnamon, garlic, onions and the stock. Taste for salt. Add only a little now; remember that both the pickled lemons and the olives are salty. The shanks should be barely covered by the stock; if not, add a little water. Bring to simmering point and then cook, either on top of the stove or in a moderate oven (180°C–350°F), until the shanks are just tender (about 2 hours).

Remove the onions from the casserole and blend them with a cupful of the stock. Return this to the pan, add the olives and the sliced lemon and simmer together to blend the flavours for a further 20 minutes or so. Shank meat must be practically falling off the bone.

We serve this with couscous, perfumed pumpkin (see page 59) and with a chutney made from fresh dates. The recipe for pickled lemons is in the chapter on citrus fruits (see page 218).

## LAMB SHANKS with CUMIN SEED and TOMATO JUICE

This recipe originally came from a little book on herb cookery written by Rosemary Hemphill, *The Penguin Book of Herbs and Spices*. I have long since mislaid my copy and now have only my handwritten version in my filing cabinet. I feel that we altered the quantities a little from the original.

- 12 lamb shanks, skinny end cut off, otherwise left whole
- 1 tablespoon cumin seed
- 2 teaspoons whole white peppercorns
- 3 teaspoons salt
- 100 g (3 oz) plain flour (approximately)
- 4 cloves garlic, finely chopped
- 3 onions, finely chopped
- juice of 2 lemons or 1 pickled lemon, sliced (see page 218)
- 3 dill cucumbers, sliced
- 2 red peppers
- 2 yellow or green peppers
- 1 litre (32 fl oz) tomato juice (maybe a little more will be needed)

Place the cumin seed, peppercorns and salt in a heavy cast-iron frying-pan and roast them for 4–5 minutes, stirring until fragrant. Grind together in a coffee grinder. Mix the ground spices with two-thirds of the flour and roll the shanks well in the mixture. Place the shanks in a cast-iron casserole and scatter over the rest of the flour and all the other ingredients. Bring to simmering point gently on top of the stove (using a simmer mat to prevent the contents sticking). Check the level of the tomato juice. The casserole should look fairly liquid at this stage. Add more juice if necessary to barely cover the contents. Simmer until quite tender and then serve the shanks with rice or couscous or barley or millet or cracked wheat with lots of the sauce.

I once made a version of this dish by using the Middle Eastern preparation kibbeh, a paste made from soaked burghul (that is, cracked wheat) and minced lamb to encase leftovers of the cooked and boned shanks. It was quite delicious.

## LAMB SHANKS, CUMIN SEED and BURGHUL PIE

- 200 g (7 oz) fine burghul (cracked wheat)
- 200 g lean raw lamb, finely minced
- salt, pepper
- 1 cup melted butter
- 2–3 cups cooked and boned shank meat from the preceding recipe, including any peppers, dill cucumbers and onion in the sauce clinging to the meat
- 1 cup jellied sauce from the shank dish (or rich stock)

Soak the burghul in 1 litre (32 fl oz) of cold water for an hour. Drain and squeeze dry. Spread out onto a flat tray. Incorporate the minced lamb into the squeezed grain by kneading it to form a soft dough. Season well with salt and pepper. Add half the melted butter. Grease a rectangular gratin dish about 25 × 15 cm (about 10 × 6 in) with a little of the remaining butter.

Use half the dough to line the dish, patting it very thinly. Roughly chop the boned shank meat and any vegetables and spread over the cracked wheat crust. Spoon or pour the jellied sauce or rich stock over the shank meat layer. Spoon on the rest of the dough and smooth it in an even layer. With a sharp knife divide the dough into portion-size squares. Brush each square with the rest of the melted butter.

Bake at 200°C (400°F) for about 30 minutes, and then lower the temperature to 180°C (350°F). Cook a further 10 minutes or so until the top is crisp.

This is a solid pie—desert or family food rather than an elegant party.

While holidaying in the Ionian island of Ithaca I was privileged to meet a Dr Vretos, a friend of my Greek friend's family. He has assembled a collection of domestic furniture and objects that provides insight into the vanished way of life of the island Greeks. Among the interesting kitchen tools was a *tserapa*, a primitive 'oven' shaped rather like a Mexican sombrero with a flattened crown. The *tserapa* was made from a mixture of clay and goat hair. The cooking fire was allowed to burn down to hot coals, the meat was skewered or placed directly on the coals and the tserapa was then placed over it so that the heat was trapped.

The relevance of this story is that back home I discovered a recipe for roast lamb with lemon in the style of Cephalonia, the neighbouring island to Ithaca. The recipe specified that the joint be cooked in a tserapa. Without a *tserapa*, the idea of roasting in a covered, very hot casserole, dribbling a little oil or lemon juice or tamarind juice down the sides of a cast-iron pot is sound. I have tried this using lamb shanks and a much-loved black pot, which has a very tight-fitting lid. The tiny amounts of liquid don't make a sauce, but caramelise on the skin of the shanks. The shanks will take at least 2 hours to become tender. I spiked the shanks with slivers of garlic first, and added a bunch of oregano to the pot. It is necessary to pre-heat the pot as well as the oven to very hot before placing the meat in it.

# BEEF & PORK

Mum's beef and potato pie was the family standby. I suspect she made it so often when we were small because the ratio of potato to meat could easily be increased without the pleasure being lessened. We grew our own potatoes, so they were cheap, and Mum always made this dish with gravy beef, that is shin of beef, and water. Recently my father and sister admitted that they never liked it much. I always found it delicious. The beef cooked very slowly on top of the stove creating a panful of 'beef tea'. Many was the spoonful I stole from the pan before the pie was lidded!

I have served my version of Mary's pie several times and have been pleased to find that it brings forth aahs and sighs from many a diner. It is true that my recipe is a little more extravagant than hers.

## MARY'S BEEF and POTATO PIE

- 1.5 kg (3 lb) chuck steak from well-aged ox beef, cut in one piece or sliced 5 cm (2 in) thick
- 3 tablespoons plain flour
- 1 large onion, finely diced
- salt, pepper
- 1 litre (32 fl oz) veal stock (if you have none, water will do, but the gravy will be less rich)

- 4 large potatoes peeled and cut into 2.5 cm (1 in) cubes (a waxy variety such as kipfler, pink fir or red pontiacs)
- 400 g (13 oz) lard pastry (recipe follows)

Cut off excess fat from the beef. Cut into 4 cm (2 in) cubes. Do not cut out all gristle and connective tissue. The meat cooks very slowly for a long time, and this gristle of course supplies the delicious gelatinous texture in the gravy. Roll the beef in the flour and place in a saucepan with the chopped onion, salt and pepper. Pour over enough stock or water to cover the meat. Mix well. The mixture should be quite liquid at this point. Bring very slowly to simmering point. Allow to *barely* simmer for about 2 hours, skimming the foam once or twice. When the meat is nearly cooked, but still has a little resilience, add the peeled and cubed potatoes. Simmer for a further hour until the potatoes are tender. Taste the gravy and adjust the seasoning. It should be a rich brown.

Tip the cooked meat and potato into a china pie-dish. I stand a traditional china pie-funnel in the centre. Mine is topped by a china blackbird, but an upturned egg cup is a perfectly satisfactory substitute.

Roll out the crust. Brush the rim of the pie dish with an egg wash made by mixing an egg with a little milk, and lift on the crust. Press the edges firmly and brush the surface with the egg wash.

Place the pie in a hot oven 200°C (400°F) for 15 minutes and then lower the temperature to 180°C (350°). Bake for a further 20 minutes. If the pastry is becoming too brown, cover with aluminium foil.

This dish seems to cry out for the traditional three veg. Try tiny brussel sprouts, cooked till crunchy and rolled in butter and parsley, steamed or baked pumpkin, and some soft leaves of rainbow chard or silver beet, picked from the garden, blanched and stewed in a spoonful of cream and a touch of nutmeg.

## — LARD PASTRY —

- 200 g (7 oz) sifted plain flour
- 200 g (7 oz) sifted self-raising flour
- pin salt
- 200 g (7 oz) lard at room temperature
- 180 ml (6 fl oz) cold water

Sift flours together with salt. Rub lard in quickly. Make a well in the centre and work in the cold water. Knead until you have a fairly soft, springy and elastic dough: 2–3 minutes. Form into a ball, cover and chill for 20 minutes before rolling.

This pastry, which is a traditional one from the north of England, cooks as a flaky, tender crust, somewhat biscuit-like.

*Boeuf à la mode* means fashionable beef. It is a splendid dish and well within the capabilities of a good cook.

There is a famous, long-established Parisian bistro, Benoit, which serves this dish every day, and has, I believe, served it every day, lunch and dinner, since the restaurant opened. The restaurant has close ties with the traditions of the Lyonnais, notably its excellent charcuterie. It serves pig's head terrine, pistachio-studded boiling sausages, greeny-brown lentil salad and, also every day, *les restes*, or the leftovers of the day before's *boeuf à la mode*, shredded as an entrée and accompanied by a procession of white bowls containing sliced pickled cucumbers, crudités, mayonnaise and warm, yellow potatoes glistening with mustard and oil.

Although I was tempted once by a braised rabbit with mushrooms, and on another occasion I passed up the pig's head in jelly for a memorable puff pastry sandwich of mushrooms, on every other visit I have had to have the *boeuf à la mode* with lots of carrots. Sensibly, a soup spoon is also served to do justice to the savoury liquid. The dish is also known as *boeuf à la cuillere*, beef with a spoon, implying that the braise should be so gentle but so thorough that the meat can be eaten with a spoon.

It is good served cold as a centrepiece for a buffet table, in which case request a large piece of a suitable cut, one that can be contained snugly in an enamelled cast-iron pot with a good lid. I have tried many different cuts of beef in Australia and feel that blade is the best. Many cookery books suggest silverside (which I find is too stringy) or topside (which I find too dry). It is a dish that needs to be planned several days before you wish to enjoy it, either hot or cold, but do try it!

# BOEUF À LA MODE

The choice of wine to use is up to you. Mostly one is advised to use red wine; I usually use white. The flavour of the final sauce will have a different nuance using red wine than it will have using white wine. Take your pick.

- 1 x 2 kg (4 lb) piece of bolar blade, roughly cylindrical in shape
- 500 g (1 lb) pork back fat
- 2 tablespoons parsley, finely chopped
- 1 tablespoon brandy, for larding strips
- butter/oil
- 1 onion, sliced
- 2 carrots, chopped
- 100 ml (3 fl oz) brandy
- 1 glass of dry wine, red or white

- 3 cloves garlic, peeled but whole
- 3 pig's trotters, split lengthwise
- 1 litre (32 fl oz) approximately of strong, veal stock
- bay leaf
- thyme
- 1 kg (2 lb) sweet carrots, of medium size (not baby carrots)
- 1 kg (2 lb) young parsnips
- butter
- salt, pepper

### TO PREPARE BEEF

Trim off any excess fat, aiming to have a roughly cylindrical piece of meat. Cut the back fat into thin strips about 1 x 1 cm (½ x ½ in). Roll the strips in the chopped parsley and the 1 tablespoon of brandy. Lard the piece of beef with these strips. A larding needle is a specialised piece of kitchen equipment like a long needle, usually with a hollow channel in which one puts the piece of fat. As one pushes the needle through the beef the fat strip is left in position as the needle is gently twisted and pulled out. Sometimes the larding needles available are too small; that is, the hollow channel cannot comfortably hold a 1 cm (½ in) strip of fat. What I do is to force some clean object through the meat. I use a kitchen steel, which makes a good-sized channel in the piece of meat, and then poke the fat into the space thus provided with my fingers. It helps a lot if the larding strips are chilled thoroughly or even frozen. Do not omit this step. It is one of the special characteristics of *boeuf à la mode*, the translucent and succulent little nuggets of larding fat in each slice of what would otherwise be very dense meat.

Tie the beef firmly into a long shape and pat over it any parsley-brandy mix left and let it rest overnight to soak up the flavours.

## To cook beef

The next day, heat some oil and butter in the enamelled casserole you intend to cook the beef in, and seal the joint very well on all sides. Remove it to a plate, re-heat the oil/butter and brown the sliced onion and the chopped carrot. When thoroughly browned, return the meat to the pan, warm the 100 ml (3 fl oz) brandy, light it and pour the flames over the meat. Turn the meat once while the flames dance. Add the wine you have chosen, the whole, peeled garlic cloves, the split trotters and the veal stock. The veal stock should barely cover the meat. Add a bay leaf and a good sprig of thyme, cover the dish with aluminium foil, then the lid, and place the casserole in a low oven (160°C–320°F) for at least 3 hours, turning it once. It may take as long as 4 hours before a skewer slips through the meat without the slightest resistance. Once this point has been reached, uncover the pot and leave the beef to cool in its juice. When cold, refrigerate overnight.

## To serve the beef cold

Next day, remove all the surface fat, remove the meat carefully to a board, scraping all the blobs of jelly back into the pot. Melt the sauce, adjust its seasoning and strain it. Discard the vegetables, but you may enjoy the trotters mixed with a little vinaigrette. Slice the beef and either arrange it in a basin or in a long terrine pan and pour over the strained, seasoned jelly. When properly set, turn it out onto a big platter, and with a cloth dipped in warm water lightly skim off any speck of fat. The beef appears as dark mysterious shapes embedded in golden bronze jelly.

I would cook thinly sliced carrots separately in diluted veal stock and season them with oil and vinegar and lots of chopped parsley. Tuck them like an orange frill around the jellied beef.

## To serve the beef hot

As I have already mentioned, the beef is so thoroughly braised that it is possible to eat it with a spoon. What this means is, of course, that it cannot be neatly sliced while hot. If you wish to serve the whole joint at the table, be prepared that a spoon will be a better implement for serving than a carving knife.

If, however, you want everyone to see how beautiful the pattern of larding is, and to receive an elegant slice, proceed as follows. Slice the beef cold into 1 cm (½ in) slices. Season and strain the juices. Separately cook the carrots in some of the sauce. Keep the carrots chunky.

Peel and slice the parsnips. Sweat them in a good lump of butter and then add a ladleful or two of beef sauce and cook them in a covered pan until quite tender. Purée in a food-processor. Taste for seasoning. You should have a very delicious, creamy purée that can be steamed hot in a minute or two.

### To finish

Place your slices of beef in a flat baking dish. Pour over the strained sauce and simmer for at least 5 minutes until the slices are shining with sauce and are very soft.

Re-heat the carrots, either still in a pan with their sauce, or in a steamer. Re-heat the parsnip purée in a steamer.

In soup plates, or pasta dishes, and using a lifter, place a slice of beef, several carrots and a spoonful of parsnip purée, and then ladle over a good measure of the sensational, sticky juices.

The buttered parsnip is of course my personal touch. No self-respecting Frenchman would ever eat a parsnip!

First cousin to *boeuf à la mode* is the Italian *bollito misto*. It is equally closely allied to the French *pot-au-feu* and the boiled beef dinner of New England. Our own corned silverside with a well-made mustard or parsley sauce is very similar and ought to be one of our proudest dishes, but it seems to have fallen from favour.

Bollito misto is well known in cooking literature and was regularly served at the old Mietta's restaurant in Fitzroy. It is quite a production, but is well suited to entertaining large numbers of carnivores. It is undeniably more dramatic when whole ribs and whole knuckles of beef are served than when one reduces the quantities. Save the bollito misto until your next big winter dinner party when you want to feed 15 people.

Several years ago we were directed to the Ristorante Ciccarelli at Madonna di Dossobuono, near to Verona, by a local food-loving resident. The *bollito misto* ceremony began with the arrival of a platter of steaming vegetables cooked in the broth: carrots, sweet flat onions and chunked zucchini. Next we were served a large bowl of soft-leaved salad, a big hollowed-out plate and three separate bowls of sauce. (An aside regarding these plates. So many of these simmered and braised meals involve delicious juices that are meant to moisten every mouthful that it is impossible to serve them on a conventional flat dinnerplate. A large pasta plate would do, although you will need to have several refills. It is a good idea to search out and invest in some of these hollowed-bowls.)

Back to the sauces. The first was salsa verde, of which there are many variations. This one had minced cetriolini (which are crunchy small pickling cucumbers preserved in vinegar), parsley, anchovies, garlic, oil and vinegar. I have given my recipe, which adds capers and has an oil-soaked slice of day-old bread in it. The sauce is good with deep-fried brains or vegetable fritters. I have also been served salsa verde as a crostini topping in Italy.

The second bowl had pungent horseradish mixed with cream. In my first book, *Stephanie's Menus for Food Lovers*, I passed on our big secret for grating horseradish. It is worth repeating, as the intensity and flavour of garden-fresh horseradish, mixed with a few drops of vinegar or lemon, salt and cream is delicious. Normally one scrapes the root and laboriously grates it with tears streaming down one's cheeks. Now we feed the peeled pieces into our electric juicer. It makes the most terrible noise, results in a few drops of juice, but when the machine is opened there is the pulverised horseradish. Stir the juice back into the pulp and do wash the juicer very well. Orange juice with a touch of horseradish is not such a bad dressing for a salad, but not too good for breakfast!

The third sauce was pearà, a speciality of Verona and absolutely delicious. I had read of it in Waverley Root's *The Food of Italy*, and although we had two other bollito misti during our holiday, this was the only occasion the special sauce was served. It is a more sophisticated version of England's bread sauce. Pearà is made by cooking slices of the chewy country bread in rich veal stock till it is smooth and porridge-like. It is then seasoned with lots of black pepper and Parmesan, and a good deal of chopped bone marrow is added. The sauce is stirred together constantly until the marrow is melted and the sauce becomes a smooth and perfect unguent for the simply boiled meats.

The waiter then arrived with the *carello* (trolley), and we chose the varieties of meat we favoured. He had a whole calf's head (the ear had already been carved to an earlier table), cotechino, a sticky, bright-pink spiced pork sausage, a poached hen of golden hue, a beef tongue, ribs of beef brisket, breast of veal and others. We pointed and he carved. Our plates looked most attractive with the pink, white and cream slices. A little broth was ladled over and away we went; a little of this sauce on this morsel, a little of that on another.

Regulations in this country make it difficult, if not impossible, to obtain a calf's head. Even if you obtain one it is a rather grisly and difficult business to scrape the skin. It is easy to obtain a pig's head, or half a pig's head, or even several pigs' ears. With a dish like this one, you are in charge. Do not be bullied by the recipe! You include what you can obtain and of course, what you would like to eat!

## BOLLITO MISTO

The cooking time for this dish will be at least 3 hours, so time the operation accordingly. Use a choice of all or some of the following meats.

- ½ beef brisket on the bone (say 4–5 ribs)
- some beef bones (including the marrow bone after the marrow has been removed; see pearà recipe)
- 1 veal brisket on the bone
- 1 veal knuckle, left whole
- 1 fresh ox tongue
- 1 × 2 kg (4 lb) poaching hen (not the worn-out old birds sold as boilers)
- 6 pigs' ears, fresh
- 1 cotechino sausage or 1 zampone (the same rich pork filling, encased in a boned trotter, rather than hog casings)

### — VEGETABLES USED FOR COOKING —

- 2 large onions, halved
- 6 cloves garlic, peeled, left whole
- 4 cloves
- 3 medium carrots, chunked
- 2 leeks, washed and sliced
- large bouquet garni: 2 bayleaves, large sprig thyme, parsley stalks
- 2 peeled, seeded tomatoes

### — VEGETABLES TO ACCOMPANY THE DISH —
#### (all or some)

- carrots
- potatoes
- onions
- zucchini
- turnips

## To cook meats

Choose a very large stockpot, one large enough to hold all the meats comfortably with room to spare. Half fill with lightly salted cold water. Place in the beef bones and marrow bones. When the water is boiling, add the beef shin and adjust the heat so that the water barely shivers. Skim the surface very well for the first hour. While the meat is simmering, heat a heavy frying-pan to very hot, film it with oil and scorch the cut side of the onions so that they are really dark-brown. After 1 hour add the browned onions to the pot with the veal brisket, veal knuckle and the tongue. Add the garlic, the cloves, the carrots, leeks, bouquet garni and the peeled and seeded tomatoes. When the liquid returns to simmering point, skim well and leave for 45 minutes. Add the hen and the pigs' ears. After a further 45 minutes check the progress of the beef and the veal. If by chance they are completely tender, remove them and keep warm in a covered casserole dish in a very low oven with a few ladles of juice poured over them. When the tongue is tender, lift it out, run under cold water and quickly skin it. Return the tongue to the covered casserole with the cooked meats.

The cotechino or zampone should be simmered in water in a separate pan for 1 hour. This is a precaution in case either one is too salty. Commence cooking the cotechino or zampone when the hen is added to the main pot or a little earlier. It can safely rest in its bath of water and will stay beautifully warm for at least 30 minutes. If you have bought cotechino, it should be skinned before being sliced to serve.

The accompanying vegetables should all be cooked in some of the broth in separate pans so that they do not get lost or submerged among the pieces of meat.

When the hen is cooked, the vegetables are cooked, and the meats are tender, prepare to serve. The sauces will all have been made beforehand. The pearà is the only sauce needing to be served warm. Make it while the vegetables are simmering and keep it warm over a pan of hot water.

Either carve the meats in the kitchen and arrange the slices dramatically or else serve the whole joints and carve in front of your guests. Unless you are very fast, this second method can result in cold meat. I would opt for pre-slicing in the kitchen onto really hot, deep platters, and ladle some of the juices, strained and at boiling point, over the slices. The vegetables should also be served in HOT, HOT bowls with more boiling broth. After everyone has been served, return all sliced meats, vegetables, etc. to the stockpot with the rest of the strained broth ready for a fast re-heat for second helpings.

Any broth remaining will make a good soup, or could be clarified to result in a rich, golden consommé.

Any of the meats remaining can be served cold as a salad with more of the salsa verde, or they can be sliced or shredded and accompanied by all the things that accompanied the leftover *boeuf à la mode* chez Benoit: hot potato salad, mustard, pickled cucumbers, sliced fresh cucumbers in wine vinegar and so on.

If the pigs' ears were not eaten, slice them really thinly, like fettuccine, and toss them in lots of parsley and a simple vinaigrette and mix with the cold tongue and the shredded beef and veal. They will add a crunch to your salad that is most appealing.

## SALSA VERDE

This sauce can be used in all sorts of ways. I have already mentioned fritters. It is also a marvellous sandwich spread on rye bread with pastrami or corned beef.

- I thick slice, good-quality white bread, soaked in 2 tablespoons olive oil
- I large handful parsley
- I tablespoon capers
- 2 cloves garlic
- 2 anchovy fillets

- I tablespoon lemon juice
- 2 pickled cucumbers, sliced (pickled in vinegar and crunchy, not sweet gherkins or dill pickles)
- pepper
- 2 tablespoons olive oil, if necessary

Squeeze bread and combine all ingredients in the food-processor, using the on/off action. The mixture should still retain a little texture and a speckled look. Decide whether or not to drizzle in a little extra oil. Store in a screw-top jar. If made the day before, it may need to have a few drops of oil stirred into it the next day.

## PEARÀ

- 4 marrow bones, sawn into 12 cm (5 in) lengths
- 1 thick slice good-quality white bread, crust removed
- 250 ml (8 fl oz) veal stock, or the broth from the bollito towards the end of its cooking time
- 2 tablespoons best-quality grated Parmesan cheese
- black pepper

Soak the marrow bones in lots of water overnight. Push out the sections of marrow and chop finely. The bones are to be used in the stockpot with the meats.

Crumble the bread into the stock and cook gently, stirring until the bread has absorbed all the stock and is smooth. Stir in the cheese and the marrow. Continue to stir until they are both melted. Taste and add pepper. The sauce should be quite peppery. Add a touch of salt if necessary. (The cheese is salty, so never add the salt until after the cheese has melted into the sauce.)

## LITTLE STEAKS with
## MARROW and PARMESAN SAUCE

I liked the taste of pearà so much that I didn't want to restrict its use only to bollito misto. I have adapted it for another dish. We have some really bad take-away food in this country, but perhaps the best is the steak sandwich. At its best (which is seldom) one gets full-flavoured beef, cut thinly, quickly seared and then slapped onto well-toasted bread, so that the juices from the steak ooze into the bread in a delicious manner.

This is our version of the steak sandwich, with some important differences.

Firstly we made a good, crusty loaf and cut thick slices from it and toasted them on the grill so that they were really crispy. Then we bought premium eye fillet from heavy ox beef, full of flavour. Then we made a quick sauté of smoked bacon, sliced parboiled potatoes, and sliced Belgian endives, and tossed them well until crusty with lots of parsley. Then we heated a non-stick pan until it was dangerously hot. In went the little steaks, three thin slices per portion. Less than 1 minute on each side, then we slapped them quickly onto the toast before one bead of juice escaped into the pan, added the sauté of vegetables and made an instant sauce by adding in rapid succession to the still very hot pan, a spoonful of veal stock, a spoonful of best Parmesan, a spoonful of diced beef marrow and a good pinch of pepper. A quick swirl and the shiny little sauce was over the meat and the plate was whisked away to the eager diner.

Our little steaks with beef marrow and Parmesan sauce are extremely well received, and each time I serve them I give a mental salute to Verona.

Before leaving boiled meats I should mention our springtime boiled dinner, which proudly features our home-made boiling sausage. The recipe for the sausage came from Lyons, the home of fine sausages. In the charcuteries in that city one is amazed to see the variety ranging from fresh links to matured sausages flavoured with fennel, garlic, truffles, wild mushrooms or pistachios. From another part of France entirely, Périgord in the south-west, I took a recipe for *la mique*, a special dumpling, served as filling and savoury food in broths and stews. It is quite unlike the usual dumpling, fluffy with baking powder. The *mique* has salt pork in it and freshly grated horseradish, and simmers for a long time in broth. In Périgord it would often be cut into sections and served instead of bread with cabbage and ham soups. We made smaller ones, one for each plate of springtime pot-au-feu.

The *cervelas aux pistaches* is the perfect sausage to make for wrapping in brioche dough. Served hot with mustard it makes a delightful beginning to a winter meal or with a green salad is an excellent lunch. And why not make your own mustard? I shall describe the dish first and then give my recipes for mustard and the cervelas.

## SPRINGTIME POT-AU-FEU
### (ample for 6, can easily be doubled)

- 2 litres (3 pints) well-flavoured chicken stock
- 2 peeled and seeded tomatoes, cooked till mushy in 1 tablespoon butter
- 1 trotter, split lengthwise
- 1 pickled ox tongue
- 1 onion, stuck with 2 cloves
- 1 carrot
- 1 leek, sliced
- sprig thyme, parsley stalks, bay leaf (bouquet garni)
- 1 teaspoon peppercorns
- 12 baby carrots
- 12 baby turnips
- 1 cup peeled and skinned broad beans
- 6 mique dumplings
- 1 cervelas sausage, cooked
- 6 chicken breasts
- chopped parsley

Simmer chicken stock with the cooked tomato and the trotter very gently for 1½ hours, strain, cool.

Place rinsed ox tongue in pan with the onion, carrot, leek, bouquet garni and peppercorns, cover with cold water, bring to simmering point, simmer approximately 2 hours until quite tender. Run under cold water until cool enough to handle, skin. Return to clean pan and pour over strained cooking liquid. Taste chicken stock and taste tongue cooking liquid. You will need to add some tongue cooking liquid to lift the quality of the broth. Add it little by little as you do not want the broth to be too salty. It will still reduce a little before being drunk.

Heat a little of the broth in a pan and just cook the peeled carrots and peeled turnips. Remove when they are still a little firm. Do not refresh them. You want them to have the flavour of the broth, not have it washed away. Return vegetable cooking broth to larger quantity of broth. Dip broad beans in boiling water for 3 minutes. Run under cold water to stop the cooking, then remove the skin from each bean exposing the brilliant green.

Make the dumplings according to the recipe.

Slice the tongue. Slice the sausage. Remove and discard skin from the chicken breasts and remove the little fillet from each breast. These tender little strips will overcook if added to the broth at the same time as the larger piece.

## T O  S E R V E

Have one saucepan of broth at simmering point. Drop in the dumplings. They should simmer for 20–25 minutes. They can come to no harm if left a little longer.

Have hollowed serving dishes very hot. Ten minutes before you wish to eat, place the sliced tongue and the sliced sausage in a flat-bottomed baking dish and pour over the rest of the broth. Bring to simmering point. Place the chicken breasts in the simmering liquid, together with the turnips and carrots. Cover the pan, with either a lid or aluminium foil. After 4 minutes, turn the chicken breasts, add the little fillets and the broad beans, turn off the heat and poach for a further 4 minutes.

Place 1 chicken breast, 1 chicken fillet, 1 slice of tongue, 1 slice of sausage, 2 carrots, 2 turnips and 1 dumpling in each hot bowl, scatter over a measure of broad beans, retrieved with a slotted spoon. Pour over some broth, not too much, it shouldn't look swamped, and scatter on the parsley. This is a truly delicious, light and fragrant meal.

## LA MIQUE-PÉRIGORD DUMPLING

- 200 g (7 oz) good-quality wholemeal bread
- 3 eggs
- 2 tablespoons melted duck or pork fat
- 60 g (2 oz) minced smoked bacon
- 60 g (2 oz) fresh, grated horseradish
- salt, pepper
- 90 g (3 oz) fine, yellow cornmeal

Cut the bread into small dice and mix with eggs, fat, bacon and horse-radish. Season and add cornmeal. The mix should be sticky, not dry. Form into balls and simmer 20–25 minutes in broth.

## CERVELAS AUX PISTACHES

Polish sausage casings are usually sold in a packet containing 10 metres of casing. Cut off the length required, soak in warm water for 30 minutes to soften, then rinse in iced water before filling using a piping bag with a wide nozzle. Poach in simmering water exactly as for the muslin parcel. This method is more work, but it is preferable. The sausage does not lose its juices.

- 1 kg (2 lb) lean, boneless pork shoulder
- ⅓ cup shelled pistachios
- 2 tablespoons cognac
- 1 tablespoon salt
- ½ teaspoon freshly ground pepper
- ¼ teaspoon freshly grated nutmeg
- 300 g (10 oz) hard back fat
- muslin or clean sheeting for wrapping or ask your butcher for a collagen sausage casing suitable for Polish-style sausage

Have the butcher lightly brine the pork for 12 hours only, or do it yourself.

Chop pistachios coarsely, mix with cognac, salt, pepper and nutmeg in small bowl. Cut meat and fat into 4 cm (1½ in) cubes. Sprinkle with pistachio mixture. Mix through well with hands. Put mixture through the coarsest blade of a meat mincer. If you do not have one, do not use a food-processor. You will have to chop the meat and fat by hand or else ask your butcher to grind it for you. Leave overnight.

The next day, fry a small patty of the meat, and when it is cool taste for seasoning. When you are happy with the seasoning, place the mixture in an electric mixer and beat it using the 'K' beater for 2–3 minutes until the mix looks really homogeneous.

Divide the mix into 4 and form each quarter into a roll. Place in a doubled piece of muslin and twist and turn the ends in opposite directions until you have a firm sausage shape like a Christmas bonbon. Tie once or twice around the circumference and at each end and then gently lower the sausages into simmering water. Simmer for 30 minutes and then turn off heat and allow to cool completely in the water. When cold, drain on a rack, unwrap and rewrap in plastic wrap. The sausages will keep really well for several days in the refrigerator or you could freeze two of them. Each sausage should be about 5 cm (2 in) diameter.

## — SIMPLE BRINE FOR PORK —

- 1 litre (32 fl oz) water
- 250 g (8 oz) rock salt
- 250 g (8 oz) sugar
- 30 g (1 oz) saltpetre

Boil all together and then leave to cool before pouring over the meat. The meat should be stored in a glass or earthenware basin.

- ¼ cup yellow mustard seeds
- ¼ cup red wine
- ⅓ cup red wine vinegar
- ¼ cup water
- ¼ teaspoon ground allspice
- ½ teaspoon honey
- ¼ teaspoon ground black pepper
- 3 cloves garlic, very finely chopped
- 1½ teaspoons sea salt
- 1 bay leaf, finely crumbled

Combine the mustard seeds, red wine and red wine vinegar in a bowl and let stand for 3 hours. Put the mixture into a blender and add the water, allspice, honey, pepper, garlic, salt and bay leaf. Whirl to a fairly coarse texture. Scrape into the upper part of a double boiler. Stir over simmering water for 5 10 minutes, or until the mustard has thickened. Scrape into a jar and allow to cool completely before capping and storing in the refrigerator.

I am sometimes asked the origins of certain dishes on our menus. They are as varied as the dishes, but here is the tale of Tante Claire and a pig's foot. In both London and Australia I had been strongly recommended to the restaurant Tante Claire in Chelsea. The only booking available was at 10 p.m. I made a silly decision to take the tube rather than a cab. The restaurant is a long way from Sloane Square, and I was nervously aware of each clip of my heels as I walked the long, dark and totally deserted length of Royal Hospital Road, looking like a mugger's dream in fur coat and grandma's gold chains (later stolen in France, so I needn't have worried on that score).

I spied listed on the main course offerings a stuffed pig's foot and, with visions of sticky pork skin, ordered it. The dish was absolutely splendid. It came glowing like well-rubbed mahogany in a sticky sauce with the flavour of star anise and soy balanced by other liquids at which I could only guess. The only bones still present were in the toes, so that it was boldly and unmistakably a foot, rather than a squarish parcel as I have seen on other occasions in other establishments. The filling was light and crumbly and full of morel mushrooms. With it came a smooth garlic and potato purée and a separate dish of braised turnips. What a dish! Succulent, melting, spicy, almost perfumed. I nearly fell off my chair with excitement. It was clearly an adaptation of Chinese red-cooking.

In Melbourne at the King of Kings restaurant, and probably at lots of other Chinese restaurants I don't know, one can order red-cooked trotters (bones intact for sucking), and ears and gizzards and other innards. They are served there at room temperature, with sometimes a bowl of pickles, and they are delicious. Red-cooking is a basic Chinese method (called flavour-potting by Irene Kuo), where ingredients are simmered for hours in a master sauce, which always includes dark soy, ginger and star anise. The sauce is kept and used over and over, acquiring great depth of flavour.

In a splendid book, Ginger: east to west, author Bruce Cost gives a recipe for pigs' feet with ginger and black vinegar and relates that this Cantonese dish is ritually shared with visitors to the household of a woman who has just given birth. Besides the benefits of the other ingredients, it is felt that the dose of ginger—over 700 g (1 1/2 lb): 1.5 kg (3 lb) pigs' feet—prevents the new mother from catching a chill, helps her reproductive cycle return to normal, and aids her digestion.

So I started plotting a pig's foot dish and sent a postcard home to the restaurant, urging a bit of practice at boning a trotter in order to keep the skin intact.

The next input to the final dish was one of our last meals in France at the wonderful restaurant Hièly at Avignon. I never need an excuse to visit Avignon, which is an enchantingly pretty town. If greed and culinary anticipation are insufficient, the Renaissance exuberance of flowers, trees and animals that decorate the walls of the stunning Palace of the Popes is a further inducement. Hièly has more character than any other equivalent restaurant in France that I have visited. Even the flowers have special character. Riotous tiger lilies, snapdragons and pink peonies fill giant faience vases. The restaurant offers a small, fixed-price structure, with several supplements, not the usual huge à la carte selection. One of the specialities was the pieds et paquets, a regional dish of nearby Marseilles. This rustic dish consists of squares of tripe, stuffed with chopped pigs' feet, herbs, onions and garlic, rolled into little parcels and braised in a rich tomato stock so that the finished dish is sticky, very tender and satisfying. The waitress expressed anxiety at our ordering this dish and queried whether we properly understood where the 'paquets' came from? Obviously they have had many shocked and horrified reactions from Anglo-Saxons. After we had scraped the plate clean with obvious satisfaction she beamed approvingly at us.

Then I recalled a meal we had at remote Estaing, a tiny village in the valley of the Lot. My companion had ordered *les tripoux*, and had received bundles of tripe stuffed with herbs and salted pork and cooked in a very soupy liquid. This dish was not successful. It was bouncy, watery and generally lacking in care and attention. The message was long cooking, plenty of flavour and succulence.

So back home we launched into it. Apprentice Anne purchased a devilishly dangerous double-sided knife and quickly became extremely competent. She researched and bought a steel mesh boning glove, exactly like chain mail, which minimised damage to her left hand and produced rows of boneless trotters, which we all felt looked like glove puppets.

I decided on a stuffing of part fresh pork and part spicy Italian cotechino sausage, studded with pistachio nuts. A pork stock was made from all the bones, rich in gelatine, and I made a separate sauce from fresh tomatoes, a little star anise, a touch of soy and a little maple syrup. One was blended with the other and the gentle and long braising started.

The trick is to coincide the moment when the trotters are meltingly tender and the sauce is sufficiently reduced to shine and coat the meat. We are serving braised witloof with the dish and slightly crunchy brown lentils.

We learnt a lot from this dish. Everyone learnt to bone a trotter, which was not easy. We found it much easier to bone them before cooking. I have included the recipe, as the construction of the sauce and the cooking process lead so readily to variations.

If you or your cooking partner happen to be surgeons, you may take it as a challenge to be able to divest each trotter of its skin in one piece. If not, there are other dishes to be made, which still offer the glorious experience of sticky sauce, gelatinous pork skin and savoury stuffings.

To make the stuffed trotters you must first make a stock from the bones of the trotters. You must also make a tomato and maple syrup glaze and you must make a stuffing. The pork bone stock could be the base for innumerable pork pies, or be clarified to set a *jambon persillé*, or an egg *en gelée* or provide the jellied layer in a fancy *pâté en croûte* and so on.

The tomato and maple syrup glaze also sauces one of our specialities, a barbecued slice of belly pork, and would be excellent with American-style beef ribs, or pork baby back ribs. The stuffing makes unusual meatballs, which can be braised quite simply in the pork glaze, either just as they are or wrapped inside cabbage leaves, which will become bronzed and succulent after the long braise, or wrapped in a thin piece of lacy caul with just enough sauce so that the top surface is exposed and turns crispy and brown.

## TOMATO and MAPLE SYRUP GLAZE for PORK DISHES

- 1 kg (2 lb) tomatoes, peeled, seeded and roughly chopped
- 1 large onion, chopped
- 3 cloves garlic, chopped
- salt, pepper
- 1 bay leaf, 1 sprig thyme
- maple syrup
- light soy sauce

Cook the first five ingredients together until soft and well reduced. Blend and measure the sauce. For every 1½ cups of tomato sauce, add 1 tablespoon light soy sauce and ½ cup maple syrup. The complete glaze keeps well in a covered container in the refrigerator.

## PORK STOCK

- bones from 6 trotters or 3 whole trotters, split by the butcher
- 1 onion, chopped
- 1 carrot
- 1 piece celery
- 1 leek, sliced
- 1 bouquet garni
- 1 glass dry white wine

Place all ingredients in a stockpot. Cover with cold water. Bring slowly to simmering point, skim. Adjust heat to steady simmer and cook for 3–4 hours. Strain and cool. The stock should set to a firm jelly when cold.

## STUFFED PIGS' TROTTERS

- 6 pigs' trotters

## — BRAISING SAUCE FOR PORK DISHES —

- 1 litre (32 fl oz) tomato and maple syrup glaze
- 1 litre (32 fl oz) pork stock

## — ADDITIONAL FLAVOURINGS —

- 2 teaspoons finely chopped root ginger
- 2 cloves garlic, finely chopped
- 4 points star anise
- 1 tablespoon soy sauce

## — STUFFING FOR BONED TROTTERS —

- 1 kg (2 lb) pork, minced
- 500 g (1 lb) crumbled cotechino sausage or other uncooked boiling sausage
- ½ cup pistachio nuts, roughly chopped
- 1 cup fresh breadcrumbs, tossed in 2 tablespoons butter until golden
- 2 eggs
- salt, pepper

### To bone trotters

Make a slit down the centre of the underside of each trotter and, using a small, very sharp knife, gently ease the skin away from the bones, keeping the knife turned towards the bone at all times. Work outwards towards one edge of the trotter, and then start from the same slit and work towards the other outer edge. Then turn the trotter over and free the remaining skin on the edge where the hock would join on (that is, not the toes!). Proceed to complete the boning by peeling the skin back from the knife until you can extract the bone. The only bones that should be still in position are the very small ones in the toes that give the trotter its shape.

Re-form each trotter by placing a portion of mince inside the skin and squeezing the skin back into its former shape. There is no need to tie it, but it is necessary to choose the baking dish carefully. The trotters should be quite firmly packed. Pour over sufficient of the braising sauce to amply cover the trotters. There should not be sufficient room for them to float about. Cover the dish and braise in a low oven (160°C–320°F) for about 3 hours.

Serve with brown lentils and braised witloof or a silky purée of potatoes, mashed with hot milk and incorporating 2–3 tablespoons of thrice-blanched puréed garlic cloves.

The trotters can be completely braised in the morning and re-heated, still in their sauce and in the same pan in the evening. Just be careful that they don't stick.

It is just possible that you may have tried to bone the trotters and failed. You now have 6 raggy trotters, skin split in all directions, bones still intact. The situation could be saved by turning the damaged trotters into pork stock. Make the tomato and maple syrup glaze as in the recipe, and then combine the pork stock and the glaze as in the recipe for the stuffed trotters.

Instead of the trotters, substitute some pork hocks, pickled or not, as you prefer. Braise them instead. They will take about the same length of time. I usually skin the hocks before serving them, as the skin is so rich and there is so much of it. I slice it up and make sure that everyone gets a few curls of the skin in their dish.

One last thought. If the sauce seems to be too thick or too rich, add a few spoonfuls of extra stock or even water. Remember you are the boss, not the recipe!

## BARBECUED BELLY PORK

- ½ fresh belly of pork, approximately 1 kg (2 lb), as lean as possible, skinned and boned
- 1 litre (32 fl oz) tomato and maple syrup glaze (see page 110)
- 1 teaspoon chilli sauce or to taste

Brush the meat liberally with the glaze. Roast the meat in a moderate oven, 180°C (350°F), by placing the meat directly on the oven rack and positioning a similarly sized baking pan with a little water in it underneath the meat to catch the drips. The meat will take about 1½ hours to be quite tender, depending on the thickness. Every 20 minutes, paint the meat with more of the glaze. When it is cooked, remove and allow the meat to cool and firm on a board. When quite cold, slice into thick (2.5 cm–1 in) slices. As this meat is so rich, one slice is enough. Any more could be dangerous! When ready to serve, light the fire or heat the griller. This is perfection if cooked over a charcoal fire, but pretty good under a fierce grill.

We simmer the slices hot in the rest of the tomato and maple syrup glaze and then sear them on the barbecue. We accompany the barbecued pork with a potato and celeriac purée and a heap of stir-fried greens, whatever is best at the time. I have mentioned elsewhere how good cos lettuce leaves are tossed in a few drops of oil until crisp but thoroughly tender.

Another vegetable accompaniment that tastes and looks good is quickly blanched slices of red, yellow and green sweet peppers, mixed with crescents of blanched and quartered onions, all tossed in a pan in a little oil, allowed to settle for a minute now and then, so that here and there the edges catch and become quite deliciously scorched.

I am aware that I am right out of step with those who caution us against eating excessive amounts of animal fats, particularly pork. Whenever I am asked about this, I still say: balance, variety and moderation. Nobody could eat a great deal of these hearty dishes, and undoubtedly, historically, they were born out of dark, cold winters and heavy manual work, but they are delicious in small quantities, and occasionally. Having said that, I intend to complete this section on pork cookery with my version of cassoulet. I have been asked over and over to publish this recipe, and I have always hesitated. It is complex, although certainly not difficult, and I wondered whether anyone would want to bother. But perhaps at a ski lodge after a hard day on the slopes, or in the depths of winter for a Sunday late lunch when one could sleep afterwards? Anyway, here it is.

## CASSOULET
### (Stephanie's Restaurant Version)

This classic of regional cuisine from the Languedoc has many variations, but it must include *confit*, that is pieces of goose or duck, salted and preserved in goose or duck fat. We make our own *confit* of duck with all the legs, which are not used when we use the breasts only of ducklings. The recipe is on page 117. It is not worth making cassoulet for a few people, so these quantities will feed 20 people.

- 1 fresh pork neck, cut into thick slices
- salt, pepper
- 2 large sprigs thyme
- 2 bay leaves
- bundle of parsley stalks
- 1 kg (2 lb) haricot beans
- 2 boiling sausages, such as the cervelas (on page 105) or Italian cotechino
- 1 kg (2 lb) skinned, boned, salted belly pork
- 3 fresh pork hocks
- 4 onions, finely chopped
- 6 medium carrots, peeled and finely sliced
- 5 litres veal stock
- 2 whole heads unpeeled garlic
- 3 peeled and seeded tomatoes, chopped
- rind from ½ a pork loin, cut into 5 cm (2 in) strips
- 500 g (1 lb) pork fat minced and worked with 1 tablespoon chopped garlic
- 20 preserved duck legs (for method, see pages 117–19)
- fresh breadcrumbs

### DAY BEFORE YOU ARE INTENDING TO COOK THE CASSOULET

Grind pepper and salt over the pork and spread the meat out on a tray. Scatter over 1 sprig thyme, 1 bay leaf and a few parsley stalks. Soak the haricot beans in a large bucket of cold water.

### NEXT DAY

Simmer beans for 10 minutes, drain. Drop sausages into simmering water (if uncooked) for 30 minutes. Omit this step if using your own pre-cooked cervelas.

Heat some of the duck fat from the preserved legs and fry the slices of pork neck until golden. Remove the pork neck slices to a plate. Add the belly pork (in one piece) and the hocks to the hot fat and sauté until golden. Place them in a stockpot. Add the onion and sliced carrot to the hot fat and sauté until golden. Remove to the stockpot. Add the heads of garlic, the tomatoes, the pork rind and the rest of the parsley stalks tied as a bouquet garni with the remaining thyme and bay leaf to the stockpot. Pour over the stock and bring slowly to simmering point. Simmer 45 minutes. Add the slices of pork neck and the drained beans and the fat worked with the garlic. Simmer another hour. Add the sausage and the duck legs. Simmer a further 30 minutes. Check that the meats are tender. If the pork hock or belly pork seem still a little resilient, continue to simmer gently for a further 20 minutes.

Using a skimmer, lift out the meats when they are tender and place on a tray to cool a little. Discard the bouquet garni. Press the whole heads of garlic through a coarse strainer so that the pulp falls back into the juices.

Slice the belly pork, roughly shred the meat from the hocks, cut the sliced pork neck into large cubes, slice the sausage. Select one or two large earthenware casserole dishes and arrange all the meats in a fashion that anyone lifting a spoonful will have a good mix of flavours. Poke the duck legs here and there, and scatter over the pork rind. Ladle over the beans, which should be dripping with slices of carrot and rich juices. Taste the juice: it should be strongly flavoured. Add more pepper and salt if needed. Spoon over some juice, reserving some. Scatter a thick layer of fresh crumbs over each pot, completely covering all pieces of meat, duck and sausage. Drizzle over some more juice.

<h2 style="text-align:center">To serve</h2>

Re-heat slowly for at least 45 minutes. The crust should be golden and bubbling. If it looks at all dry, with the back of a serving spoon push some of the crust into the cassoulet and drizzle over another layer of juice. The bubbles at the edges of the pot should be a rich golden brown and very sticky.

Several years ago we were visited by a diner who was born and bred in Toulouse, right in the centre of cassoulet country. My heart sank when he ordered the cassoulet, but he loved it. I was intrigued when he ordered a little red wine vinegar, which he said was customary to pour *couter la graisse*—a bit like the British way of dousing their chips with vinegar. He poured his vinegar into the dregs of the dish and spooned enthusiastically. It is also customary in the south-west to pour a little of one's red wine into the bowl. *Faire chabrol*, it is called.

# CONFITS & BIRDS

— F E A S T S  &  S T O R I E S —

Many cookbook authors talk of *confit* of pork, duck or goose as if their readers are quite familiar with this process. I have given several examples of confit in my earlier book with, I hope, adequate explanation. Since publishing *Stephanie's Menus for Food Lovers*, however, I have read a most comprehensive article by Paula Wolfert published in January 1983 in *Cuisine* magazine. Her explanation of the method is very clear, and the selection of recipes she includes is truly typical and mouth-watering. The next few pages are a paraphrase of the essential steps as outlined by Paula Wolfert in this article.

Confits (from the French *confire*, to preserve) are simply preserved meats that have been salted to draw out the moisture, then cooked and stored in fat.

> In past generations, it was an intrinsic and thrifty part of the farm kitchen routine, a way of making use of every part of the animal from good pork shoulder and meaty duck legs to such humble odds and ends as duck and goose gizzards, wings and necks, or the tongue and ears of the pig.

Despite the large amounts of rendered fat used in the preparation and storage of *confit*, there is nothing fatty—or dry, salty or stringy—about the effect of properly made *confits*. Rather, they are nutty, silky, delicate and surprisingly fat-free. The secret is gentle heat and patient cooking. Alain Dutournier, a Gascon chef and owner-chef of the Carré des Feuillants in Paris and owner of Au Trou Gascon in Paris has suggested to Paula Wolfert that a good principle to follow is to raise the fat temperature gradually along with that of the pieces of meat, let the confit cook evenly, and then cool it in the fat as slowly as it heated.

The slow initial heating allows all the fat under the skin to melt out, the slow cooking inhibits stringiness, and the slow cooling prevents the meat from falling apart or losing its shape. Like all animal fats, *confit* fats are fragile and burn much faster than oil. Once the fat gets hot enough to smoke it is 'spent' and is not usable in cooking again.

On its home territory, *confit* was intended to last for months without refrigeration, hence in traditional recipes the ducks, or other meats, are salted more heavily and for a longer time than is necessary with our smaller ducks and refrigeration. In Paula Wolfert's master recipe she has reduced the salt and the initial salting period accordingly. The amount of salt recommended is based on an expected maturing time of at least 1 week and up to 3 months. For storage of less than a week, the amount of salt should be halved, since the full ripening reaction won't have had time to take place.

## PAULA WOLFERT'S CONFIT of DUCK

- 6 duck legs
- 3–6 tablespoons kosher salt or sea salt (smaller amount if to be used within a week)
- ½ tablespoons coarsely chopped shallot
- 1½ tablespoons chopped fresh parsley
- 2 teaspoons black peppercorns, lightly crushed
- 1 bay leaf, crumbled
- 1 teaspoon coarsely chopped garlic
- 1 sprig fresh thyme
- 4–6 cups extra rendered fat (good quality lard or rendered goose fat)
- 1 whole head garlic
- 2 cloves

Remove any loose fat from duck. Mix salt, shallot, parsley, peppercorns, bay leaf, garlic and thyme. Toss duck pieces with this seasoned salt mixture.

Cover with plastic wrap. Refrigerate 12 hours. Render any cut-up duck fat and extra skin in a pan with 1 or 2 spoonfuls of water over low heat for about an hour. Strain the fat into a heat-proof container. Reserve any crispy bits of skin for cracklings.

Remove marinated duck pieces from bowl and rinse briefly under cold water. Pat dry. In a crockpot or heavy enamelled cast-iron pan, heat the rendered fat with the extra fat until it has just melted. Slip in the pieces of duck and the split head of garlic with a clove stuck into each half.

Bring the fat, uncovered and very slowly, to a temperature of 90°C (190°F). This should take about 1 hour. Maintain this temperature for another 30 minutes or so and then test the thickest part of the thighs for tenderness. If done, remove the pan from the heat and let the duck legs cool in the fat for 1 hour.

To ensure that the *confit* does not spoil, ladle the clear fat carefully into another clean, enamelled cast-iron container, leaving any meat juices behind. Simmer the fat for 5 minutes until the spluttering stops and the fat is clear and golden. Allow to cool a few minutes. *Confit* that is to be used within a week can simply be stored in any convenient-sized plastic bowl covered in fat. When the fat has congealed, pour a thin layer of oil over the surface and store in the refrigerator.

*Confit* to be kept longer, up to 3 months, needs to be potted more carefully. Glazed earthenware crocks, the traditional storage containers, are perfect. Place ¼ teaspoon of salt in the bottom of each crock. This prevents meat juices that may seep from the duck during the ripening process from turning sour. Ladle warm fat into the crock to half-way mark. Slip in the pieces of duck *confit* without crowding. Ladle in additional fat to cover completely and leave a generous 2 cm (1 in) space. Let cool, uncovered, to room temperature. Store, covered, overnight until fully congealed. Seal with a 1 cm (½ in) layer of melted fat (preferably butcher's lard, which is more impenetrable to air than duck fat). Cover with kitchen paper held with string or a rubber band.

To use *confit*, it is necessary to warm the vessel sufficiently to soften the fat. Place the crock in a pan of warm water and remove the pieces that you need. Make sure remaining *confit* is well covered. Once the seal is broken, the *confit* is more perishable. Use within a week.

It makes sense to store *confit* in several containers rather than one large one if you have prepared a large amount. Even if you wish to serve the *confit* as part of a cold platter or a salad, it should be heated first. If crisp skin is not necessary, steam the *confit* pieces for 5 minutes. Usually, however, one desires the skin to be crisp. Lift the pieces from the crock. Scrape the fat clinging into a heavy non-stick pan and heat till rippling. Add the *confit* pieces, skin down, cover tightly and cook over medium heat for 5–10 minutes. Shake pan once or twice to make sure *confit* is not sticking. Once the skin is brown, remove from the heat and let rest for 1 minute, still tightly covered, so that the meat can be loosened from the skillet without tearing the flesh. Uncover, pour off fat and gently turn each piece skin side up, cook a further minute.

Paula Wolfert continues her astonishly definitive article with delicious recipes for *confit* of pork; garbure, which is a cabbage and ham hock soup and is a meal by itself, a *pot-au-feu* from Albi, made special by the inclusion of duck *confit*, a croustade of duck *confit* with apples, and a dandelion salad with gizzard *confit*. I suggest readers who are as tantalised by these country dishes as I was purchase a copy of her book *Cooking of South-west France*.

I was once invited by the late Jean Troisgros to spend a week observing in the kitchens of the restaurant Troisgros. He had been a guest at a special dinner in our Hunter Valley, an important wine-producing area, and was a most charming and delightful man. M. Troisgros frequently had duck gizzards for his light evening meal before service, and showed me how to skim a few from their just-warmed fat, slice them, sauté them with a sliced clove of garlic for 30 seconds, toss them onto a bowl of frisée lettuce and sauce them with a few drops of red wine vinegar swished in the still hot pan. A slightly fancier version of this salad, using duck skin cracklings, is on page 152.

One of the things I have always loved to eat is a well-roasted chicken. It surprises me that one of the dishes that rarely 'sells' in the restaurant is a buttery, tarragon chicken, while almost any duck dish will be ordered in huge numbers.

I imagine the answer is that families don't buy ducks to cook at home as they are very expensive and give very poor yield for the dollar. And I suppose that, whether I like to admit it or not, the mass-produced take-away chicken businesses have convinced people that chicken is ordinary.

Ironically, ducks in Australia are nowhere near the quality of French ducks. Cooks hoping for deep-breasted and tender birds are doomed to disappointment. We can provide birds that are deep-breasted and chewy, or shallow-breasted, tender and flavourless. Asian cooks succeed best with our ducks as their spicing, roasting and crisping methods do not depend on a thick layer of breast meat. French magret-style dishes can be attempted with any hope of success only with the very few properly fed Pekin ducks available, or with the bigger Muscovy, which is really a goose, and is mostly very chewy, especially when grilled rare. There are one or two suppliers of excellent cross-bred mallard and Pekin ducks, which I use as often as possible.

I feel that I get good results with the fresh chickens I buy. Most often they are not corn-fed or free-range, but they still respond well to lemons, tarragon, garlic, fennel and so on. Very recently I purchased chickens that had been fed on corn and were free-ranged. They were marvellous.

Here, then, is a small collection of poultry recipes from near and far. Enjoy them, but don't forget the simple butter-roasted chicken.

## ROAST CHICKEN for HOLLY and LISA

- 1 × 2 kg (4 lb) chicken, corn-fed if possible
- salt, pepper
- 3 good sprigs of tarragon or lemon thyme or fennel tops
- 1 thick slice of lemon
- 1 clove garlic, crushed with a knife
- 60 g (2 oz) butter
- 1 glass dry white wine
- 1 tablespoon cream

Wipe chicken inside and out. Remove any giblets and neck (reserve them for stock). Season chicken inside and out. Place herbs, lemon slice, crushed garlic in cavity of bird. Rub half the soft butter all over the breast and legs and put the rest inside the cavity.

Truss the bird if you wish. Lightly oil a baking pan and place the chicken on its side in a hot oven 220°C (430°F) for 20 minutes. At the end of this time, turn the chicken to the other side and set timer for a further 20 minutes. Turn chicken breast uppermost for 20 minutes. Remove from oven. Tip bird so that all juices, herbs, lemon, garlic fall into the baking pan. Place bird on a hot serving plate and return to turned-off oven while you make the simple sauce.

Tip off excess butter, leaving solids in pan. Place over fast gas jet. Press on garlic, lemon and herbs, allow to sizzle for 1 minute. Add glass of wine and scrape and stir until all little brown bits have floated free. Strain this juice and bubble with the spoonful of cream.

I prefer to cut the chicken into joints in the kitchen, and slice the breast meat. I then pour the sauce over, together with any other juices that have collected while I was carving. Serve with a green salad, or, a special summer treat to accompany this chicken would be a bowlful of freshly picked and 6-minute boiled green beans. If there is room, you could tuck some small potatoes around the chicken at the start of the cooking time.

## GRILLED CHICKEN PAILLARD

Attempt this dish only if you are able to obtain really flavoursome chicken. Remove the skin, turn the small fillet to the outside, place a sheet of heavy plastic over the meat and gently flatten it with a meat hammer or cutlet bat. Season, paint with olive oil, and grill in exactly the same manner as for the lamb paillard on pages 87–8, allowing an extra 2 minutes per slde.

I serve this with some sliced cooked artichoke hearts tossed in butter with gnocchi made from one of Australia's finest products—Gippsland blue cheese made at Neerim South in Victoria.

### — BLUE CHEESE GNOCCHI —

- 200 g (7 oz) blue cheese, rind removed and at room temperature
- 2 eggs
- 1 clove garlic, chopped to paste
- 60 g (2 oz) plain flour
- pepper

Combine cheese, eggs, garlic in the food-processor until a smooth paste. Stir in the flour by hand. Add pepper to taste. Allow to firm in the refrigerator before forming into shapes with two spoons and poaching in lightly salted, barely simmering water for 4–5 minutes.

This series of recipes is an excellent example of the way in which I design dishes at Stephanie's. They are often multi-part, as this is. Often they are intended to combine very loosely, so that if there is no okra in the market, I am able to turn easily and without trauma to an equally delicious alternative, the green bean and cashew side dish.

## SPICED INDIAN QUAIL with CURRY NOODLES, QUAIL EGGS in COCONUT SAUCE, FRIED COCONUT, OKRA CURRY

### — SPICE MIXTURE FOR QUAIL —
#### (sufficient for 6 quail)

- 1 tablespoon whole coriander seeds
- 20 whole peppercorns
- 12 cardamom pods
- 1 teaspoon whole cloves
- 1 teaspoon salt
- 1 teaspoon cumin seed
- 1 teaspoon curry powder
- 60 ml (2 fl oz) melted butter
- 30 g (1 oz) finely chopped ginger

Grind together the spices and salt in a coffee grinder until they form a powder then mix with the melted butter and ginger.

### TO PREPARE QUAIL

Cut out backbone from each quail, make a cut on either side of the breastbone so that the quail will open out flat. This is called *crapaudine* in French, to resemble a toad. If you remember the flattened out, squat shape of the last cane toad you saw in north Queensland, it will help with the shape of the quail.

With the fingertips, loosen and separate the skin from the breast meat and work 1 teaspoon of the spice mixture over the entire breast surface. Smooth the skin back into place and press a little of the spice mixture towards the thighs. Brush the birds with melted butter and set aside until time to grill them.

### TO GRILL

I use a ridged cast-iron grill plate, either over two gas jets, or on the outside barbecue. An open barbecue grill is quite suitable, providing the bars are close enough to prevent the little birds falling into the fire.

Place birds carcass side down to the heat source and grill for about 8 minutes. Turn and briefly seal the skin side. Do not leave them more than 1 minute this side, as the spice mixture will burst through the skin and be lost in the fire. Remove quail after grilling to a warm resting tray.

To test the quail prick the thickest part of the thigh to see if the juice runs clear. If still undercooked, return to the grill for 2 more minutes, carcass side down to the fire.

We remove the breastbone and ribcages before serving, but this is really a measure designed to protect silk dresses, and is unnecessary *en famille* or with friends.

Serve scattered with fried coconut, and set out bowls of lukewarm hard-boiled quail eggs in coconut sauce, okra curry, pickled limes and fresh lime wedges. All or some. The curry noodles are delicious if the quail dish is the centrepiece of your party, but could be forgotten if the little birds are the entrée. (That is, forget them on this occasion, but not entirely, as they are fantastic with prawns and mussels tossed through them, or curried beans) I have given a recipe for curried beans with raw cashew nuts, which I serve with the quail on the frequent occasions when I am unable to get baby okra.

## — FRIED COCONUT —
### (Senonding)

- 2 tablespoons grapeseed or other light oil
- 4 cloves finely chopped garlic
- 4 spring onions, finely chopped, including most of the green tops

- 1 teaspoon ground coriander
- 1 teaspoon ground cumin
- 125 g (4 oz) desiccated coconut
- pinch of salt

Heat oil in a heavy-bottomed pan. Fry garlic and onion 1–2 minutes. Add the spices and then the coconut and salt. Lift and stir really well to mix all the flavours through and continue to cook until the coconut is a rich brown. Allow to cool completely, and then the coconut can be stored in a screw-top jar.

I also like this scattered over a salad of cucumber, or one can roll deep-fried carrot or corn fritters in the coconut.

## — HARD-BOILED QUAIL EGGS IN —
### SPICY COCONUT SAUCE

- 12 hard-boiled quail eggs, peeled
- 2 teaspoons turmeric
- 4 cloves garlic, finely chopped
- 1 dessertspoon ground coriander
- 1 teaspoon ground ginger
- 1 teaspoon ground cumin
- 400 g (13 oz) finely chopped onion
- 1 stalk lemongrass, finely chopped
- 400 g (13 oz) peeled and seeded tomatoes, finely chopped
- 250 ml (8 fl oz) coconut milk
- 1 tablespoon lemon juice
- 1 tablespoon desiccated coconut, lightly toasted (or use the fried coconut from the preceding recipe)

Cook all ingredients except the eggs together over moderate heat for 20 minutes. Stir from time to time to prevent sticking. Add the hard-boiled eggs and cook for another 10 minutes. The eggs taste better the longer they are left in the sauce. The whole dish could be made the day before and gently re-heated. It is also good cold.

## — OKRA CURRY (BHENDI KARI) —

This recipe comes from Charmaine Solomon's wonderful and ency-clopaedic work, *The Complete Asian Cookbook*. I have three copies, one at my beach house, one upstairs in my study for reading and reference, and one in the kitchen downstairs. When my elder daughter moved into her first flat, I gave her a copy as a house-warming gift.

- 500 g (1 lb) fresh, tender okra
- 1 large onion, thinly sliced
- 2 fresh green chillis, slit and seeded
- 1 tablespoon clarified butter
- 1 clove garlic, finely sliced
- ½ teaspoon finely chopped ginger
- ½ teaspoon ground turmeric
- ½ teaspoon ground coriander
- ½ teaspoon ground cumin
- 1½ cups coconut milk or buttermilk
- 1 teaspoon salt, or to taste

Wash okra and cut off stem ends. If they are large, cut into convenient lengths. Fry the onion and chillis in butter over medium low heat, until onions are golden. Add garlic, ginger and turmeric and fry, stirring for a minute longer, then add okra and fry for 3–4 minutes. Add the coriander and cumin, coconut milk or buttermilk and salt. Simmer uncovered until okra is tender, 10–12 minutes.

## — CURRY NOODLES —

- 300 g (10 oz) plain flour
- 2 tablespoons curry powder
- 3–4 eggs

The extra egg will probably be needed, as the curry powder absorbs quite a lot of moisture. Follow method for pasta making on page 7 and cut the pasta on the fine blades. After cooking (following basic method on page 7), toss in either a little clarified butter or coconut milk, or toss with some of the sauce from either the quail egg dish, or the okra curry.

## — CURRIED BEANS WITH RAW CASHEWS —

- 500 g (1 lb) green beans, topped and tailed and left whole if young and garden-fresh, cut into 7.5 cm (3 in) pieces if they are standard supermarket beans
- 1 small onion, finely chopped
- 60 g (2 oz) raw cashew nuts
- 30 g (1 oz) clarified butter
- 2–3 teaspoons curry powder, or more to taste
- 1 cup coconut milk

Blanch/cook the beans in lots of boiling salted water until just tender. Refresh quickly under running cold water.

Fry onion and cashews gently in butter until the onion is soft and golden. Add the curry powder and the coconut milk and simmer together for 5 minutes. Add the beans and simmer for a further 5 minutes. Taste for salt.

Although this quail dish (overleaf) is certainly designed to appeal to spice lovers, I do not wish to make it a palate-numbing experience. The chillis and curry are flavourings to be used with discretion.

# GRILLED ITALIAN-STYLE QUAIL,
## with LIVER CROSTINI and
## PARSNIP CHIPS

This is another example of a multi-part dish. Each component could combine equally well with other things, and frequently does in my kitchen.

## — MARINADE FOR QUAIL —
### (sufficient for 6 quail)

- ¾ cup dry Madeira
- ½ onion, finely chopped
- 6 juniper berries, bruised

- 6 peppercorns, crushed
- 3 sprigs parsley, chopped

## — SAUCE —

- (a) reduction of the liquid from the marinade OR

- (b) 500 ml (16 fl oz) strong poultry stock, including the trimmings from the quail

- 2 teaspoons tomato paste or 1 tablespoon fresh purée of tomato
- 1 cup very well-browned chopped vegetables (1 small carrot, ½ onion, 1 stalk celery, 2 cloves garlic)

### To prepare quail

Cut out backbone of each quail, reserve. Cut off wingtips, reserve. Cut off necks (if still present), reserve. Make a cut on either side of the breastbone so that the quail will open out flat. I have commented further on this on pages 122–3. Place all the bits in a small baking dish, add a few drops of oil and brown well in the oven. Transfer browned bones to saucepan with the well-browned vegetables and pour off any fat from the baking dish. Deglaze with the strong poultry stock, pour over bones and vegetables in pan, add tomato paste and bring all to simmering point. Simmer for 1–2 hours, skimming off any debris once or twice.

Meanwhile, combine all ingredients for marinade and pour it over the wiped quail and leave for at least 6 hours or overnight.

### To finish sauce

Remove quail from marinade, draining well. Pour all strained marinade liquid into a pan and reduce until the base of the pan looks syrupy. Pour on the strained rich stock you have made and boil hard to reduce by about half. Taste to see that flavour is good, but not over-reduced. Remove l/2 cup for chicken liver mixture. Set sauce aside for later re-heating; or, if you are to proceed at once with the grilling, keep the sauce hot in a stainless jug sitting in a pan of very hot water.

### To roast whole cloves of garlic

Select fat, large cloves of garlic.

Prick each one with a fine skewer to prevent explosions. The most painful burn I have ever experienced in my years in the kitchen was once when a clove of garlic exploded as I was prodding it to see if it was cooked. The soft (it was cooked!) meat of the garlic shot out of its skin and stuck to my finger like toffee. I literally saw stars!

Rub the garlic cloves with a little olive oil and put in a moderate oven with 1 or 2 bay leaves and a sprig of thyme. Once soft, the garlic is delectable to eat, either still in its papery, oily skin, or else squeezed out onto hot toast. The garlic stays warm for at least 30 minutes out of the oven.

### To toast breadcrumbs

Melt 60 g (2 oz) of butter until foaming in a heavy frying pan. Tip in 1 cup of fresh breadcrumbs and continually spoon the crumbs over and over until they are uniformly golden brown and have become like golden sand. Spread crumbs on a plate to cool and then store in a screw-top jar. Use within a day or two or they will taste stale.

I often mix them with lots of freshly chopped herbs and serve the lively green-gold mixture in saucers alongside some asparagus with a lightly coddled egg.

### Liver crostini

One slice of crusty bread per quail sliced crosswise about 1 cm (½ in) thick, toasted one side, with the untoasted side painted with olive oil.

## — LIVER MIXTURE —

- 8 chicken livers
- 125 g (4 oz) smoked bacon, cut into small dice
- a little olive oil
- 4 medium onions, coarsely chopped
- 3 cloves garlic, finely chopped
- ½ cup of the quail stock
- 2 tablespoons dry Madeira
- 1 teaspoon salt or to taste
- pepper to taste
- 2 tablespoons finely chopped parsley

In a heavy frying-pan, cook the bacon until crisp and golden brown, about 5 minutes. Remove bacon with a slotted spoon and add cleaned chicken liver. Sauté quickly and remove from pan when still pink in middle. Add a few drops of olive oil to the pan and then add onions and garlic to the pan. Cook for 1–2 minutes until onions have softened, stirring. Then cover the pan, reduce heat and cook for at least 30 minutes, stirring once or twice. When the onions are really golden, return the bacon to the pan, turn heat full up, add stock and Madeira and boil until the liquid has evaporated and the sauce is thick. Adjust seasoning and stir in chopped parsley. Stir in coarsely chopped sautéed chicken liver and warm together for 1–2 minutes.

### To grill quail and serve

The procedure is identical to that described on pages 122–3 for the Indian spiced quail. Once the birds are cooked, remove them to a warm resting tray. You should now have at the ready:

(a) toasted crumbs

(b) hot, roasted garlic cloves

(c) hot sauce

(d) crostini slices piled high with liver mixture: place crostini in an oiled baking dish and bake in a very hot oven about 5–6 minutes at 200°C (400°F).

Serve the grilled quail half resting on the crostini, scatter 2 or 3 garlic cloves around, sprinkle on a heaped teaspoon of golden crumbs and drizzle over a spoonful of hot sauce. The final, delicious touch is to pass a shallow basket piled with parsnip chips (recipe page 59).

I have visited Bali twice, once as a penniless student many years ago and once more recently when I was lucky enough to have an introduction to Kichen, guide extraordinaire. Kichen understood that different visitors have different interests, and he made it his business that I saw as many culinary-related sights as possible, and tasted the best dishes. I had wonderful memories of *babi guling*, suckling pig roasted and sold at a roadside stall in the tiny village of Gianyar. Kichen took me, not to Gianyar this time, but to the night market at Denpasar for a feast of *babi guling*. This dish is not for those who hate fat.

Two women presided over a table on which were four enormous green enamel basins. The jointed pig reposed in two basins, shiny and crackling. In another was chopped innards of some sort, and in the fourth crisply fried bubbles of pork fat and the pig's intestines, encasing more chopped-up and highly seasoned special bits. The women were doing a roaring trade. The Balinese came, ordered, ate, paid and left with great efficiency. Another stream of people had take-away service, their pig, rice, stuffing, sausage and crispy skin all wrapped in a banana leaf.

While I think it unlikely that many people will wish to tackle roasting a whole pig, the same spicing was evident in the delicious *ayam tutu*, Balinese chicken. In Balinese restaurants one was required to give one day's notice for *ayam tutu*. I ate it several times, the best version at a roadside lunch stall where the chicken was served steamed with a mound of rice, sliced fried chicken giblets, a bowl of tiny potatoes and snake beans in a richly flavoured chicken and chilli broth, with a handful of freshly roasted local peanuts and a salad of sliced cucumber in sweet rice vinegar.

The dish I ate was accompanied by steamed white rice, but I had been offered a sweet pudding the day before, made from intensely blue-black rice. The dish was startling and dramatic. Kichen said that in Bali black rice is always used for sweet dishes, either this pudding or for sweet cakes or to make the beautiful edible free-standing sculptures that are constructed as offerings in the temples.

Back home and musing over how to recreate my memory, while browsing through our Vietnamese markets I found the same rice. It looks dusty brownish-black when raw, long-grained and quite reminiscent of wild rice. In fact the flavour and nuttiness of the cooked black rice is quite close to wild rice, and also reminds me of pearl barley. It is a fraction of the price of wild rice.

## STEPHANIE'S BALINESE CHICKEN

Coconut cream is sold as a solid block and is ideal for melting into soups and broths. In Bali this would be fresh coconut oil. Coconut oil must be bought very fresh as it goes rancid very quickly and would then completely spoil the dish.

- 6 × 350 g (12 oz) spatchcock (1 per person)
- 5 cm (2 in) piece of ginger, very finely chopped
- 4 cloves garlic, finely chopped
- 1 stalk lemongrass, stripped of its outside leaves and chopped very finely
- 2 hot red chillis, slit and seeded, chopped finely
- 2 teaspoons turmeric
- 2 tablespoons finely chopped coriander stalks

- 6 spring onions, finely chopped, including most of the green part
- 100 g (3 oz) solid creamed coconut, not coconut milk
- 3 cups well-flavoured chicken stock for the sauce
- 1 litre (32 fl oz) light chicken stock for cooking the rice
- 2 cups black rice or wild rice or wild rice mixture or brown rice

### — FOR GARNISH —

- 1 hot red chilli, slit, seeded and cut into very thin slivers
- leaves of fresh coriander
- some raw peanuts

### — VEGETABLE ACCOMPANIMENT —

- snake beans, or any vividly green Chinese vegetable suitable for serving in soup
- a little oil
- 1/3 cup chicken stock or water

#### To prepare the spatchcock

Cut out the backbone from each spatchcock, make a cut on either side of the breastbone so that the bird will open out flat as for the two preceding quail recipes. In my version I grill the birds after stuffing the breasts with a spice mixture, once again exactly as for the Indian quail. (At the end of the recipe I have suggested an alternative preparation, which would be a more authentic recreation of the dish as I had it in Bali.)

Combine all the ingredients listed from the ginger down to the spring onions. Melt the solid coconut cream and stir it into the spice and herbs. You should have a fairly thick paste.

With the fingertips, loosen the neck skin and ease the skin away from the breast meat and the upper part of the legs. Work a heaping teaspoonful of the mixture all over the entire breast surface and over the thighs. You must leave 1 teaspoon of the mixture per person to use in the broth. If you have excess, label and freeze it for another day. Brush the birds with melted butter and set aside until time to grill them.

### To cook rice

The time and amount of stock needed will, of course, vary considerably depending on the variety of rice used. If you are using either black rice or wild rice, wash it well in a colander and then allow three times the volume of light stock to rice.

Place the rice in a pan that has a tight-fitting lid, add the stock and salt and bring very slowly to simmering point. Place a folded clean towel over the rice, to absorb the steam, jam on the lid, turn the heat to very low and continue to cook the rice for at least 30 minutes, by which time it should have absorbed all the stock. When it is ready, either keep it in a warm place, or be prepared to steam it hot again when the birds are cooked.

### To make sauce

Bring your well-flavoured chicken stock to the boil. Add the reserved coconut/spice paste and stir until simmering again. Taste for salt. It should be spicy, aromatic and delicious. Keep hot in a bain-marie, or re-heat when needed. If reheating, do not let it boil for a long time, as it will reduce unnecessarily and the lovely fresh taste of the coriander will change.

### To grill birds

Follow the instructions exactly as given for the Indian spiced quail on pages 122–3. The spatchcock will need to cook for 15 minutes carcass side down to the heat source, and will need 3–5 minutes to crisp and brown the skin side. ▶

Have ready a large pot of boiling water and boil the snake beans.

If you are using Chinese greens, they are better if stir-fried, using a wok and a spoonful of light oil. Have the oil very hot, swish and tumble the greens until shiny, reduce heat, add a dash of chicken stock or water, cover the wok and cook until crisp-tender. They will be shiny and cooked in about 4 minutes. When they are ready, distribute the leaves among your serving dishes. The ideal bowls for this dish are wide soup plates. If using beans, divide them up into the bowls.

Despite my remarks about not boning the quail in the other grilled poultry dishes, in this case it is a good idea. The bird will be served in soup, and it is much harder to pick up and deal with anything other than the drumsticks. It is very easy to lift out the ribcage bones and with a small knife separate the flesh from the breastbone and then pull the bone firmly away from the flesh.

Place a mound of black rice in each dish, a boned spatchcock, ladle over your fragrant broth, float a few coriander leaves and a wisp or two of red chilli, scatter in a few peanuts, and there it is, quite delicious and quite different.

## — ALTERNATIVE AND MORE — AUTHENTIC COOKING METHOD

- 1 × 2 kg (4 lb) fat roasting chicken
- 3 litres (5 pints) light chicken stock (1 litre–32 fl oz–is for the rice)

Divide the spice mixture in half. Rub half under the skin as for the spatch-cocks. Place the other half inside the chicken, sew up the vent and the neck skin and let the bird sit overnight to absorb the flavours.

When required, poach the bird in the chicken stock in a suitable-sized cast-iron pot with a well-fitting lid. It will take about 1¼ hours. Cook the rice and beans as for the other method. Carve the chicken into serving bowls and ladle over the broth. Ensure that all the spices from inside the chicken are allowed to escape into the broth before it is served.

The garnishes would be the same.

## CHICKEN in ALMOND GREEN SAUCE
### (a Mexican-inspired dish)

I don't know where I first read of this dish. Chickens cooked in almond sauce of one sort or another occur in many books on Mexican cookery. None is exactly like this one, and certainly by the time I had made it several times and had various thoughts about the tastes I would like to see linked with it, I wonder whether any Mexican would recognise its origin.

It is a very quick and easy dish and the fresh taste of the sauce is appealing after a hot day.

I use chicken breasts for this dish, poach them and then spoon over the bright green thick sauce. I serve wild rice with it and a hollowed-out, crisped potato skin filled with chunky guacamole. I toast some flaked almonds and scatter a very few over the chicken, and on the side of the plate put either a pickled banana pepper or other home-made pickle or chutney.

• 6 good-sized chicken breasts, skinned

### — ALMOND GREEN SAUCE —

• 1 onion, finely chopped
• 6 large lettuce leaves from the outside of a cos or iceberg lettuce, shredded
• 1 cup coriander leaves, roughly chopped
• 1 cup flat-leaf parsley, chopped
• 2 cloves garlic, chopped
• 3 hot chillis, slit, seeded, chopped
• 1 cup blanched almonds, finely ground
• 1 cup chicken stock
• salt (optional)

### — FOR POACHING —

• 1 litre (32 fl oz) chicken stock

### — FOR GARNISHING —

• 6 medium potatoes baked in their jackets, flesh scooped out and the shells returned to the oven for a few minutes to dry
• coriander sprigs
• flaked almonds, toasted
• chutney or pickled banana pepper

First make the sauce. Place the first six ingredients in the food-processor and process until a fairly fine purée. Add the ground almonds and ½ cup of chicken stock. Season with salt. Tip this thick purée into a heavy-based pan and gently cook for 5 minutes. It must be stirred constantly or the almonds will stick and scorch on the bottom of the pan. You will probably need to add the remaining ½ cup of chicken stock to adjust sauce to consistency of thick porridge. Taste again for salt and spiciness. Leave aside until needed. It will keep at this stage, covered in the refrigerator, for 2–3 days.

### To cook wild rice

Follow instructions for cooking wild rice on page 131.

### To poach chicken breasts

Bring 1 litre (32 fl oz) of chicken stock to simmering point. Place the chicken breasts in the stock in a single layer. Avoid overlapping. Cover the pan. Turn after 3 minutes. After a further 3 minutes the breasts should be cooked and will feel slightly springy under the touch of your fingertip. Remove the cooked breasts to a warmed plate, cover and proceed to finish and serve the dish.

### To finish and serve

Measure ½ cup of poaching stock for each chicken breast. (This may be all the poaching liquid.) Place this measured portion of poaching stock into a small pan over high heat and stir in your green purée. Stir until well blended and bubbling.

Place a heap of wild rice in the centre of each plate, press the crisped potato shell into the centre of the rice.

Slice the chicken breast diagonally two or three times, place around the rice, spoon over the steaming sauce, scatter over the almonds, and fill the potato shell with guacamole. Drop on a few sprigs of fresh coriander. Place the pickled banana pepper on the plate.

Diana Kennedy, an authority on Mexican cooking, has very firm ideas about guacamole. She says that it is usually eaten in Mexico at the beginning of a meal with a pile of hot, freshly made tortillas and other snacks, such as crisp pork skins, or a plate of tacos, or tostados variations based on the classic tortilla, a paper-thin disc of yellow cornmeal dough.

It is often served puréed as a smooth dip, and I agree with Diana Kennedy that this homogenous mess is not what guacamole should be. The word means a concoction or mixture of avocado and so it should be. Chunky, pale green and pretty with the darker green of the coriander and the red of the tomato.

This is the recipe given by Diana Kennedy in her book *Mexican Regional Cookery*.

## GUACAMOLE

- 2 tablespoons finely chopped white onion
- 2 fresh, hot green chillis, finely chopped
- 4 large sprigs fresh coriander
- salt to taste
- 2 avocados
- 1 large red tomato, peeled and chopped into small pieces

### — GARNISH —

- ¼ small onion, finely chopped
- 6 sprigs coriander, roughly chopped

In a mortar and pestle, grind the onion, chillis, coriander and salt together until almost smooth. Cut the avocados in half. Remove the pit, scoop out the flesh with a wooden spoon, and mash roughly into the ingredients in the mortar. Mix well to incorporate, then stir in tomato. Adjust salt if necessary. Sprinkle with extra salt and coriander, and serve immediately.

Diana Kennedy disapproves, but I add a little lime juice and sometimes substitute a few drops of tabasco for the hot chillis.

She also recommends serving guacamole in the molcajete in which she would make it, a Mexican mortar shaped as a shallow thick bowl supported by three short legs, made of porous volcanic rock. It looks lovely, and I certainly will serve it this way when I find one! I did recently buy a rustic and beautiful stone mortar from one of our Asian specialist shops. It came from Thailand.

The next recipe is from the south-west of France; or, rather, the idea is. A chicken and potato pie cooked with duck fat and wrapped in bread dough sounds very heavy, and indeed it is rustic fare. The recipe I have given for the crust is a very light bread dough, and the whole pie is marvellous for a picnic. And while on the subject of picnics and poultry, I had to include my favourite pasty filling: lots of vegetables, pigeon and cumquats. The pasty pastry is the one I have given in my earlier book with the recipe for my grandmother's blackberry pie, and it is also used for Mary's beef and potato pie on pages 93–4. It is a very versatile dough.

## CHICKEN and POTATO PIE in OLIVE BREAD DOUGH

### — BREAD DOUGH —

- 500 g (1 lb) plain flour
- 200 g (7 oz) mashed potato
- 1 tablespoon yeast (dry Fermipan variety)
- 300 ml (10 fl oz) water
- 100 ml (3 fl oz) olive oil
- 1 teaspoon salt
- 1 cup pitted, chopped olives

Mix to a soft dough. Allow to rise (45 minutes). Handle with hands rubbed with oil.

### — FILLING —

- 500 g (1 lb) waxy potatoes, sliced 1 cm (¼ in) thick
- 2–3 tablespoons duck fat
- 10 cloves garlic, whole, peeled and blanched in water
- 1 large onion, finely chopped
- 5 chicken breasts, skinned or 3 chicken breasts and 2 confit duck legs
- 3 tablespoons flour
- 1½ cups good chicken stock
- 2 tablespoons parsley
- 2 teaspoons chopped rosemary or tarragon
- salt, pepper

Fry potatoes in 2 tablespoons of the duck fat until golden and just tender. Lift out slices, drain and place in a deep bowl. Fry blanched garlic cloves in same duck fat until golden (3 minutes, approximately). Drain and place in bowl. Fry chopped onion gently in same fat until golden, drain into bowl. Add extra tablespoon of fat and re-heat the fat. Seal the chicken breasts 2–3 minutes on each side and then remove. They will still be quite rare.

Add the flour to the remaining duck fat and stir the roux until it is pale-gold. Add the hot chicken stock and the chopped herbs and whisk till you have a smooth, thick sauce. Simmer for 5 minutes. Season.

Chop the chicken into bite-sized chunks and add to the bowl with the vegetables. Cut the *confit* from the bone and add if using. Stir in sufficient sauce to make a moist mix but not a sloppy one.

### To assemble and cook

Knock down the dough and press and pat it into a 26 cm (10 in) springform tin. The excess should hang over the edges of the tin. Pile the filling gently in and then cover it with the excess dough. Sprinkle with olive oil and scatter over a few grains of rock salt. Allow to rise 10–15 minutes.

Bake at 220°C (430°F) for 10 minutes and then 180°C (350°F) for a further 10 minutes. Allow to settle for 5 minutes before releasing the tin and cutting into wedges.

## PIGEON and CUMQUAT PASTY

The quantities given will make 8 good-sized pasties.

### — LARD PASTRY —

- 100 g (3 oz) sifted plain flour
- 100 g (3 oz) sifted self-raising flour
- pinch of salt
- 100 g (3 oz) lard at room temperature
- 90 ml (3 fl oz) cold water to mix

Sift flours together with salt. Rub lard in quickly. Make a well in the centre and work in the cold water. Knead until you have a fairly soft, springy and elastic dough, 2–3 minutes. Form into a ball, cover and chill for 20 minutes.

- 2 turnips, peeled thickly and cut into ½ cm (¼ in) cubes
- 1 medium carrot, peeled and cut into ½ cm (¼ in) cubes
- 1 medium onion, peeled and cut into ½ cm (¼ in) cubes
- ¼ bulb fennel, cut into ½ cm (¼ in) cubes
- 3 cumquats, pickled, halved, pipped and finely chopped
- 1 medium potato, peeled, cut into ½ cm (¼ in) cubes
- 4 pigeon, skin removed, flesh minced or chopped
- 4 pigeon livers, sautéed 1 minute in 1 teaspoon oil, chopped
- salt, pepper
- 1 tablespoon chopped parsley

- 1 whole egg
- 1 tablespoon water
- a pinch of salt

Mix all pasty ingredients together. Season well. Roll out pastry and cut circles 12 cm (5 in) diameter. Divide the mixture between the pasties. Egg wash the exposed pastry. Bring edges together and crimp tightly. Egg wash the pasties.

Cook 10 minutes at 220°C (430°F) and then for a further 30 minutes at 180°C (350°F).

Serve the pasties hot with braised fennel or warm or cold at a picnic with a good chutney.

Over 15 years ago I visited Lung Wah Restaurant at Shatin in Hong Kong's New Territories to eat the speciality of the house, roast pigeon. It was memorable. I have made many attempts, but never managed to reproduce exactly its glossy, thin, brown skin, its crispness and succulence. In 1986 I visited Hong Kong as one of a panel of international judges to participate in a Hong Kong culinary festival: The Flavour of '86. The Hong Kong Tourist Association was happy to arrange for me to revisit Shatin and to visit the Lung Wah kitchen to observe the pigeon performance. They did tell me that an official lunch had been arranged at Lung Wah later in the program and that I might perhaps risk a surfeit of pigeon. Not likely, I said, being a pigeon addict.

Shatin was once the countryside. It is now heavily built up with high-rise flats, new roads, hotels and shopping complexes. Happily the Lung Wah restaurant is still tucked into a green hillside, and the main eating area is still a large, open pavilion with slowly turning fans. On weekends the restaurant serves 500 pigeons a day, for most patrons order at least one.

In the kitchen the woks were heated by diesel, and each wok station was well-insulated with firebrick as the flames surged and glowed with a terrifying roar, like an ironworker's furnace. Flames shot high as a wok's contents were flipped. Each cook worked unconcernedly in singlet and shorts, frequently with a lit cigarette in his mouth.

Alongside were huge, bubbling cauldrons of water and stock. Spice bags dangled in the bubbling brew as dozens of pigeons swam desperately (or so it appeared, as they all still had heads intact). Another nonchalant cook was in charge here, poking and prodding and skimming the oil from the surface. This pigeon oil was later used to fry the birds. Once they were completely cooked (about 15 minutes), the birds were swished into a bath of mysterious ingredients and put to rest until ordered. When ordered they were deep-fried over unbelievable heat for 3–4 minutes, and then rushed to the table to be enjoyed with the saucers of spiced salt, light soy and chilli sauce. This is the Lung Wah pigeon experience at its most elemental. One tears at the birds, relishing the crispy skin, the crunchy neck, the splintery beak, and, if you are really Chinese, the brains, before getting to the juicy, rich flesh.

The cooks had prepared us some special dishes to follow our roast king pigeons. We next had the popular dish of minced pigeon stir-fried with mushroom, bamboo shoots and water chestnuts to roll in lettuce leaves, followed by a special white fungus and pigeon-egg clear soup. The pigeon egg had been simmered for 20 minutes, which causes a curious phenomenon. The yolks had become particularly creamy, and the whites translucent and jelly-like. These textures were particularly appreciated by the Chinese, and the Chinese photographers were particularly impressed by this dish. Pigeon eggs, they said, are very costly.

We then had an excellent pigeon-liver sausage with a little dice of pork fat, which had been lightly fried before including it in the sausage to add a crunchy texture. The final dishes were a stir-fry of pigeon giblets with chilli and black beans and a dish of the marvellous, vivid greens, in this case, mustard greens. We didn't taste them, but I had noticed a tub of duck webs soaking in the kitchen, already boned and ready to be stir-fried. I must try this at home some time, as I really enjoy cartilage. The braised chicken feet with chilli and black bean I had eaten the day before at a yum cha had been delicious, but the feet had no flavour of their own. Rather they provided crunch and a vehicle to carry the delicious sauce to the mouth. Altogether a delicious lunch, and it provided an interesting contrast to the dishes chosen by Willie Mark, Hong Kong's extrovert, knowledgeable gourmet, for our official lunch three days later.

A table was prepared for us inside, in air-conditioned splendour and away from the ordinary mortals tearing at their pigeons. The first course was the excellent caviar from the Amoy River in China. Gold-grey in colour, like oscietra, it had an excellent flavour, the grains large and separate like beluga. We then had a delicious soup, carried sealed to the table in a porcelain pot. This soup was made from blanched pigeon, herbs, tangerine peel and fresh ginseng. As everyone knows, ginseng controls stamina and blood pressure, relieves fatigue, enhances physical constitution and replenishes vital energy! It certainly was a splendid soup.

It is fascinating for a Western visitor to realise how seriously the Chinese link foods to health, not necessarily as a medicine, but the health-giving qualities of an ingredient are considered along with its texture and flavour.

We then had the minced pigeon dish again and a platter of cold, roast pigeon legs. The French judge, Michel Piot from Le Figaro, was disappointed. I had been telling him all morning how delicious his whole roast pigeon would be. I was also curious to see how he would react to this completely cooked bird, accustomed as he was to the blood-rare pigeon flesh in France. Perhaps it was considered a little low-class to ask all these VIPs to gnaw at their food? It seemed impolite to Willie to ask. I was just secretly delighted that I had visited Lung Wah on the previous occasion. Once again we were served the pigeon-egg delicacy, this time deep-fried and served with silver fungus.

After lunch, our energy replenished by the ginseng, we returned to the Royal Hong Kong Jockey Club to eat our way through another 12 dishes!

# LUNG WAH PIGEON
(our best effort so far)

- 3 squab pigeons, 375–400 g (12–13 oz), head and feet still attached
- 3 litres (5 pints) chicken stock
- 1 cinnamon stick, splintered
- 3 whole star anise
- 1 × 5 cm (2 in) knob ginger
- oil for deep frying
- salt and pepper for dipping

## — COATING SAUCE —

- 1 cup water
- ½ cup rice vinegar
- ½ cup maltose or honey
- ½ teaspoon bicarbonate of soda

Boil all the ingredients for the coating sauce together.

Simmer the chicken stock with the cinnamon, star anise and ginger for 30 minutes. Stick a butcher's hook firmly through the neck of each squab pigeon and lower them into the stock. Return to the simmering point and simmer up to 10 minutes, depending on how rosy you like your pigeon. 8 minutes would do me, but the Cantonese would leave them much longer. Lift the birds out and hang in a draughty place to rapidly drain and cool. After 2–3 minutes dip the birds into the coating sauce and then hang again to dry completely, for at least 2 hours.

Heat about 5 cm (2 in) of light oil in a wok and, when it is very hot, carefully lower the birds into the oil. Spoon the oil over and over–be careful, they will spit. When the birds are a rich brown, remove them and serve at once with salt and pepper dip; or allow them to cool, slice the flesh and combine with white-cooked chicken as a salad with a soy dip.

### SALT AND PEPPER DIP TO ACCOMPANY DEEP-FRIED DISHES

Place salt and ground pepper in a clean, heavy cast-iron pan and heat until they become aromatic. The proportions are up to you. Szechuan peppercorns can be used for a specially aromatic dip. They should be dry-roasted whole in the pan and then ground finely in a coffee grinder.

# WHITE-COOKED CHICKEN

- 1 × 2 kg (4 lb) corn-fed, free-range chicken
- 2 spring onions, sliced
- 1 × 5 cm (2 in) knob ginger, sliced
- ice for chilling chicken

Remove any inside fat from chicken. Wipe dry inside and out. Bring water, spring onions and ginger to simmering point in a pan sufficiently large to allow the chicken to be completely submerged in the liquid.

Plunge in the chicken, breast down. Allow the liquid to return to boiling point, skim the surface carefully, adjust heat to a gentle simmer, put on the lid and time the cooking for 10 minutes exactly. Turn off heat, do not lift lid and time for 1 hour.

Have ready a large tub of water into which you empty lots of ice-cubes. The aim of the next exercise is to chill the chicken quickly, thus causing the juices to solidify in a thin layer under the taut, shiny chicken skin.

Lift chicken, using a strong lifter, drain liquid from the cavity and then plunge the bird into the icy water, breast down. Leave until completely chilled, at least 1 hour. At this point the chicken can be removed to a plate, wrapped in a clean cloth, or covered in plastic and will be sensational at any time over the next 4 or 5 days.

## To serve white-cooked chicken

With a sharp knife, remove the legs. Separate the drumstick from the thigh with a sharp cut through the joint. Using a cleaver, cut through the leg and thigh into round sections. The bone will still be quite red—the meat will be incomparably delicious. If you have never used a cleaver, remember two things. It must be sharp, and you must be bold and decisive. Keep your left hand out of the way and sharply and firmly bring the blade down. Most satisfying.

Next, remove each breast fillet, gently keeping skin and, most importantly, the layer of jellied juices intact. Slice the meat into neat long slices across the grain.

Serve the meat with one of the following easy sauces or else combine it in a more Western-style salad, perhaps with melon or fresh lychees.

## — CHILLI SAUCE DIP —

- 3 teaspoons chilli sauce
- 3 tablespoons light soy sauce
- 1 tablespoon light oil

## — GINGER SAUCE —

- 1 tablespoon finely minced ginger
- 4 tablespoons soy sauce
- 1 tablespoon light oil
- pinch of sugar

## — SEARED SPRING ONION DIPPING SAUCE —

- 4 spring onions, finely chopped
- 1 teaspoon finely chopped ginger
- 1 teaspoon finely chopped garlic
- 3 tablespoons light oil
- 3 tablespoons light soy sauce
- 1 tablespoon rice wine or dry sherry
- 1 teaspoon sesame oil

Mix spring onions, ginger and garlic in a bowl. Heat oil until smoking hot. Instantly pour over the contents of the bowl. They will hiss and sizzle. Stir. Add the rest of the ingredients.

This last sauce is one of my favourites and is an excellent seasoning for rice or egg noodles that have been briefly boiled (4–5 minutes).

## YAM of ROSES

A rather more exotic use for white-cooked chicken is this Thai-derived, rose-petal salad.

- 1 long, ridged cucumber or 3 small, Lebanese cucumbers
- salt
- 1 cup water
- 2 large, fragrant red roses (not sprayed)
- breast meat from a white-cooked chicken
- 2 teaspoons palm or brown sugar
- juice of 3 limes
- 2 teaspoons fish sauce
- 4 spring onions, chopped finely
- 2 hot, red chillis, slit, seeded and chopped finely
- 3 tablespoons roasted peanuts
- 2 spring onions, slit lengthwise and slivered (soak slivers in a bowl of cold water for 1 hour to curl)

## To prepare cucumber

Slice cucumber thinly, leaving skin on unless it seems to be tough (taste a slice). Place in a bowl, sprinkle with 2 teaspoons salt and 1 cup water. Mix lightly. Soak for 30 minutes and then drain very well.

## To assemble salad

Line 6 small plates with about half of the rose petals, using the most perfect for this. Tear the rest of the petals into smaller pieces. Slice the chicken meat into small strips. Mix the cucumber with the torn petals, sugar, lime juice, fish sauce, spring onion, chillis and peanuts. Stir gently until the sugar has dissolved. Mix the chicken in lightly and divide the salad between the 6 plates. Decorate with a few curls of spring onion.

Melbourne is a convincingly multicultural city to a degree that many of its citizens fail to realise. Our Chinatown is a working, vigorous centre for the extensive Chinese community. There are few products and delicacies that are not available here, and it is not surprising that Melburnian food lovers appreciate many Asian tastes. A stroll through Little Bourke Street on Sunday is a stimulating, nostril-twitching experience. Yum cha is enjoyed by growing numbers every week, the roast duck and noodle shops and the steamed-bun makers do a roaring trade in take-outs, and it is possible to banquet on the most rarefied of delicacies, from superior shark's fin, to fish lips, to stuffed conch, braised baby abalone and so on and so on. If only I had nine stomachs!

## BLACK SATIN DUCK TERRINE

This terrine is totally Asian in its ingredients, but quite Western in its presentation. It seems to appeal to both East and West. I usually serve it with a bowl of pickled watermelon rind, spring onion brushes and hot, steamed onion and sesame oil buns.

- 1 duck, dressed weight 2 kg (4 lb)
- 10 dried Chinese mushrooms
- 2 pieces dried tangerine peel
- 6 points star anise
- 2 cloves garlic, finely chopped
- 1 teaspoon finely chopped ginger
- 1 tablespoon rock sugar or 1½ tablespoons honey
- 1 tablespoon sesame oil
- 60 ml (2 fl oz) light soy sauce
- 60 ml (2 fl oz) dark soy sauce
- 1 litre (32 fl oz) well-flavoured, fat-free chicken stock
- 30 g (1 oz) sugar
- 12 leaves gelatine per litre (32 fl oz) of finished juice

Soak Chinese mushrooms in warm water to soften for 30 minutes. Remove and discard hard stems. Simmer all ingredients together, other than the duck. Remove any visible fat from the duck and simmer it in the liquid in a covered pan until the duck is completely tender. This will take around 1 hour. The duck should be well cooked. Allow it to cool in the liquid until you are able to handle the duck.

Remove all flesh from the carcass. Discard carcass. You will have some small shreds of meat as well as the larger pieces from the legs and breasts. Strain the liquid into a bowl. Do not discard mushrooms and tangerine peel. Cut duck meat into even-shaped pieces and drop the pieces into the bowl of liquid to keep moist until all the meat is cut up. Slice peel finely. Keep mushrooms whole.

Pack the solids into a Le Creuset, or similar, cast-iron terrine pan, distributing orange-peel slivers and whole mushrooms evenly. Pour all the liquid into a tall, clear jug. Allow to settle and skim off all fat. Measure.

Soften the appropriate number of leaves of gelatine in cold water. Squeeze and drop into 100 ml (3 fl oz) of flavoured juices, which you have brought to simmering point in a small pan. When completely dissolved, stir the gelatine mixture into the balance of the juice. Pour juice over terrine. Move terrine to the refrigerator and do not disturb until quite set. Overnight is safest. The solids will float, and when the terrine is sliced will appear to be suspended in clear, dark 'satiny' jelly.

I slice the terrine with A VERY SHARP KNIFE dipped in hot water, using a sawing motion, not pressing down.

## PICKLED WATERMELON RIND

This old-fashioned pickle is very well known, and I have included a recipe for it in my first book, *Stephanie's Menus for Food Lovers*. It is repeated here for convenience.

As a variation, add 1 or 2 slices of ginger to the syrup, or add ½ cup grenadine syrup if you prefer a pink pickle.

- 1 kg (2 lb) watermelon rind
- ¼ cup salt
- 1 litre (32 fl oz) water

### — PICKLING SYRUP —

- 1 kg (2 lb) sugar
- 600 ml (20 fl oz) white wine vinegar
- 600 ml (20 fl oz) water
- 1 lemon, thinly sliced
- 1 tablespoon cinnamon bark
- 1 teaspoon whole cloves
- 1 teaspoon whole allspice berries

Cut the rind with just a blush of pink left on and trimmed into even-shaped pieces, approximately 6 × 1 cm (2 × ½ in) thick. Soak rind overnight in the ¼ cup salt and 1 litre (32 fl oz) of water.

Next day, drain the rind, put it in a pan, cover with cold water and simmer for about 30 minutes, until the head of a pin will easily pierce the skin.

Make up the pickling syrup by combining all the given ingredients and simmering for 10 minutes. Add the drained rind and boil rapidly until the rind is translucent. Fill hot clean jars with the rind and syrup and leave for about a week. It is even better if you can bear to leave it for a month.

## SPRING ONION STEAMED BUNS

The recipe is taken from my favourite Chinese authority, Irene Kuo, *The Key to Chinese Cooking*. She also gives instructions for plain buns, flower rolls and meat-filled buns, with a variation on plain buns that uses finely chopped spring onions. I add some finely chopped ginger to the spring onions.

## — BASIC DOUGH —

- 1 teaspoon dry yeast
- 2 tablespoons lukewarm water
- 500 g (1 lb) plain flour, sifted
- 1 tablespoon sugar
- 1 cup lukewarm water
- 1 teaspoon baking powder

## — FILLING —

- sesame oil
- 6 spring onions, finely chopped, using most of the green part
- 1 x 5 cm (2 in) piece ginger finely chopped

Dissolve the yeast in 2 tablespoons lukewarm water, or mix it directly with the flour if using the Fermipan variety.

Mix the flour and sugar in a bowl. Make a well in the centre and pour in the dissolved yeast and the water. Stir until you have a lumpy mass. Press together into a ball. Turn out onto a floured work surface and knead for 5 minutes. At the end of this time the dough should be smooth and springy.

Place dough back in the bowl and leave in a warm place to double. When doubled, lightly knock back and tip the dough onto the floured work surface. Flatten into an oblong shape. Scatter over the baking powder and knead again for a further 5 minutes until the dough is smooth, satiny and firm, with plenty of bounce.

### TO FORM AND STEAM

Pat the dough into a rectangle, roll it out lightly. Paint the surface with sesame oil, salt lightly (optional) and scatter over the spring onions/ginger. Roll up the dough as if rolling a roulade. Cut into sections and roll into smooth round buns, or refer to *The Key to Chinese Cooking* for very clear instructions on how to form flower rolls.

Transfer the buns to a lightly floured tray. Cover with a dry, floured cloth and allow to rise in a warm place until doubled (approximately 45 minutes). The buns should be puffed and taut and feel light.

Line the steamer with a damp cloth and place the buns so that they do not touch. Steam for 15 minutes over high heat. Turn off steam and allow steam to subside for at least 5 minutes before removing the buns. Once steamed the buns will keep, wrapped in plastic, for a week or more in the refrigerator. To re-heat, steam as above.

My last cooking story in this section concerns an all-Australian bird, the magpie goose. I set out for Kakadu National Park, 200 km east of Darwin in the top end of Australia in a 4-wheel drive vehicle to search for bush tucker. Kakadu is unique in Australia in that it is owned by the Aboriginal people of the Alligator River and is jointly managed by the Australian National Parks and Wildlife Service and the tribal elders.

My interest in Aboriginal traditional food had been stimulated by the fascinating paper given by archaeologist Betty Meehan at the second symposium of Australian gastronomy held in Adelaide in September 1985, detailing the varied diet and the cooking and gathering traditions of the Anbarra people of Arnhem Land.

I had as companion and guide an officer of the Northern Territory Tourist Commission, who had previously spent some years living in Arnhem Land and was knowledgeable, interested and very willing to point out to me all that was edible.

Driving the Arnhem Highway, Chris frequently stopped and pointed. We saw Australia's only stork, the jabiru, in pairs absorbed in courtship. An elegant brolga preened, three free-ranging water buffalo moved off at our approach, wallabies bounded alongside, and frequently there was the lapis blue flash of the forest kingfisher.

He showed me the screw palm (*Pandanus spiralis*). Its centre tender shoot can be eaten and has a nutty flavour reminiscent of the heart of an artichoke. Its outer leaves are used for weaving, and the roots and tougher leaves as a fuel. Another palm, *Cycas armstrongii*, is used by the Aboriginal as a source of flour. The kernels must be soaked to rid them of a poison before use.

We were travelling during the wet season, and the lush green floodplains were a-flower with large, starry white lilies with red stamens (*Crinum asiaticum*) and an edible bulb, Chris said. At our approach and after repeated use of the horn, we were rewarded by the dramatic sight of dozens of long-necked magpie geese rising in flight and settling a little farther away to continue their grazing for insects, frogs and bulbs.

We arrived at our destination, Cooinda, a motel and camping-area owned by the Aboriginal community. Next day we travelled to see the rock paintings at Nourlangie dating from 20,000 years ago. These paintings are cared for and parts are repainted by Bill Neiijie, known as Kakadu Man. He is greatly concerned that the next generation will not care for the traditions as he does. As we walked, Chris pointed out many plants and fruits.

I renewed acquaintance with *Grevillea pteridifolia*. I once used these flowers to make a delicate honey-like sorbet for an Australian dinner. The Aboriginals suck the flower bracts to enjoy the nectar. We gathered billygoat plums (apparently there are several varieties) or bush 'banana (*Planchonia careya*), which I found sticky and meaty like a banana and very pleasant. Bush 'apples' abounded, the fruit of *Eugenia suborbicularis*, related to our common lilly pilly. They are bright rosy-pink, sharp, crunchy and refreshing. We dug for yams, which are a highly prized food. Chris says that Aboriginals will refer to some yams as 'cheeky', which means unfit to eat, or slightly toxic. When yams are dug, a little bit is always replaced to ensure continual renewal. Among the sandstone rocks at Nourlangie we met a yellow-bellied goanna and other smaller lizards. These reptiles are highly regarded traditional foods, usually eaten lightly roasted.

The next highlight was an excursion on the flooded Yellow Waters in a flat-bottomed boat. We were floating over an area that, the boatman said, was the camping-ground during the dry season. Before the end of the Wet there would be 8 metres of water expected here. We nibbled on peeled water-lily stalks fished from the water. They were a little like celery, but more like several Asian vegetables I remember from Hong Kong. The boatman pointed out the freshwater mangroves (*Barringtonia acutangula*). Aboriginal fishermen pound its leaves, pods and seeds and throw it into the water to stun the fish. The poison apparently doesn't affect the eating quality of the fish. The majestic white-breasted sea eagle watched us slide by, all around us fish were jumping, and the Christ-bird was walking on the water. The rain fell steadily, creating a rather eerie atmosphere as the boat slid slowly and silently among the paperbarks.

Bill Neiijie gave Chris a present of a magpie goose, which I was delighted to cook. For most of the year the goose is regarded as traditional Aboriginal food, as is the case with green sea-turtle, goanna and dugong. However, there is an annual open season, which in 1985 was from August to November.

It was a fitting farewell to the Territory to feast on such a dish. Aboriginals roast the goose in an earth oven. I treated it more convention-ally, as for wild duck, and its flesh was rich, gamy and very tender.

## ROASTED MAGPIE GOOSE
### (or wild duck)

- 1 magpie goose weighing approximately 1 kg (2 lb) dressed
- salt, pepper
- 2 cloves garlic, smashed
- 1 onion, finely chopped
- 1 carrot, finely chopped

- 2 stalks wild fennel
- 2 tablespoons olive oil
- 1 glass dry white wine
- 500 ml (17 fl oz) simple stock made from the neck, wingtips and giblets of the bird

Wipe the bird inside and out. If there are any feathers still present, pass the bird over a gas jet to singe them. Season it with salt and pepper, lightly crush one of the cloves of garlic and put it inside the bird. Rub all over with the olive oil.

Thoroughly brown the vegetables in an extra tablespoon of oil, place the goose on its side on the vegetables in a hot oven (240°C–460°F) for 10 minutes, then turn it to the other side for a further 10 minutes. Turn the bird breast uppermost for 5 minutes and then remove it from the oven. Cut the legs from the carcass, and return them to the oven in a clean pan to continue cooking after lowering the temperature to 180°C (350°F) while the sauce is made. Keep the breast section warm by covering it loosely with foil.

Pour off any fat that has accumulated in the pan, deglaze with the white wine, scraping well to dislodge any bits of caramelised vegetables. Add the stock and boil fiercely for 5 minutes. Strain sauce, taste for strength and seasoning and keep it bubbling gently while you carve the breast meat onto very hot plates. If the legs still need further cooking, serve them as a separate course with a green salad and accompany the breast meat moistened with its simple sauce with roast sweet potatoes in lieu of yams.

It intrigues me that the only recipe in this poultry section that could be said to be classically French relates to a bird that has been cooked for thousands of years by the Australian Aborigine in an earth oven. And yet I am continually described as a French cook and my restaurant as a French restaurant .

# SNIPS, SNAILS & OXTAIILS

— FEASTS & STORIES —

So much has been written recently about the pleasures of offal eating that the battle may be already won. I hope so, as from the cook's point of view the world of 'snips' or variety meats or offal opens up a whole world of new possibilities. For this chapter I have had to be very strict and to restrict myself to recipes that seem to be original (as far as I know), and those that are my very, very favourites. I have taken liberties with the definition of offal and include here my recipes for garden snails. At the present time the idea of catching and preparing the common garden snail fills most people with incredulity at best, and more frequently with horror. Fortunately, once the dish is described and prettily presented, a gratifying number of diners eat and enjoy them.

First a return to the world of *confits* for a salad using gizzards and hearts. I have earlier described *confit*-making in general. In the restaurant, we used goose gizzards and goose hearts for this salad. Duck gizzards and hearts are just as delicious and much easier to obtain. The goose giblets came our way as a by-product of a dish featuring goose breasts. The price of the birds was high, so that it made good sense to use every morsel. The neck skin was eased off the neck, turned inside out to clean, and then frozen for a later occasion, when it was stuffed with a savoury mix of poultry liver, fresh pork, minced duck, a little cognac and herbs and seasonings. All loose fat from inside the bird and around the thighs and all the excess skin was carefully put on one side to be rendered with a clove or two of garlic. Goose fat is superb as a frying medium for potatoes or for sauerkraut, even if you do not decide to use if for *confit*.

The legs were prepared in the manner described on page 118, with the important difference that we boned them before the initial salting. The leg bones and carcass, of course, went straight into the stockpot to create a clear, well-skimmed stock.

---

## SALAD of DUCK CONFITS with SAUTÉED DUCK HEARTS, LIVERS and APPLES

- 6 duck legs, boned
- seasoned salt mixture, as for Paula Wolfert's confit of duck (pages 117–9)
- 6 sprigs thyme
- 6 duck gizzards
- 4 cups rendered duck fat (see also pages 117–9)
- 6 duck hearts
- 6 duck livers

- 3 tart cooking apples, each peeled and cut into 8 wedges
- 60 g (2 oz) butter
- 1 teaspoon red wine vinegar or cider vinegar
- selected washed and dried salad greens, hopefully with some peppery varieties, such as rocket, frisée, radicchio or watercress

### — TO COOK HEARTS AND LIVERS —

- 1 tablespoon butter
- 1 tablespoon olive oil
- 1 tablespoon brandy or Madeira or port

- 4 tablespoons good poultry stock or water
- 2 tablespoons cream
- duck cracklings (see page 154)

### To prepare duck legs

Bone the legs and leave overnight in the salt and seasonings as described on page 118. Next day, rinse, place a sprig of thyme in each one and tie in a cylindrical shape, like a small sausage. Cook in the manner described in the basic method. This preparation can be done weeks before you wish to serve the salad.

## To Prepare Duck Gizzards

The gizzard will have been cleaned by the poulterer and will look like a hard, muscular lump covered in tough skin and gristle with at either side a smaller lump. With a sharp knife, cut each of the smaller lumps away from its enclosing skin. It is really very easy to do this. Then slit the larger lump down the centre, and, working your knife along the base of the lump and then up the side, you should free the gizzard of all skin and gristle. (If the duck leg bones are simmering away for your poultry stock, toss in the gizzard skins as well.) You should have 4 roughly almond-shaped pieces of meat from each gizzard.

Now season these and leave overnight, proceeding exactly as with the duck legs. The gizzards could be cooked in the same fat and at the same time as the legs, if this is convenient. The legs may be tender first. In this case, ladle off enough fat to cover the legs as they cool slowly, and continue to cook the gizzards until they can be easily pierced with a skewer.

Alternatively, you may decide to prepare a larger quantity of gizzards, and they would therefore need to be cooked and stored separately. It is quite likely that you will want to do this after you have first tasted these delicious morsels. A jar of this *confit* in the refrigerator is a splendid resource.

## To Prepare Hearts and Livers

Trim off all the fat and gristle from the flat end of the acorn-shaped heart. Score a small cross on the pointed end of the heart to ensure even cooking. Like the duck liver, the hearts are best sautéed until they are just pink inside.

Trim the duck livers of all threads and blood vessels. Check carefully to ensure that the bile duct is no longer attached to the liver. Any greenish stain on either lobe must be cut away to avoid a bitter taste.

## To Serve

Fifteen minutes before serving, remove the duck legs from their fat in the manner described on page 118. Snip and remove the strings, and then proceed to cook and crisp the legs in a tightly covered frying-pan as described in the basic method. The gizzards are best warmed gently in the fat still clinging to them and then left in a covered pan until needed.

Melt the 60 g (2 oz) of butter in a non-stick pan and fry the apple wedges. While they are cooking, arrange 6 piles of greens on 6 heated plates. When the apples are golden, increase heat and add the splash of vinegar. Divide the apples among the 6 plates and the juices.

Return the frying-pan to the flame, add the tablespoon of butter and of oil, heat. Toss in the livers and the hearts. Sear well, then pour on the alcohol. Allow to burn away, add the stock and the cream. The sauce will form almost instantly. Divide the livers and hearts among the plates. Finally, slice the duck legs and arrange on each salad and scatter over each plate the 4 pieces of gizzard together with a few drops of the well-seasoned fat.

Serve at once. The *pièce de résistance* with this salad is to have available some crispy duck cracklings to add a rich crunch.

### DUCK OR GOOSE CRACKLINGS

A bonus from making *confit* is the crispy cracklings that result from rendering fat and skin. Even if you are not making *confit* you may have a supply of duck skin. For instance, many cookbooks give recipes these days for sautéed duck breast, without the skin.

Cut skin and fat into small strips and place in a heavy saucepan with a few spoonfuls of water. Cook over a moderate flame until all the spitting and hissing has stopped. Stir from time to time to prevent sticking. This will take at least 1 hour before the fat looks clear. Watch closely at this point. When the skin is browned and crispy, lift out the cracklings with a slotted spoon and drain on kitchen paper.

### A VARIATION ON THE SALAD

Replace the salad greens with cooked chickpeas, tossed in a sharp vinai-grette while warm, or replace the sautéed apples with red cabbage braised with apples and red wine vinegar in the well-known European manner.

## SAUTÉED SWEETBREADS, served with MUSHROOM TERRINE

It is not easy to get excellent quality sweetbreads in Australia. The best are exported, mainly to France, where they are rightly appreciated as a delicacy. Ask your butcher for export-quality veal sweetbreads. They are usually packed in 500 g (1 lb) packs, and arrive frozen, complete with labelling in French. Their appeal is their richness and creaminess, and the fact that they combine well with other meats and all manner of flavours.

Lamb sweetbreads are to be avoided in my opinion. They are so small and fiddly that they do not justify the time spent in their preparation. They are, however, much cheaper.

### — BASIC PREPARATION —

Soak sweetbreads overnight in cold, salted water to draw out the blood. The next day, drain the sweetbreads, rinse, and place in a pan with cold water and bring just to simmering point. Drain again, rinse under the cold tap and then pull off as much as possible of the loose membrane and pieces of fatty tissue. The sweetbreads are now ready to be braised, a necessary step before using them in a salad, or before sautéeing them. Drop the cleaned sweetbreads into a bowl of cold water until ready to braise them to avoid discoloration.

### — TO BRAISE —

- 1 kg (2 lb) sweetbreads
- butter or oil
- 1 carrot, chopped
- 1 small onion, chopped
- 1 leek, well washed and sliced
- thyme, bay leaf, parsley stalks
- ½ stick celery, chopped
- ½ cup Madeira or late-picked white wine or port
- 1 litre (32 fl oz) veal or chicken stock

Heat the butter and oil in a cast-iron casserole and sauté the vegetables until well coloured. Add the sweetbreads, and turn them in the butter. Increase heat and pour on the wine. Allow to bubble fiercely for 3–4 minutes until it has all but evaporated. Pour on enough stock to barely cover the sweetbreads, bring to the simmering point, turn down heat to maintain a gentle simmer. Cover the pot and cook until the sweetbreads are tender, about 30 minutes. Allow to cool in the stock until they are able to be handled.

Strain some of the stock into a bowl and then, piece by piece, remove the sweetbreads from the liquid. Check for any membranes not removed previously, and drop each piece back into the bowl of stock. When all have been checked, place them on a cloth-covered tray, cover with another damp cloth to prevent their drying, and press with another board topped with some weights (jam jars, tins). Allow to become quite cold. Strain the rest of the stock and use as the base of the sauce.

Bubble the stock and taste it for strength and character. It will probably need to reduce by about half. Reduce it and keep it warm if you are to proceed directly with the recipe.

### To cook sweetbreads

Cut any very large sweetbreads into bite-sized pieces. Season. Roll in seasoned flour and then shake the pieces in a sieve to remove the excess flour.

Heat a mixture of olive oil and butter in a large frying-pan until it stops foaming. Pan-fry the sweetbreads without crowding until they are golden brown and crisp on the outside. If the pieces are too small, they will not be creamy inside.

In another pan heat the sauce and swirl a nut of butter into it to thicken it lightly. Season well with pepper. A very extravagant but sensational result is achieved by adding 1 tablespoon of truffle juice to the sauce just at the moment of service. At the time of writing the price of truffle juice means that the flavour will have to become a taste memory for me!

At Stephanie's we serve our golden sweetbread fritters with a slice of mushroom terrine (see pages 65–6), steamed hot for 1–2 minutes, half a poached pear, warmed through in the sauce with its hollow filled with the sharp freshness of a purée of sorrel.

In my earlier book, *Stephanie's Menus for Food Lovers*, I have given the recipe for two of my favourite offal recipes using sweetbreads, the first a salad in which the braised sweetbreads are separated into small pieces and mixed with a dressing based on some of their braising juices, orange juice, walnut oil and pistachio nuts. The salad is served either on crisp salad leaves, or sliced, simmered Jerusalem artichokes or pink radishes. The second dish is one of our most famous, the stuffed tripe sausage, where the filling of chicken mousse holds lots of surprises, sweetbreads being one of them.

Frequently one encounters pieces of sweetbread, cut very small, heavily disguised in creamy sauces and stuffed into pastry cases. I dislike these dishes very much. But, instead of being negative, I shall progress to my other enthusiasm: tripe. Practically all tripe sold in Australia is pre-cooked. In fact, if you are looking for the beige, uncooked variety to make *les tripoux* (pages 161–2) or another long-simmered dish, you may have difficulty locating it. Apart from Dany Chouet's recipe on page 161, all tripe recipes presume blanched tripe, which has been pre-cooked. One is usually offered either blanket tripe or honeycomb tripe. Test tripe after 30 minutes' cooking. It should be tender, but still al dente. There is nothing more certain to turn people off than serving tripe with the texture of wet rags.

I have read that in the bistrots of Lyons a commonly encountered dish is the *tablier de sapeur* (fireman's apron). I have visited only two bistrots in Lyons and it featured in neither, but that proves nothing, of course. The dish itself is very simple. Squares of pre-cooked tripe are seasoned and rolled in egg and breadcrumbs and are then fried in clean oil until golden, and are served with a sauce having sharp, vinegary ingredients such as *remoulade* (mayonnaise-based) or *ravigote* (vinaigrette-based). This is fine, but I felt that it could be improved.

## STEPHANIE'S TRIPE and CUMQUAT FRITTERS on a GREEN PEA SAUCE

- 1 kg (2 lb) blanched honeycomb tripe
- 1 litre (32 fl oz) veal stock or chicken stock
- 10 pickled cumquats (see page 159)
- 2 tablespoons chopped parsley
- salt, pepper
- 1 cup plain flour
- 2 eggs
- 2 cups fine, white breadcrumbs
- clean oil for deep-frying or shallow-frying

## — SAUCE —

- I cup sweet green peas, shelled
- I tablespoon butter
- strained stock from the tripe
- I teaspoon sherry vinegar (approximately)
- salt
- white pepper

## — GARNISH —

- I tablespoon pickled capers
- 3 spring onions

### TO PREPARE SPRING ONIONS

Split spring onions lengthwise. Wash well and, with a very sharp knife, sliver them on the diagonal. Include lots of the green tops. Each sliver should be 4–5 cm (2 in) long. Drop the spring onion slivers in a bowl of cold water to curl. Store in the refrigerator.

### TO COOK TRIPE

Place the uncut tripe into a pan and pour on the stock. Dilute with water if the stock is insufficient to cover the tripe. Simmer for 30 minutes, then test for tenderness. When cooked, lift out the tripe and spread it on a tray to cool quickly. Cut into squares of about 4–5 cm (2 in).

Finely chop the pickled cumquats, flicking out the seeds. Marinate the tripe squares in the cumquat, cumquat liquid, chopped parsley, and salt and pepper for at least 1 hour. The tripe should be very well seasoned.

Arrange three trays in front of you: (1) plain flour; (2) well-whisked eggs; (3) fine breadcrumbs.

Dip each square of tripe into tray (1), then (2), then (3). Ensure that each square has a good coating of crumbs. Refrigerate the tripe to set the coating until needed.

### TO MAKE SAUCE

Sweat the peas in the hot butter over low heat for 2–3 minutes. Add sufficient of the strained tripe stock to cover the peas generously. Simmer until the peas are tender, but do not overcook. The bright green colour is one of the charms of the sauce. Blend the sauce or use a food-processor. Pass through a strainer to ensure that the texture is quite smooth. Add the sherry vinegar, salt and pepper. The sauce should taste sharp, but mustn't lose the sweetness of the peas.

## To serve

Heat the oil to very hot. Fry the squares of tripe without crowding. Drain on kitchen paper. Spoon some pea sauce onto a plate, pile on the tripe fritters and scatter over the capers and the frilly, green onion slivers.

## — SPICED (PICKLED) CUMQUATS —

- 500 g (1 lb) cumquats
- 1 teaspoon salt
- 600 ml (20 fl oz) water
- 150 g (5 oz) castor sugar
- ½ cinnamon stick
- 1 teaspoon whole cloves
- 600 ml (20 fl oz) white wine vinegar

Dissolve the salt in the water. Bring to the boil. Pour over the cumquats in bowl or basin and allow to stand for 12 hours. Drain. Simmer sugar and spices in vinegar for 5 minutes. Pour boiling vinegar over cumquats, bottle and store in a cool place.

## TRIPE cooked in an ITALIAN MANNER

Balsamic vinegar is wine vinegar produced in Modena. It is aged for at least 5 years in wooden barrels made of juniper, mulberry and chestnut woods. It has a special perfume acquired from its long ageing in wood, its colour is a warm brown and it is syrupy in texture. Balsamic vinegar is very powerful, and should always be used sparingly in salad dressings, in some meat dishes, and sometimes sprinkled on berries.

- 1 kg (2 lb) honeycomb tripe, cut into 2.5 cm (1 in) strips
- 200 g (7 oz) smoked bacon or pancetta
- 2 tablespoons olive oil
- 2 onions, finely chopped
- 1 tablespoon balsamic vinegar
- 2 tablespoons tomato paste
- 1 slit, seeded hot red chilli, left whole
- 1 bay leaf
- 1 tablespoon chopped oregano leaves
- 1 cup dry white wine
- 1 cup well-reduced veal stock
- salt
- chopped parsley

Sauté bacon in olive oil for 3–4 minutes. Add the onions and cook until soft and golden. Add tripe strips and increase heat to full. Cook rapidly for a few minutes to evaporate moisture from the tripe. Add balsamic vinegar, stir and allow to evaporate. Add tomato paste, chilli, bay leaf, oregano, white wine and stock and reduce heat to maintain a steady simmer. Cook uncovered to reduce sauce. Taste for tenderness after 30 minutes. Remove hot chilli before serving. Adjust salt and sprinkle with lots of chopped parsley.

Sometimes I peel and halve some potatoes and cook them in the saucepan with all the other ingredients. I have also served the tripe with a separately made dish of simmered dried butter beans, dressed while still warm with a spoonful of the tripe sauce.

I consider that I have a cast-iron stomach and the constitution of an ox, but occasionally things go wrong. Some years ago I was staying in Albi, a beautiful rose-brick town, famous as the birthplace of Toulouse-Lautrec. Lunch had been miserable, so in the evening we decided to visit a very typical Albigeos tavern. I took one look at my companion's hot sautéed radishes with salted pig's liver, and had one mouthful of my own tripe cooked with pork knuckles in a saffron and bean broth and had to leave. I really regret it, as whenever I read my notebook I am intrigued by the sound of the combination. I'm sure the dish must have been wonderful, and I think in retrospect I must have been liverish. I know that one extra bottle of vinegary Gaillac primeur had been drunk at lunch.

More recently I was treated to a marvellous tripe dish, cooked by a French woman, but this time in Australia, at Cleopatra, a fairyland retreat from the world in the Blue Mountains in New South Wales. The quilted, ruffled huge bed was like sleeping on a powder puff, the huge pillows invited one to loll and read or simply to gaze out the window to the wide veranda with its wicker armchairs facing a massed wall of pink, white and rose-coloured rhododendrons.

Lunch was served in the garden, each table under its own shade umbrella with its own cloth of tissus de Provence. Dany makes special breads and breadsticks for every meal, and this day we feasted on tripe cooked in rich stock with pork and onions and peppercorns. After this, a bowl of soft-leaved lettuces, a pyramid of peaches and cherries and a delicate bavarian cream in a pool of intense passionfruit juice. This time I have the recipe and have been able to recreate the flavours of the lunch.

---

## DANY'S TRIPE as served at CLEOPATRA

---

Dany's recipe depends on obtaining uncooked tripe. It is not easy to get, and must be ordered a week in advance from most butchers. My butcher advises me that this tripe is often called 'hard' tripe. It will look greyish when you obtain it. In Périgord, this dish would have been made from veal tripe and calves' feet. I vouch for the fact that Dany's compromise version is a delight for any tripe lover.

- 1.5 kg (3 lb) 'hard', uncooked tripe, preferably honeycomb
- 1 pig's trotter, whole
- 1 litre (32 fl oz) dry white wine
- 1 whole peeled onion stuck with 2 cloves
- 4 medium carrots, washed, whole, unpeeled
- 4 large leeks, washed, split lengthwise, green part separated from white
- 1 stick celery
- 1 bouquet garni (fresh thyme, 1 bay leaf, parsley stalks)
- ½ small head of garlic, skin left on
- 1 teaspoon salt
- 10 white peppercorns
- 1 tablespoon pork fat or duck fat
- 2 tablespoons flour
- 3 cloves garlic, very finely chopped
- 1 tablespoon flat-leaf parsley, very finely chopped
- 60 ml (2 fl oz) brandy

Soak tripe and trotter in cold water for 2 hours, changing the water 2 or 3 times. Check trotter for any hairs remaining and scrape off.

Place whole tripe and trotter in a large pot. Cover with the white wine. Add onion, carrots, green part of the leeks, celery, bouquet garni, garlic head, salt, peppercorns. Bring to the boil and cook, covered, slowly on top of the stove or in the oven for 6–7 hours or until the tripe is tender. Let the contents of the pot cool for 30 minutes. Strain through a colander into a deep bowl. Discard and throw away all the vegetables.

Chop very finely the white part of the leeks. In a heavy, deep pan cook the leeks in the pork fat very slowly, so that they soften and melt. Stir in 2 tablespoons flour and make a roux. Cook for 3–4 minutes and then gradually mix in half of the reserved stock. Let the sauce come to simmering point and simmer gently while you bone out the trotter and cut the trotter meat and skin into very fine pieces. Cut the tripe into 5 cm (2 in) squares. Add the tripe and the trotter meat to the sauce. Add more of the stock if the sauce is too thick or there is not enough sauce. Three-quarter cover the pot and simmer for a further hour.

Fifteen minutes before serving, check the seasoning and add the chopped garlic mixed with the parsley and the brandy. Serve boiling hot in an earthenware pot, which will retain the heat, and accompany the tripe with lots of hot toast.

A quick mention of brains. Fritters are my favourite, although a childhood memory of brown bread sandwiches filled with crumbed brains and crumbled, crispy bacon has just flashed through my mind. I also love poached brains served cold as a salad, either in a vinaigrette or in a cold cream-and-mustard sauce. Then there is tongue, mentioned in the spring-time *pot-au-feu* (page 104), and delicious when braised and served in the classic manner with Madeira sauce, creamed spinach and steamed potatoes. I have detailed recipes for trotters and for ears in the bollito misto (see pages 99–101).

I shall leave the 'snips' here and move on to snails. I have to tell another French story.

Wonderful as Paris undoubtedly is, it is always a relief to leave the traffic behind and hit the blessed 'D' roads through green, green Burgundy. The sight of peach and apricot trees in full, frilly bloom and blindingly yellow fields soothes and smooths jangled nerves. We stayed in Mailly-le-Château (*le haut*), with its thirteenth-century church, and from the ramparts of this old village marvelled at the vista of the river Yonne sliding through a landscape of such astonishing lushness. It had rained that afternoon, so that our pre-dinner walk became very exciting. The lanes were bordered with a low, mossy stone wall, which was alive or rather a-crawl with elegantly striped *Helix aspersa*, the *petits gris* —garden snails to us! Suitably titillated, we dined on snails prepared with a hazelnut, parsley and garlic butter. I was delighted at the cook's jest: each shell was 'closed' with a toasted hazelnut.

A few days later, still in Burgundy, we had an excellent meal at La Côte d'Or, at Saulieu, owned by the talented chef Bernard Loiseau. Here again I had snails, this time in a rich soup of nettles, a lovely rustic dish. I was becoming more and more excited by these snails.

My enthusiasm was encouraged a week later when I spent an evening with Richard Olney in the south of France. Richard is a passionate and inspiring cook whose culinary writing essentially describes his way of life. The conversation turned to snails. Richard was up in a trice and returned with a large bucket. One glance was enough. These were the same as our snails! I was determined. We would start collecting. And we have.

## GARDEN SNAILS

This simplified snail cooking method is basically that suggested to me by Richard Olney.

First gather your snails. Gather as many as possible on the same day and store them together in a large, airy bucket with a tight lid with lots of small air-holes or stretch fine chicken wire over the bucket. Keep the bucket in a cool place for 3–4 days. Never underestimate snail pushing power: the lid needs to fit firmly.

Rinse snails under cold running water for 3–4 minutes. Plunge snails into a large pot of boiling, salted water. Boil them for 1 minute. Drain and refresh under cold water. Remove snails from their shells, using a fine skewer and a spiralling action. Meanwhile make a flavoursome court-bouillon.

## — COURT-BOULLON —

- 1 onion, sliced
- 1 handful wild fennel tops
- 1 stick celery, sliced
- 1 carrot, sliced
- 1 bay leaf

- parsley stalks
- 1 sprig thyme
- 1 cup white wine
- 1 litre (32 fl oz) chicken stock or water

Simmer all together for 45 minutes, then strain. Place shelled snails in the court-bouillon and simmer until tender. This will take a minimum of 2 hours, and may take 3. Cool and store snails in their court-bouillon. They can be frozen quite satisfactorily in their court-bouillon.

---

## POT of SNAILS with NETTLES, SPINACH and MUSHROOMS and a PUFF PASTRY LID

- 6 dozen snails, prepared as above
- 250 g (8 oz) young nettle leaves, picked while wearing rubber gloves
- 100 g (3 oz) butter
- salt, pepper
- 1 bunch spinach, washed and stemmed
- freshly grated nutmeg

- 2 tablespoons butter
- 100 g (3 oz) button mushrooms, sliced finely
- 4 cloves garlic, finely chopped
- 250 g (8 oz) puff pastry
- beaten egg for egg wash
- 6 oven-proof dishes, such as egg en cocotte or soufflé types

### TO PREPARE NETTLES

Wearing heavy gloves, wash the nettles well and then transfer them dripping to a pan and cook, stirring 5 minutes. Drain extremely well, pressing hard with the back of a spoon or a saucer to extract the moisture. Transfer to the food-processor or blender while still warm, and purée, adding one-third of the butter, salt and pepper to taste. Remove to a bowl.

### TO PREPARE SPINACH

Place washed, stemmed spinach in a pan and cook briefly in the water clinging to the leaves. Drain, process and add the remaining butter as for the nettles. Combine with the nettle purée, taste for seasoning, add the nutmeg.

Heat the remaining 2 tablespoons butter in a frying-pan and sauté the mushroom slices over high heat until the slices are golden and a little crisp. Add the garlic, stir and toss for 1 minute, and then add the mushroom slices to the bowl of puréed buttered greens.

## TO ASSEMBLE

Cut puff pastry rounds to fit the top of each dish. Pastry should be 5 mm (¼ in) thick.

Drain the snails of their court-bouillon. Strain the court-bouillon through a fine strainer. Rinse the snails quickly in cold water to ensure there are no fragments of shell. Divide the snails among the pots. Add 1 or 2 spoonfuls of the strained court-bouillon to the mushroom/greens mixture. The consistency should be softly spoonable, not liquid. Spoon the mixture into the pots and stir lightly to mix. They should not be more than half full, as the filling will bubble away under its pastry lid, and if it is in contact with the pastry the lid will be soggy not crisp. Brush the rim of the pot with beaten egg and firmly fit the lid. Do not make a vent in the top. The lid should puff into a dome.

Cook in a hot oven 220°C (430°F) for 15 minutes or until the crust is well browned and crisp.

Serve with a spoon and fork. Take care when cutting into the domed lid, as a gush of steam will emerge.

The amount of garlic is, of course, variable. Snails are traditionally cooked with quite large amounts of garlic, as it is thought to help the digestion. I once made this dish using the fat pine forest mushrooms we find in the autumn. Their meaty texture was delicious. It added a very rustic note to the dish.

# SNAILS in LITTLE POTS with SPICY TOMATO SAUCE and GARLIC CROUTONS

- 6 dozen snails, cooked as in basic method
- olive oil
- 3 shallots, chopped very fine, or 1 onion
- ½ cup smoked bacon, cut into very fine dice
- 1 stalk celery, finely diced
- 4 cloves garlic, finely chopped
- ½ small hot chilli, seeded and chopped very fine (optional)

- 2 teaspoons red wine vinegar or 1 teaspoon balsamic vinegar
- 1 kg (2 lb) ripe tomatoes, peeled and seeded, finely chopped
- 1 bay leaf
- large sprig fresh thyme
- salt, pepper
- melted butter for the croutons
- 36 rounds of mixed-grain bread cut to sit like lids on each pot
- 6 porcelain snail pots per diner

### TO MAKE SAUCE

Heat olive oil and sauté the shallots or onion, the dice of bacon, the celery and the garlic and the chilli, if used. Cook for 4–5 minutes and then increase heat and pour in the vinegar. Stir once or twice and then add the chopped tomatoes, the bay leaf and the thyme. Adjust heat to a comfortable bubble, stirring from time to time as sauce thickens. Taste and adjust seasoning. The sauce should be rich, thickish and warmly spicy.

Drain the snails from their court-bouillon, rinse (as described on page 165) and mix into the sauce. Divide snails and sauce between the pots. Two snails should end up in each pot.

Warm the melted butter and brush each crouton lightly. Place a bread round on each little pot, buttered side up. Stand pots on a steady tray and place in a hot oven 220°C (430°F) for 5–7 minutes until the croutons are brown and you can hear and see that the sauce is bubbling.

Remove each little pot to a serving plate most carefully. They are very hot, and you don't want any to spill. I use reliable kitchen tongs, as I find that with a cloth I am far more likely to knock one pot against the other and someone has to go one short.

The bread croutons could be brushed with garlic butter, if you like garlic as much as I do, or you could leave out the thyme and use the roasted garlic and rosemary butter (see page 84) as the spread.

The more usual presentation of snails is to serve them in their shells. Mostly this is either because the restaurant has bought their snails already stuffed with garlic butter from the nearest charcuterie (in France), or because the tinned snails they use are sold with the cleaned shells as part of the packaging (in Australia).

It can be done with your own gathered snails, but you must select snails with large shells. After you have extracted the snail, rinse the shells and place them in a saucepan with a teaspoon of salt and cold water and bring to the boil. Rinse well and dry in a low oven.

One simply places a little garlic butter (or garlic and hazelnut butter) in the snail shell, adds the snail, small end first, then packs in a little more butter, pressing firmly with one's thumb.

To serve snails in this manner you will need snail oven plates, which have hollows to cradle the snail so that they cannot wobble and spill the juice. One also needs special tongs to hold each shell steady while extracting the snail with a special snail fork. The shells are, of course, red-hot after their 5–7 minutes in a hot oven. If you develop a passion for snails, it will be a good idea to buy this special equipment.

The snails plus garlic butter can also be packed into a mushroom cap and baked.

One final word. Some pesto mixed with a very little butter makes a superb snail sauce, either served with snails in the shell or combined with either the spinach and nettle mixture or the tomato and chilli sauce in the two preceding recipes.

While picnicking in France I was intrigued to notice that each stalk of long grass in the fields was hosting dozens of minute white snails, the stalks bending and swaying under the extra weight. Not a suitable variety for the kitchen.

I have not included any recipes for veal in my section on meats and poultry. I hesitated over a rather good dish of brisket of veal, which we stuff with a ham, pinenut and lemon stuffing and braise, and we have served many roasted loins of veal. But the truth of the matter is that in Australia we cannot easily obtain veal of the quality that one dreams of. Firm-grained, milky-pink veal is practically never available. Animals such as this are milk-fed, but are around 12 weeks old. The more usual veal is what is known in Australia as 'bobby veal'. These calves are sold as soon as they can stand. Their flesh has no muscle and no fat. In times long past, they were sold for a 'bob' a calf, hence the name. A 'bob' was a slang term for a shilling in pre-decimal days.

My butcher tells me that a quality veal industry is developing, but that it will take time. In the meantime, the good stuff is in very short supply. When I am able to anticipate a regular and adequate supply of best-quality, milk-fed veal, I shall use it with enthusiasm.

In the meantime I have not been able to ignore my two favourite recipes for calf's liver. I select liver of about 1.5–2 kg (3–4 lb) weight that is glossy, firm and a pale beige-pink. Liver is not expensive in this country, so I am ruthless when slicing it. All tubes and membranes are saved for a staff member's cat. My customers get only the smoothest and choicest slice. The liver that I select is very rich. Just as the liver of force-fed goose is paler and richer than the liver of the common barnyard goose, so too with the calf's liver. The pale colour is an indicator of fat content, so one should not serve too much.

The dish is sauced with butter, so one should exercise restraint and certainly begin this meal with something totally without fat. Perhaps the orange, pinenut and basil salad described on page 193.

---

## PAN-FRIED CALF'S LIVER with BRUISED and BUTTERED SAGE

This is a recipe that takes 4 minutes to execute. Guests must be ready, plates must be hot, accompanying vegetables must be ready before you start. I prefer to serve a side-dish of a classic potato dauphinois, or a gratin of chard stems with a blue cheese and cream sauce, or steamed broccoli crisped under a layer of fresh buttered crumbs and Parmesan. Any one of these dishes can be already at the table while you sear, sizzle and serve the liver. Guests can either serve themselves at the table or the gratin can be served separately as a following course.

- 6 thin slices of calf's liver, trimmed of all skin, tubes, blood vessel
- salt, pepper
- 12 freshly picked sage leaves
- 1 tablespoon butter per slice
- non-stick frying pans

Heat two or three non-stick pans to very hot. Season the liver slices with salt and pepper and slap them in the pan. Cook for 2 minutes, turn. Cook for a further 2 minutes. This is all done over high heat. Transfer the liver slices to your hot plates. They will rest there just long enough for you to toss the sage leaves into one of the pans, wait for the leaves to crisp and shrivel a little, and then toss in the 1 tablespoon of butter for each slice. While the butter is still foaming and frothing, spoon it over the meat and place the sage leaves on top. Serve at once!

## CALF'S LIVER TERRINE
### in COGNAC JELLY

I first read of this dish in Michel Guérard's *Cuisine gourmande*. I have made it many times, and our recipe is now so altered that it is quite legitimate to claim this as our own recipe. Michel Guérard cooks his liver in flavoured goose fat, as for a *confit*. The original version used raw foie gras, a prohibited import in this country. Select the liver with the same care as in the preceding recipe. Skin it but do not trim it, as it will be done later. The thicker the liver the better, as after the considerable trimming there still needs to be a respectable slice.

- 1 kg (2 lb) calf's liver in one piece
- 1 bay leaf
- 1 clove garlic, smashed lightly
- salt, pepper
- 3 tablespoons cognac
- 2 litres (3 pints) veal stock

- 12 leaves or 1½ tablespoons powdered gelatine per finished litre (32 fl oz) of veal stock
- peppercorns
- muslin, kitchen twine
- a cast-iron terrine

Combine the crumbled bay leaf, the clove of garlic, the salt and pepper and 2 tablespoons of the cognac and rub it over the liver. Place the liver in a dish and in the refrigerator overnight, covered with plastic wrap.

### TO COOK LIVER

Next day, wipe the liver lightly, wrap it firmly in muslin and tie lightly in a sausage shape with the twine. Drop the garlic and the bay leaf into the stock with any liquid and bring it to simmering point. Place the liver in it and adjust the heat to a gentle simmer. Simmer the liver for approximately

15 minutes. Test by plunging a fine skewer into the centre of the meat, leave it there for 1 minute and then touch it to your mouth. If warm, it is cooked. If completely cold, replace the liver and test after another 3 minutes. Let liver cool for a few minutes. then unwrap it and wipe the outside with a cloth.

To achieve an absolutely sparkling dish, clarification is essential. For easy reference I have included a method for clarification at the end of this recipe.

### To assemble terrine

After the clarification, measure 1 litre (32 fl oz) of veal stock. Adjust its seasoning, adding the third tablespoon of cognac. Soak 12 leaves of gelatine in cold water. Bring 200 ml (7 fl oz) of veal stock to simmering point. Squeeze the gelatine and swish it into the stock until it has completely dissolved. Add this to the rest of the veal stock. Stir to mix. Pour a 1 cm (½ in) layer into the bottom of the terrine and chill until set. When set, scatter over some coarsely crushed peppercorns.

Trim the liver of the worst of its pipes and tubes and place it, best side down, in the terrine. Carefully pour over the rest of the well-seasoned liquid jelly. Remove the terrine to the refrigerator and do not move it until the terrine is quite set.

### To serve

Dip terrine briefly into hot water and turn out onto a flat board. With a thin-bladed and sharp knife dipped in hot water, cut into 1 cm (½ in) slices. Each slice of liver should be framed with golden jelly. Serve the terrine with a large slice of crusty toast and a salad dressed with a touch of sherry vinegar and walnut oil. I like to use lamb's lettuce (*mâche*) with this for its pleasant, lightly peppery flavour. Grind some pepper over the terrine or ensure that the peppermill is near by.

### — TO CLARIFY STOCK —

- 3 egg whites
- 2 slices carrot
- ½ stick celery
- ½ onion, sliced
- 2 parsley stalks
- 1 litre (32 fl oz) stock

Combine all ingredients except the stock in the food-processor. Process until the vegetables are chopped and the egg whites are light and frothy. Tip this mixture into cold stock and stir continuously until the mixture is just about to simmer. Allow to simmer gently for 1 hour. Turn heat off and leave for 5 minutes. Line a colander with a damp, clean cloth and suspend it over a bowl. With a wire skimmer, gently lift part of the 'raft' of coagulated egg and vegetable and discard it. Ladle the clear broth through the damp cloth. Make any final adjustment to seasoning.

Once upon a time, one of my most faithful customers, who is also a good friend, ate our braised oxtail with red wine and olives, and he sighed and mumbled, 'Stephanie, I'd tell you how good it was if only my lips weren't stuck together!' We both agreed that braised oxtails are sticky perfection.

There has been a bit of a vogue for boned and stuffed oxtail, which I have cooked myself. In retrospect I feel that the appeal of the dish may have been in the challenge to bone an oxtail without making lots of holes in it. It is a devilish thing to attempt. What one gains in delicacy, one loses in stickiness. The divine gelatine, the lipsticking quality, is greatly diminished. Even less successful are dishes where the meat is stripped from the bones and presented as a heap of tatters, sometimes wrapped in spinach or cabbage. Shredding the cooked meat can be successful if served cold, as either a type of potted meat or rillettes. I have included here a recipe for oxtail rillettes, which is cooked with surprising amounts of pork back fat. Do not omit the fat. The back fat provides the smoothness missing in those wrapped balls of shredded oxtail.

Another favourite oxtail dish is oxtail consommé served with little puffs of oxtail and bone marrow in the manner of Russian piroshki.

# OXTAIL BRAISED with BLACK OLIVES

- 6 oxtails sawn into sections (freeze the very skinny pieces and thaw them when you wish to make oxtail consommé)
- seasoned flour
- butter or olive oil
- 100 ml (3 fl oz) brandy
- 1 large onion, sliced
- 4 medium carrots, sliced
- ½ bottle sound red wine
- bouquet garni
- 6 cloves garlic, peeled but left whole
- 6 cm (2½ in) piece orange peel
- salt, pepper
- 1 cup pitted black olives

Trim any excess fat from the largest pieces of oxtail. Roll oxtail pieces in seasoned flour and pat off the excess. Brown well in the mixture of butter and oil. Do not rush this stage and do not crowd the pan. When all the oxtail is browned, place the pieces into a cast-iron enamelled cocotte. Place the cocotte over low heat and shake until warmed through. Flame with the warmed brandy, shake and stir until all the flames die out.

Wipe out the pan in which the pieces were browned, add a little fresh oil/butter and thoroughly brown the onion and carrot slices. Pour over the red wine and let it bubble fiercely. Stir to ensure that the de-glazing is complete, and then pour the vegetables and red wine over the oxtail. Add the bouquet garni and the garlic cloves. Add the orange peel. Pour over just enough stock to cover the meat, bring to simmering point on top of the stove, then cover the meat with a piece of buttered paper, place the lid on firmly and transfer the casserole to the oven, temperature 160°C (320°F), to cook gently for a minimum of 2½ hours.

Oxtail should be about to fall from the bones before it is ready. When this stage is reached, strain the sauce into a tall jug and allow the fat to rise. Rinse out the cocotte, and replace the pieces of oxtail, discarding any bits of orange peel or carrot still sticking to the meat. Protect the meat with buttered paper until the sauce has been degreased. Ladle off as much fat as possible from the sauce and then pour it back over the meat. Leave in the refrigerator overnight.

TO SERVE

Scrape off any further congealed fat. Scatter over the olives and re-heat gently. This will take about 1 hour. Taste the sauce for seasoning. If the sauce is a bit thin, ladle some off and boil it hard. Return to the cocotte to blend with the rest of the dish.

I think a potato and something purée is the perfect accompaniment (potato and celeriac, potato and turnip, potato and garlic). The shiny dark sauce flows like a river through the creamy purée, and a spoon is definitely necessary. Thin slivers of blanched orange peel look and taste good.

## OXTAIL RILLETTES

- 2 kg (1 lb) oxtail, sawn into pieces
- 500 g (1 lb) pork back fat, cut into large cubes
- pepper, salt
- 1 pinch of ground allspice
- 1 bay leaf
- 6 cloves garlic, peeled but left whole
- 1 cup water
- 1 large sprig thyme
- 1 teaspoon green peppercorns (optional)

Season the oxtail and pork fat well with the salt, pepper and allspice and leave overnight in an enamelled cast-iron casserole with the bay leaf and the garlic cloves tucked around the meats.

Next day, add the water and thyme and place the lidded casserole into a slow oven 150°C (300°F) for approximately 4 hours, or until the oxtail is falling from the bone and the pork fat is totally soft. Remove the bones from the pieces of oxtail, transferring each boned piece of meat to a bowl as it is handled, so as not to miss a piece. (The bone makes an absolutely horrendous noise in the food-processor and may well break the blade.) Combine the pork fat, oxtail meat, garlic cloves and thyme and process with the on/off action very briefly until you have a coarsely shredded mix. Alternatively and more traditionally, shred the rillettes with two forks. Stir in the green peppercorns, if you are using them. Rillettes should always be very highly seasoned.

Either pack the mix into a cast-iron terrine pan to serve in elegant slices with a salad, or pile the rillettes into a deep salt-glazed bowl for a more homely look. In either case a jar of cornichons should be alongside.

## PIROSHKI with OXTAIL FILLING

- I cup cooked, shredded oxtail (saved from the rillettes preparation)
- I tablespoon shallot or onion, very finely chopped
- I tablespoon butter
- ¼ cup finely chopped beef marrow
- I hard-boiled egg, finely chopped
- I teaspoon chopped dill
- few drops sherry vinegar
- salt, pepper
- I tablespoon of good stock
- 250 g (½ lb) pastry

### TO MAKE FILLING

Sauté the onion or shallot in the butter until quite soft. Add all the ingredients and mix well. The texture should be soft but not sloppy. Allow to cool before using.

Roll the pastry very thinly and cut into circles about 8 cm (3 in) in diameter. Put a heaped teaspoonful of the filling on each round and fold over, pressing the edges well to seal. Brush with beaten egg.

Bake in a hot oven 220°C (430°F) for about 15 minutes until golden. Serve 1 or 2 with a bowl of soup. Any extra can be eaten cold, or freeze them uncooked and bake directly from the freezer as an appetiser.

# SALADS & TRACKLEMENTS

Summer means salads and olives and oil and lunch on the grass. It also means fresh herbs and tomatoes and young, floppy lettuces. Mind you, iceberg lettuce is in for a comeback! I read it in an American food magazine. I do dislike this style of journalism. For most of the population iceberg lettuce never went away, but, more importantly, the wholesale embrace of one variety and the equally wholesale rejection of another seems to have everything to do with fashion and nothing at all to do with good taste. Better to rely on one's tastebuds and common sense to choose the best available produce and use it in a way to achieve its maximum potential.

Some salad plants are best in the winter months—such as radicchio. There are many, many varieties, of which only three or four are commonly available in eastern Australia. Some are large and floppy, others are smaller and have hearts, some are streaked with red only, some are quite purple, and other more unusual varieties are cream, streaked with pink. I have mentioned already that large, outside radicchio leaves are excellent brushed with oil and grilled. One can also roll them up, shred them and stew in a spoonful of butter. Use this to make an omelette. Without changing the pan, well-whisked and seasoned eggs are poured onto the softened leaves, and the whole cooked like a flat Italian frittata. Or mix the stewed leaves with a béchamel sauce, cheese, and bake between layers of pasta.

Bunches of curly endive, or frisée or chicorée as these varieties are called in France, need to be heavily trimmed as the outside leaves are really suitable only for Christopher Robin's friend Eeyore and will certainly bite the back of your throat. The hidden, blanched, frilled curls in the centre are crunchy and delicious.

All the soft-leaved varieties of salad, red and green mignonette and butter lettuce, are quite delicious. They bruise easily and cannot be whirled in salad dryers with the same impunity as can the sturdier iceberg or cos. These delicate salads should be rolled gently in a minimum of dressing so that the leaves are just shiny, certainly not dripping, and they must be dressed at the very last minute. They are also delicious placed naked and unadorned on a platter underneath a roasted chicken to soak in its buttery juices. Sometimes one sees bunches of spinach where every leaf is small, supple and in just-picked condition. A salad of such spinach leaves, served raw and turned in a dressing of crisp bacon, the warm bacon fat mixed with a few drops of a mellow wine vinegar, is a very special treat.

In the south of France one can buy *mesclun* and also at Fauchon in Paris. Correctly, it consists of a variety of wild leaves and grasses, which are all picked while very tiny. In fact it is usually a mixed collection of cultivated greenery, gathered at seedling stage and consisting of such things as corn salad, cresses, mustard leaves, dandelion, rocket and baby lettuce leaves. In Italy a similar mixture is sold as *insalata di campo* or *verdura trovata*. It is possible to make your own mixture of salad seeds and plant a patch of *mesclun*. Don't plant too much at once, but shake a few more seeds in the ground when the first patch is around 6 cm (2½ in) high.

A French friend who takes his food very seriously insists that a *mesclun* salad should be first soaked in iced water before trimming away any damaged or bruised leaves. Never add parsley or chives, he said. And use the very best virgin olive oil and not hazelnut or walnut oil, and never mustard. Mustard, he says, smothers the pepper of the rocket and assassinates the delicate aniseed of chervil. And always serve this salad on a flat plate: it will be crushed in a salad bowl.

There is quite a family of delicate and wonderful salads known as salad bowl or oak-leaf (*feuille de chêne*). Their great advantage is that one gathers individual leaves from the outside of the plant leaving the centre to keep on growing. A most authoritative book, *The Salad Garden* by Joy Larkcom, goes into considerable detail for interested gardeners on how to grow and cut these and several other varieties.

But one must not forget the humble iceberg. If home-grown and picked while the heart is still loose, one has one of the best of all possible salads. Unrivalled crispness, excellent flavour and cupped leaves perfectly suited to transport a prawn, squid or niçoise salad to a picnic spot. Big, round leaves of iceberg lettuce are frequently used in Chinese and South-east Asian restaurants as containers for minced pigeon or dishes of pickled fish, or to accompany the well-known fiery Thai rare-beef salad, yam neau.

While browsing through my library, I found this recipe—a traditional farmhouse idea from the area around Lyons.

Roll freshly shelled almonds in small, crisp lettuce leaves, and dress the rolls at the last minute with almond milk, chopped hardboiled egg and fresh herbs chopped with a garlic clove.

After the leaves have been selected, washed and gently dried comes the moment for the oil. Lawrence Durrell has written of olives in *Prospero's Cell*. The passage is quoted at the beginning of Maggie Blyth Klein's extraordinary book *The Feast of the Olive*.

A taste older than meat, older than wine.
A taste as old as cold water.

Maggie Klein's book contains everything one could ever wish to know about olives and olive oil. It is fascinating to read and includes many interesting and exciting recipes.

She firmly states that there are two basic rules for producing fine olive oils: the olives must be of the highest quality, and as little as possible must be done to them to extract their oil. She helps us to recognise and distinguish the special characteristics of oils from different regions. The cold-pressed extra-virgin oils of Tuscany have a 'peppery' flavour, the more ladylike, 'sweet' oils are from Provence. Before 'tasting' an oil, rub a little on the back of your hand and smell it. Like wines, preference is subjective.

I was overwhelmed by the quality and diversity of the olive oils in Italy. In several serious restaurants, many different bottles of extra-virgin oil were brought to the table so that the diners could choose and dress their salad at the very last minute. I loved the Italian way of simply mixing together some oil and vinegar on the plate with a little seasoning. It was so immediate, and the special character of the oil could be appreciated as a condiment. Since Italy I have become more and more intolerant of the French custom of mixing salads with an emulsified mess of poor-quality oil, too much vinegar and an excess of garlic and salt. In even the simplest Italian eating place the oil and vinegar stood on the table in glass jugs. Quite apart from the pleasure of the ritual anointing of the green leaves, there was an extra delight in the green-gold colour of the oil and the ruby tint of the vinegar.

Of course in Italy the oil was used for far more than dressing the salad. Many soups and pasta dishes had a thread of oil poured into them. Grilled fish and shellfish were finished with olive oil at the table. Sometimes a special bottle of oil was brought for the fish. It would contain whole red chillis or thick sprigs of rosemary. Oven-baked bread slices were served moistened with oil. We were offered olive oil with a portion of an aged Parmigiano–Reggiano, and it was a revelation to eat crunchy fennel strips dipped in olive oil, seasoned with salt and black pepper.

My French friend may well exhort me not to use walnut or hazelnut oils on a salad of *mesclun*, but I have done so, and I certainly use these two wonderful flavoured oils in other salads. The range of flavourings and condiments grows ever more varied. I enjoy making some flavoured oils and vinegars for special dishes, and I have included recipes for a few. Similarly I have included in this section recipes for some special preparations that can improve and expand your salad repertoire. I always have on hand the following:

— OILS —

- Extra-virgin cold-pressed olive oil. It has no more than 1 per cent acidity—its flavour diminishes when heated to more than 60°C (140°F), so it is pointless using this quality oil for sautéeing food.
- 'Pure' olive oil. I use a Spanish oil of this grade, which I find has a good flavour.
- Grapeseed oil. It has a neutral flavour, is a fine textured oil, which flows readily in the pan. Very little is needed to achieve a good result.
- Walnut oil.

- Hazelnut oil.
- Roasted sesame oil.
- Chilli oil (obtainable from Asian stores or else one can make one's own).
- Home-made spiced oils, depending on my current interest. I have included the recipe for an oil with North African flavours.

## — VINEGARS —

- Red wine vinegar. The best I know is made in Australia by Yalumba, a well-known wine company from the Barossa Valley in South Australia.
- White wine vinegar, mainly for use in court-bouillons and pickling.
- Herb vinegars made in our kitchens. Our favourites are the classic tarragon, rosemary and basil. I prefer to add freshly snipped chives, freshly crushed garlic, and quickly prepared fine dice of shallots or onions to salads than to infuse these in vinegar.
- Chinese rice vinegars, both the black variety and the mild vinegar.
- Cider vinegar, to use in Asian dipping sauces if I have run out of rice vinegar.
- Fruit vinegars. Usually raspberry, but I have made strawberry.
- A few specialty vinegars, for example, balsamic vinegar (see page 159); sherry vinegar from Spain, fruit-flavoured pickling vinegars (that is, sweetened) left after the pickled fruits are long gone.

## — OTHER BOTTLED CONDIMENTS I FIND — ESSENTIAL FOR SALADS

- Fish sauce.
- Tabasco.
- Mirin and/or Chinese rice wine.
- Light soy sauce.
- Dark soy sauce.
- Sambal oelek or other Asian chilli paste.

## — SPICES —

Pointless to list these. Buy small quantities, so you can use them before they lose their potency. Wherever possible, buy the spices whole and be prepared to grind them in a coffee grinder reserved solely for this purpose.

## — AN EVER-CHANGING COLLECTION OF — CHUTNEYS, RELISHES, SPICED FRUITS, ETC.

I have not included many recipes for these, as there are so many anthologies of these preparations already in print. The recipe for Noel's green tomato pickle is on page 86.

## FLAVOURED VINEGARS

Choose thick bottles or preserving jars and sterilise them by immersing them in boiling water for 5 minutes. Use any fruit or herb you wish. Ensure that the fruit is not damaged. Wash the herbs well.

Heat the best white wine or red wine vinegar you can buy to boiling point, leave it for 1 minute. Pack the fruit or herbs into the sterilised bottles and pour over the hot vinegar, using a clean, sterilised funnel. The amount of herb or fruit used will determine the strength of the vinegar. Obviously if you pack the jar with pears there will be less pear vinegar (or a greater strength), than if you had used only one pear. Cover the jars or bottles to prevent dust or anything worse falling in until they are quite cold and then seal properly.

Leave to stand for at least 6 weeks. Some people strain out the fruit or herbs. I don't, as I enjoy looking at the waving stalactites of tarragon or rosemary.

A different technique is used to make raspberry vinegar. I have given the recipe already in *Stephanie's Menus for Food Lovers*, but I repeat it here for convenience.

## RASPBERRY VINEGAR

- 500 g (1 lb) raspberries
- 2 cups castor sugar
- 2 cups white wine vinegar or red wine vinegar

Lightly crush the berries, sprinkle on a little of the sugar and let stand for 12 hours to start the juices flowing. Next day, strain the juice through a fine sieve into a heat-proof, sterilised preserving jar. Add the sugar. Stand the jar in a preserving pan or other pan with water two-thirds of the way up the sides of the jar. Stir with a clean metal spoon until the sugar is completely dissolved and the water comes to the boil. Maintain the steady boiling for 1 hour. Filter through a very fine strainer into sterilised bottles for storage. Store in the refrigerator.

I have used this method and the same proportions to make redcurrant and strawberry vinegar.

Incidentally, a few drops of strawberry vinegar on fresh strawberries makes a piquant salad, or use it in the same way with chunks of water-melon. Not only does it taste good, but the colours of either fruit salad look very pretty with sliced raw or smoked salmon.

One hardly needs a recipe for spiced oils. Here are two which give the idea.

## CHILLI and CORIANDER OIL

- 10 small fresh, hot chillis (red or green)
- 1 tablespoon lightly crushed coriander seeds
- 600 ml (20 fl oz) neutral flavoured oil

I would use grapeseed oil. Many cooks like peanut oil or safflower oil. I don't like the flavour of these oils, but the choice is a personal one.

Sterilise a suitable sized bottle. Ensure that it is big enough to permit you to shake the oil to mix it. Put the chillis and coriander seeds into the bottle and funnel in the oil. Cap the bottle tightly and allow to stand in a cool, dark place for at least 3 weeks before using it. Shake the bottle from time to time.

The inclusion of the coriander seeds means that I would use this oil on spicy foods, where the emphasis would be on the spice. If I had replaced the coriander seeds with bruised stalks of oregano or rosemary, I would have filled the bottle with my finest extra-virgin olive oil and used the oil to pour over barbecued whole fish.

## MOROCCAN SPICED OIL

This spiced oil is very hot and should be used very sparingly as a seasoning on grilled lamb or fish. The flavour of the oil is an important part of this condiment, so use a good one.

- 1 teaspoon caraway seeds
- 1 tablespoon cumin seeds
- 1 clove garlic
- 2 teaspoons finely chopped hot chillis, seeds removed
- ½ teaspoon salt
- 1 cup olive oil

Grind the spices in the spice grinder. Transfer the ground spice to a blender and blend with the garlic, chilli and salt for a few seconds. With the motor running, slowly add the oil. Keep this mixture in the refrigerator and use within a few days or the garlic will commence to taste rancid.

There are occasions where something other than oil and vinegar is called for. Whole books exist describing the gamut of cold sauces, but these are the ones I find myself using over and over again.

## AILLADE TOULOUSAINE
### (or walnut and garlic sauce)

- 3 cloves garlic
- ½ teaspoon salt
- 250 g walnut pieces, best quality
- ¼ cup walnut oil
- ½ cup cream
- 2 tablespoons finely chopped parsley

Never attempt this sauce if you cannot obtain fresh, sweet walnuts. Bitter, rancid walnuts will make a bitter, rancid walnut sauce. The sauce is very quickly made in a blender or food-processor.

Crush the garlic to a paste with the salt. Place in the food-processor bowl with the walnuts and process, using the pulse action, until the nuts are finely ground. Gradually add the oil and then the cream. Stop the machine once to scrape the sides and ensure that there is not a layer of nuts stuck to the bottom of the bowl. When all the cream is added and the sauce is thick and smooth, transfer the sauce to a bowl, stir in the parsley and season.

This sauce is excellent with crudites, or cold, poached fish or most cold meats, as is the following version of skordalia.

Ithaca has a long history as an island of travellers. Its most famous son, Ulysses, travelled for seven years while the faithful Penelope wove all day and unpicked her work at night to delay choosing a new husband from among her pressing suitors. (She promised she would choose when the cloth was finished.)

Our ferry approached the island late one morning. The sea was a spread turquoise shawl, the shoreline rim its silken edge. The bare, stony hills rose in the background, and Vathi, the principal village, clustered around the port, its houses apricot-pink in the brilliant light.

For the next 10 days we spent an enchanted time; listening to stories where myth and history blurred together, eating island food and even foraging for some of it, swimming in the bay at Polis where the water was as clear as glass, walking to the next village for dinner at night and returning along stony lanes under a black and starry sky hearing the occasional quiet greeting 'Yassous' from another walker.

The island has few tourist facilities, so that the life we observed had a timeless quality. We were woken each morning by the sobbing, hiccuping bray of a donkey. If one stood quietly on a path and listened, from somewhere would come the quick patter and tinkle of bells from the goats on the mountainside, just like the night-time tinkle of a Balinese gamelan orchestra.

Ithaca's own story is a sad one. Its harsh and difficult terrain required strong men and women to cultivate the stony hills. Two hundred years ago Ithaca exported currants, olives and honey, but still the men had to leave the island in order to support their families. In 1952 the island was devastated by an earthquake, which flung villages to the ground. The strewn bleached stones today look like ancient monuments. The young continue to leave, for Melbourne, for Adelaide and many for South Africa. Those left behind are old and cannot work the fields. Many olive groves are untended, the *ginesta* (wild broom) has seeded what were once terraced vineyards with its thorny bushes. Ruined windmills stand on the hilltops, abandoned as there is no longer wheat to grind.

Property is passed on to the children, rarely sold. More and more the children live in faraway lands. They may visit, but few come to pick the olives or tend the overgrown land, no matter how they yearn for their island. It is this sad dilemma that I think of when I hear the music of the bouzouki with its crying magnificent melancholy.

It was very hot and the air was strongly scented with wild broom and the wild oregano *rigani*. Melita delightedly undertook to be my culinary guide on our many walks. I saw my first caperbush with its spectacular mauve flower and sampled some freshly pickled capers, still crunchy and bright green. Sage leaves were added to the wash-up rinsing water to leave the plates sweet-smelling, I was told. Wild savoury and spearmint grew rampantly. Melita picked some small starry pink flowers to infuse in olive oil. They would be left in the oil all summer and by winter the oil would be ready to use as a general purpose healing oil.

During World War II, many people starved in Ithaca. Some hid what wheat they had in abandoned windmills in remote villages. There was not much of culinary value to forage—some dandelions and salad 'weeds' and wild garlic. The *barbarosica* grows everywhere, prickly pear to us. The young pads are peeled and steamed in Mexico, no one in Ithaca ever eats them. They seemed very juicy when I tried piercing one with my thumbnail. I wondered if they might be like eating a peeled broad bean? Intriguing when one culture uses something and another does not, even when the alternative is starvation.

One afternoon Melita went in a small boat to an uninhabited islet 100 metres off the coast of Ithaca and returned triumphant with a basket of *kritama* picked from the water's edge. We ate some of these 'weeds' (as she called them) at lunch as a salad, and the rest that evening, lightly boiled and accompanied by the Ithacan version of skordalia, a cold garlic and potato sauce. They were tender, crunchy and had a delicate aniseed flavour. The stems were swollen like samphire (*Salicornia eurowaea*), but the leaves were tapered, more like the tarragon it resembled in flavour.

Our last walk was to Arnogi, a village high in the hills, to view a Byzantine chapel, the Chapel of the Sleeping Madonna, and to search for wild asparagus. Along the road were many wild pear trees with small fruits. Melita pointed out the carob tree with its long pods. The fruits are dried and then eaten in the winter as we eat dried apricots.

The chapel has stood in this spot for 800 years and, until it was happened upon by a visiting Italian art scholar five years ago, its frescoes were completely covered with grime and candle smoke. The Italians have restored this chapel to become a jewel of Byzantine art. To view it one must ask at the Cafeneon. The owner's wife takes a massive iron key, opens the door and lights up the walls in all their magnificence.

Ithaca may be a poor island, but for one as interested in food and culinary custom as I am, there was plenty to see and taste. The staple diet does not vary greatly. Everyone has fetta cheese, probably sheep's milk cheese as well, olives, olive oil, onions garlic, bread and dried beans. In the summer, tomatoes, cucumber, zucchini and green beans are added. The quality and the provenance of these staples are striking. Practically every day we lunched under the shade of a huge tree at Polis with some of the local fishermen, near to a caravan kiosk run by an ex-staff member of Stephanie's. (He proudly claimed that he served beer in the best-polished glasses on the island.)

Melita brought small island olives preserved by her mother. Ari brought a litre bottle of his grandmother's oil. The fetta, freshly made, not brined, was a gift to Melita's mother in return for goat agistment on a piece of family land. The tomatoes and incomparable cucumbers were home-grown. The wine, potent and pink-gold in colour, was made by her father. All was local food, except for a marvellous rusk flavoured with oil and aniseed, which was a speciality of a nearby island, Lefkas, the kularakia.

One day we watched a fisherman bashing his freshly caught octopus. The next day Ari's grandmother had pickled some octopus to offer as a snack. And yet another day a swarthy moustachioed man riding sidesaddle on a donkey clattered into the clearing and offered us a bunch of fresh chick peas. I had never tasted these before. Not surprisingly like eating fresh young peas!

Melita gathered some sea urchins to show me how to select a good one. The good one had shorter, thicker spines than the other and had a dark red line around the mouth with a piece of seaweed attached.

Meat is a luxury but readily available. The first morning I was startled when I happened upon the local abattoir. The butcher had just slaughtered an ox, which was hanging from an olive tree. Its hide was spread out to dry and was being heavily salted when I inadvertently arrived on the scene. There was much squawking from the golden hens all pecking at I know not what.

Goats, of course, are everywhere, and each taverna has a spit-roasted goat or lamb on a Saturday night. The roasts are prepared with the island flavourings—garlic, lemon and mountain herbs. Traditionally the meats were a bit scrawny and were well cooked to be tender. My friend offered this as the reason for the Greek preference for thoroughly cooked meat. And if your evening meal is to be bread, green beans and cheese, it feels more substantial if the beans are stewed in a sauce of onion, garlic and tomato than if rapidly boiled, as I might prefer in a different environment.

In the evenings we ate at village restaurants, all sited at the water's edge. Customers came from the locals, the Greek summer visitors, and tourists from the sleek yachts cruising the Greek islands. We ate grilled fish or baby squid or cuttlefish, always superbly fresh. While it was cooking, a dip would appear made with the local thick yogurt and a basket of bread.

Like most other Mediterranean countries Ithaca has fewer fish these days, and it is very expensive. In a community where everything is so inexpensive, fish is $20 a kilo. As one eats, the circle of watching cats gets larger and larger and they eat every discarded bone.

## MELITA'S SKORDALIA

Melita explained that this sauce is often eaten with fish, either saltfish, grilled or poached fish. In these cases if there was any fish juice available in the household a little would be added to the sauce for extra flavour. The recipe is a Lenten brandade. Milk instead of cream, and the flavour of fish without the fish, but to be eaten with fish. Melita also believes that the milk makes the sauce more digestible. She believes that the walnut–garlic version of skordalia is so indigestible as to be considered dangerous!

- 4 cloves garlic
- a pinch of salt
- 3 medium potatoes, washed but not peeled
- juice of 1 lemon
- 1 cup Ithacan olive oil (or other variety!)
- $1/4$–$1/2$ cup milk
- a little fish juice (optional)

Crush the garlic with the salt and work until it dissolves to a cream.

Boil the potatoes, peel them, mash them. In a food-processor (but not on Ithaca) or a mortar, combine the potatoes with the creamed garlic. Add the olive oil and the lemon juice alternately. Adjust the consistency with the milk, adding it little by little. The consistency should be like a thick mayonnaise.

# TOMATO VINAIGRETTE

A tomato vinaigrette is most versatile. I use it most often with salads of shellfish or squid. Sometimes I season this sauce with tabasco, sometimes with a small amount of sambal oelek (chilli paste), if I want a more fiery flavour.

- 500 g (1 lb) ripe tomatoes
- 2 teaspoons red wine vinegar
- 3 tablespoons virgin olive oil
- 1 teaspoon chopped tarragon leaves
- 2 teaspoons finely chopped parsley
- salt, pepper

Peel and then seed the tomatoes by squeezing each half in the palm of your hand. Transfer to the food-processor or blender and purée. Slowly add the vinegar and then the oil. Stir in the herbs and taste for seasoning.

# SAUCE VIERGE

One of the best sauces of the nouvelle cuisine is the sauce vierge, which uses the same ingredients as the tomato vinaigrette, but combined in a different manner. This sauce is spooned around a quickly steamed or dry-sautéed fish fillet and is one of the most summery of fish dishes. As it is so simple, its success lies in the quality of the tomatoes, the oil and the herbs.

- 500 g (1 lb) ripe tomatoes
- 1 teaspoon coarsely chopped tarragon leaves
- 1 teaspoon chervil pluches (the little feathery section of each leaf nipped off and left intact)
- 1 tablespoon chopped parsley, chopped finely but not to dust
- ½ cup virgin olive oil
- juice of 2 limes or 1 lemon
- salt, pepper

Peel the tomatoes by dipping briefly in boiling water. Slice in half and with a small spoon remove all the seeds. Do not squeeze the tomato halves as for the vinaigrette. Chop the tomatoes into neat, small cubes and place in a bowl with the herbs. Warm the oil carefully and stir it into the tomato–herb mixture. Add the lime juice and salt and pepper.

## ORIENTAL BEAN CURD DRESSING

This sauce is decidedly different. Its Asian flavours go well with fritters of aubergine or zucchini, or with cold, rare roast beef. Try it with an Asian salad of quickly blanched bean sprouts, shredded crisp lettuce, toasted sesame seeds, white-cooked chicken (page 142) or prawns. The sauce is heavy in texture, so it should be ribboned around a mound of salad rather than tossed through it.

- 3 tablespoons fresh bean curd
- 1 clove garlic, chopped
- 3 tablespoons light soy sauce
- 3 tablespoons rice vinegar or cider vinegar
- $\frac{1}{4}$ teaspoon finely chopped hot chilli, seeds removed
- 2 teaspoons sesame oil
- $\frac{1}{2}$ cup light oil (my choice would be grapeseed)

Combine the bean curd and the garlic in the food-processor. With motor running, add the soy, vinegar, chilli and sesame oil. Slowly add the oil in a steady stream until the dressing is smooth and thickened. Taste for salt. It almost certainly will not need any. Store the dressing in the refrigerator. It will keep for several days if covered.

It is very satisfying to make jars of special treats in order to create personal salads. I first saw sun-dried tomatoes in the super palatial food halls of Dean & DeLuca in New York. One purchased them loose, like dried apricots. Back home I bought the Italian version, which is sold in jars layered with capers, herbs and oil. Little snips of sun-dried tomatoes have become one of my favourite summer flavourings for a leg of lamb, inserted here and there in the meat as one does with garlic slivers. When I came across this recipe for drying tomatoes I had to try it. I include it here for interest, although I imagine that most readers will still prefer to buy ready-prepared sun-dried tomatoes.

To dry foods successfully requires a temperature of between 49°C (120°F) and 66°C (150°F). One wonders how much actual 'sun' drying goes on.

# 'SUN-DRIED' TOMATOES

Sun-dried tomatoes are excellent in pasta sauce, or slice them thinly and add them to sandwiches or to fresh tomato and mozzarella salads. I have tried and enjoyed one of the simple appetisers from The Feast of the Olive, made by combining equal quantities of fresh ricotta and chopped black olives with a touch of brandy and a spoonful of chopped sun-dried tomatoes.

- 2 kg (4 lb) ripe, egg-shaped tomatoes
- salt
- fresh basil or rosemary or tarragon
- cloves of garlic, whole but peeled (optional)
- olive oil

Heat oven to 60°C (140°F). Cut the tomatoes in half lengthwise. Scoop out the seeds. Sprinkle the cut sides with salt. Arrange the tomatoes, cut sides up, on the shelves of the oven. If the spaces are too wide, place stainless steel or other non-ferrous cake racks over the oven racks and place the tomato halves on these.

Dry in the oven with the door propped open slightly until the tomatoes are leathery, but not hard, about 12 hours. No liquid should ooze out if you cut one piece in half. Never try to hurry the process. Drying of fruit should take place slowly in order to keep the maximum flavour. They can be eaten as a snack quite plain, or stored in the Italian manner.

Fill sterilised jars with dried tomatoes, layering them with sprigs of the chosen herb and the garlic cloves, if you are using them. Cover completely with olive oil, pressing down hard on the tomatoes to allow any trapped air to escape. Store tightly covered in a cool cupboard. Allow about 4 weeks for the flavours to develop.

Although I would usually char and peel peppers as I need them, it is very convenient to have a prepared jar ready to create an instant antipasto. Roast the fattest, fleshiest peppers you can buy over an open flame until the skin is quite black. Allow the peppers to steam under a dry cloth for a minute or so, and then rub off the charred skin, using as little water as possible. The peppers will probably need a fast rinse at the end of this operation, as there will be little flecks of black skin left. Remove the seeds, slice in half or in wide strips and layer the peppers with some peeled, lightly crushed garlic cloves in glass preserving jars and cover completely with excellent olive oil. Store in the refrigerator.

The jars will look particularly spectacular if you have layered the red with the brilliant gold. The olive oil will take on the magical flavour of roasted peppers, so use it to dress other salads after the peppers are all eaten. One of the quickest and nicest antipasto is made from watercress sprigs, crisped in a bath of iced water, roasted, peeled peppers and a couple of fillets of anchovy served with a big slice of hot, toasted crusty bread over which you have drizzled a spoonful of oil from the pepper jar.

Part of the display of fine foods in the windows of our best Italian deli-catessens is often a super-large jar of verdure sotto aceti or vegetables in vinegar. They are often works of art with carefully cut pieces of carrot wedged up against triangles of brilliant green cucumber and strips of celery forming geometric bands and stripes. Most of these preparations are ruined by having been prepared with extremely poor-quality vinegar: the sort that clutches at your throat and leaves you speechless. I prefer to make my own pickled vegetables. I also enjoy using some rather unusual vegetables.

## VEGETABLES in VINEGAR

These vegetables are delicious served with pre-dinner drinks and are, of course, far less ruinous to the appetite than nuts or other starchy titbits. They are also a splendid accompaniment to boiled meats, either to be served hot or cold. The jars look more enticing and the pickles are more interesting to eat if the vegetable selection has been thoughtfully made. I can strongly recommend the pickled corn, which is great tossed with all sorts of salad combinations.

- 1 kg (2 lb) vegetables
- 500 ml (16 fl oz) white wine vinegar or cider vinegar
- 500 ml (16 fl oz) white wine
- bay leaf

- 1 tablespoon white peppercorns
- 1 stick celery
- 2–3 parsley stalks
- 1 small onion, peeled
- 1 carrot, sliced

- extra peppercorns or 2 peeled cloves garlic
- 6–8 attractive sprigs parsley
- 1 bay leaf
- olive oil

If using sweetcorn, cut into 3 cm (1 in) sections right through the cob. I also like using broccoli romanesca when it is in season (this is a special variety of broccoli, which has green conical spears that are most attractive), slices of young choko, cut right through the delicious seed, round golf-ball carrots and pink shallots. The pickle seems always to need a few old faithfuls, such as cauliflower flowerets, small pickling cucumbers and sweet pepper strips. You could include whole hot chillis, but this will dramatically reduce the uses of the pickle jar.

Bring the vinegar, wine and all other ingredients to the boil. Simmer gently for 5 minutes. Strain. Lightly pre-cook any vegetables that need it (corn, carrots, pickling cucumber) in this liquid. Add one variety at a time and time appropriately. The vegetables must still be crunchy. Layer the vegetables into the jars together with the peppercorns, peeled cloves of garlic and the parsley sprigs. Tuck a bay leaf in each jar and then pour over the liquid. Pour a 5 mm (¼ in) layer of olive oil on the top of each jar and seal. Leave the pickles one month before eating.

Here and there in the book are a few other pickle recipes, which seem appropriate when describing other dishes or other topics. The last one I want to mention doesn't seem to fit anywhere else, so I shall include this pineapple-and-rum pickle here as it can legitimately be said to relate to salads. Indeed, the pineapple pickle is superb with a smoked ham salad or sandwich.

## PINEAPPLE-and-RUM PICKLE

- ½ cup brown sugar
- 6 tablespoons white wine vinegar
- 6 tablespoons dark rum
- 2 yellow mustard seeds
- 6 cloves
- 2 cups ripe pineapple, chopped into chunks

In a heavy pan combine the sugar, vinegar, 4 tablespoons of the rum, the mustard seed and the cloves. Bring slowly to the boil, stirring to ensure that all the sugar is dissolved. Simmer for 5 minutes. Add the pineapple and cook, stirring occasionally (until the syrup is slightly reduced) for 10–15 minutes.

Remove from the heat and stir in the rest of the rum. Transfer to a preserving jar and allow to cool before sealing. Store in the refrigerator for at least overnight and use the pickle within a month.

So much for the greens, the oils, the vinegars and the special pickled and spiced touches. This section was to have described my favourite salads, and I seem to have taken a long time to get to them.

Some salads exist just to celebrate one wonderful ingredient in combination with one other. For me that will always be tomatoes, olive oil and basil. Add a flake of sea salt and a grinding of pepper, let the sliced fruit settle in the oil for at least 30 minutes and one has heaven on a plate! It is possible to expand this salad successfully with olives, or fresh mozzarella, or thin slices of red onion, but I usually just leave it plain, and when I am with my best friend we almost fight to mop up the oil left in the dish.

A colleague of mine, chef Bill Marchetti of the Latin in Melbourne, introduced me to *pinzimonio*. He serves a platter arranged with thinly shaved raw artichokes, fennel ribs, raw mushroom fans, red, gold and green peppers and so on, with a bowl of extra-virgin olive oil, some sea salt and a pepper grinder, and one dips and enjoys. The earthy flavour of the raw artichokes is quite addictive. Here is another salad, using raw artichokes.

## RAW ARTICHOKE SALAD

- 1 large, fresh artichoke per person
- shavings or crumblings from a piece of matured Parmigiano–Reggiano
- lemon wedges
- extra-virgin olive oil
- freshly ground pepper

Snap off all coarse outside leaves from the artichoke to expose the tender heart surrounded by the very palest leaves. Remove the cone of pointed violet-tipped leaves and the hairy choke, and then slice the artichoke into fine slices and then into julienne, using a stainless steel knife.

Heap the artichoke shreds onto individual salad plates and sprinkle with a similar amount of shavings and crumblings of the very best Parmesan (Parmigiano–Reggiano if you can get it). Sprinkle with a few drops of lemon juice to delay the darkening of the artichoke and serve at once with a glass jug of wonderful oil and the pepper grinder.

---

## ARTICHOKES preserved in
## THYME-FLAVOURED OLIVE OIL

The varieties of artichoke available in Australia are not the same as the giant ones eaten in Europe. I have never seen an artichoke heart or bottom that is more than 5–6 cm (2 in) in diameter in this country. They are ideal for preserving. I love artichokes, and am always dismayed that the season doesn't last longer.

Snap off the tough outside leaves of baby artichokes (no bigger than an egg). Rub them with a cut lemon and cook in an enamelled or stainless pan until tender in lightly salted water in which you have put a few slices of lemon and several sprigs of thyme.

When tender, remove artichokes to a glass preserving jar, layering them with more thyme sprigs, some whole, peeled cloves of garlic (optional) and some slivers of preserved (or fresh) lemon. Cover with best-quality virgin olive oil and seal the jar.

Make lots, as you will find so many ways of using them. The recipe for the pickled lemons is on page 218.

---

## ORANGE-BASIL SALAD
## with PINENUTS

Basil is practically always mentioned in the same breath as tomatoes, unless one is talking about pesto. I like this salad that teams basil with oranges. It looks so attractive that I have often served it as a first course when I intend to serve a rather rich or substantial main course.

- ½ cup toasted pinenuts
- 1 tablespoon finely chopped basil
- 4 tablespoons best olive oil
- 2 tablespoons orange juice
- salt, pepper
- 6 navel oranges, peeled of all pith

Place pinenuts in a moderate oven on a flat tray and roast for about 10 minutes until evenly golden. Check after 6 minutes as pinenuts burn readily.

Reserve 3 tablespoons of the pinenuts and coarsely chop the rest. Mix the chopped pinenuts with the basil. Stir in the oil and the orange juice. Add seasoning to taste.

Slice each orange crosswise and arrange the slices on individual flat plates. Spoon some of the basil—nut mixture in the centre of each slice and scatter over the reserved pinenuts.

If you prefer, you could use half hazelnut oil in the dressing.

Basil leaves can be preserved in a glass jar filled with olive oil. Keep a jar in the refrigerator right through the winter months. The leaves will lose their bright colour, but not their flavour. The basil will impart its perfume to the oil, so that if you were to make this salad in the winter with new season's oranges, the dressing would use the basil-scented oil.

There are two attractive summer salads both based on bread. Panzanella is a popular dish in both Rome and Tuscany, and one can buy a pan bagnat at beach stalls all along the French Riviera.

Panzanella uses a thick slice of one-day-old solid, country-style bread. It is soaked in water, squeezed, and then mixed with anchovies, capers, sweet peppers, onion, cucumber and tomato. The salad is flavoured with lots of oil and a little vinegar and left to mingle and mature for 30 minutes or so before eating.

For the pan bagnat, much the same ingredients are combined with the crumb of the bread, but this time obtained from a French breadstick, a much lighter bread. The bread is saturated with oil, not water, and the salad is returned to the breadstick shell, wrapped tightly, weighted and chilled for a few hours. It is then sliced into thick slices. At least this is how I make it. The versions I have bought on French holidays have usually been no more exciting than the most dreary salad roll.

## SALADE NIÇOISE
### (Stephanie's version)

The real triumph of the south of France is the salade niçoise. Contrary to my remarks regarding the authenticity of the pan bagnat along the tourist routes, my experiences with salades niçoises have usually been excellent. There are no hard and fast rules, but I have given the recipe as I like to eat it.

- 2 slices of fresh tuna, poached or 1 × 200 g tin of tuna in olive oil
- 12 tiny new potatoes
- 3 anchovies packed in salt or 6 fillets of anchovy packed in oil
- 1 cup freshly picked garden beans or best stringless variety
- 1 soft-leaf lettuce, well washed and rolled in a towel and crisped in the refrigerator
- 6 ripe egg-shaped tomatoes
- 3 hard-boiled eggs
- ½ cup small, shiny niçoise olives (black)
- 1 cup small croutons of bread, fried in fresh olive oil
- extra-virgin olive oil
- 2 cloves garlic, finely chopped
- red wine vinegar
- chopped parsley

Poach tuna in a court-bouillon made by simmering together a pan of water with a glass of white wine, a sliced onion, a few peppercorns and a parsley stalk. When cooked, flake the fish and moisten it with a spoonful of olive oil until the moment of assembly.

Cook the potatoes and when tender halve or quarter them and place in the bowl with the flaked fish. Spoon a little oil over them also.

Soak the anchovies in milk for 30 minutes, if brine-packed. Rinse under cold water and strip the fillets from the bones. Place on a saucer.

Cook the beans in lots of boiling, salted water until cooked. Drain and add to the bowl with the fish and potato. Do not refresh! I believe that freshly cooked beans taste wonderful lukewarm and *dreadful* after being soaked in cold water.

Line individual plates with the lettuce leaves, and arrange the fish, potato, beans, tomatoes, halved eggs in a pleasant manner. Scatter over olives, croutons, pieces of anchovy fillet and make a dressing with olive oil, the garlic and the red wine vinegar. Spoon over the dressing and scatter over the parsley.

Sometimes in France I have been served a salade niçoise as a first course, and it has been presented in a very large bowl in the centre of the table. One helps oneself to all the special bits and pieces with some salad greens and the bowl is left on the table throughout the meal so that the rest of the greens can be enjoyed as a simple green salad after the main course.

For special parties or picnics, bake round loaves of crusty bread to use as a salad bowl. When the bread is cool, cut a small lid, pull out the crumb, brush the inside of the shell with olive oil and crisp it in the oven for 5–10 minutes.

After crisping the bread, rub a cut clove of garlic lightly around the inside and pile the niçoise into the centre. In this case do not add any croutons, as most guests will break off a little of their salad bowl and enjoy it.

The olives from Nice are absolutely delectable. The flavour is intense, although the olives themselves are very tiny. We have similar varieties of olives in Australia. They grow wild in many parts of South Australia. I have cured them myself, but I have never seen them available commercially.

The sliced pear, watercress and niçoise olive salad described by Maggie Klein has become a great favourite. I also make it with sliced yellow nectarines.

The last salad in this section stars the much-abused beetroot. As a teenager I had tea each Sunday evening with my boyfriend's family. I don't recall that the menu ever changed. We had cold rolled sirloin (well cooked), shredded lettuce and sliced beetroot. Later, as a live-in student at a university college, lunchtime always brought a bowl of sliced, tinned beetroot, heavily vinegared with the rawest, sharpest vinegar imaginable. I thought there was not much to be said for beetroot, but of course I was quite wrong.

One can now buy beetroot that are the size of golf-balls. The best way to prepare boiled beetroot is to wash them but do not cut off the root end or slice too close to the top as the colour will bleed most dramatically. The skins rub off easily when the beets are cooked and are still warm.

## BABY BEETROOT and CORIANDER SALAD

- 12 or 24 baby beetroot, depending on size
- 2 teaspoons coriander seeds
- 8 tablespoons best-quality olive oil
- 3 teaspoons balsamic vinegar
- salt, pepper
- snipped chives (optional)

Heat coriander seeds in a small, heavy frying-pan. Grind the seeds in a coffee grinder that you reserve for spice grinding.

Simmer the beetroot in lightly salted water until tender. Rub off the skins, slice off the tail and the top. Depending on size, halve, quarter or slice the beetroot into a flat serving dish. Scatter over the coriander seeds. Mix the oil with the vinegar, and taste it. Adjust the dressing with a few extra drops of the balsamic vinegar, if necessary, and season to taste. Pour the dressing over the beetroot.

Allow to marinate for at least 30 minutes at room temperature. Scatter snipped chives over the salad just before serving, if you have decided to use them.

# A FEW NICE TARTS

— F E A S T S  &  S T O R I E S —

These tart recipes are gathered from near and far. I have chosen them firstly for their good taste, the ultimate criteria for inclusion in this book, but also because each dish has its story.

In the mid-eighties I revisited England after an absence of over five years with the intention of visiting some good pubs, some country hotels and a few restaurants to see the state of the art as it was being practised. A dear friend collected me at Heathrow and we motored off to his oatmeal-coloured stone cottage in Midford, a sleepy village outside Bath. It was early spring, and I noted with pleasure the perfection of the pink, white and blue hyacinths circling the bright green lawn of Bath Circus.

The next day the food odyssey began with lunch at the Churchman's Inn in the minute village of Rattery. We had driven along stone-walled country lanes past signposts pointing to villages with names such as Jack-in-the-Green. England was experiencing a very late budburst, and the beech hedgerows were still quite bare in April. Devon cream, honey and farm eggs were for sale along the wayside.

The Churchman's Inn was built in the eleventh century and one had to stoop to enter the snug (the small bar just big enough for one table). I had a ploughman's lunch of local cheddar with pear and ginger chutney followed by a sublime treacle pie served with clotted cream. I could have had it with crusty cream, which was described as clotted cream mixed with crushed meringue. I have made this pie with great success. It should be eaten after a long and vigorous walk, as it is very filling.

The clotted cream also brought back memories. As a child we had an Aga solid fuel stove and my mother left the milk from our Jersey cow on the hotplate overnight in a wide, shallow enamel pan so that the crusting of the cream coincided with the ebbing away of the fire. In Jane Grigson's excellent book *The Observer Guide to British Cookery* she gives a recipe for making clotted cream that requires that cream be added to the milk. There was never any need to add cream to our milk. It was so rich that a glass left standing for 5 or 10 minutes developed a leathery, creamy skin, which we children found quite disgusting. If one makes clotted cream regularly, it is necessary to find a use for lots of skim milk.

## TREACLE TART

In the Churchman's Inn this was described as a tart, even though it had a top and a bottom crust. It can be made in a pie plate without the top crust. Cover the filling with a lattice of pastry strips.

- 950 g (8 oz) shortcrust pastry (see page 214)
- 1 egg white
- castor sugar

### FILLING

- 2 cups golden syrup (better than treacle, in my opinion)
- 3 cups fresh white breadcrumbs
- juice and grated rind of a large lemon
- a few pieces of candied orange rind, chopped fine

Select a pie pan with edges 4 cm (2 in) high and with a diameter of 20 cm (8 in). Line the pan with half the pastry. Warm the golden syrup and add all ingredients for the filling. Pour into the pan. Smooth the top and cover with the second piece of pastry. Seal the edges very well and crimp them if you wish.

Bake in a hot oven 220°C (430°F) for 30 minutes. Remove the tart, brush the top crust or the lattice strips with the egg white and scatter over castor sugar. Return the pie to the oven for a further 5 minutes to glaze the top. ▶

Serve warm or cold with clotted cream or rich farm cream. In Australia this means King Island cream, the superb cream with 45 per cent butter fat produced on a remote island in Bass Strait from contented cows. The produce from this dairy has created a sensation in our best restaurants. The butter tastes of the pastures.

## CLOTTED CREAM
(recipe from *The Observer Guide to British Cookery* by Jane Grigson)

Mrs Grigson makes the point that, although the method works quite well with pasteurised milk and cream, untreated Jersey or Guernsey milk and cream give a softer, mellower result.

Choose a wide-mouthed bowl or stainless steel basin with sloping sides. Fill it with milk, leaving a deep enough rim free to avoid spillage. Add 300–600 ml (10–20 fl oz) double cream. Leave in the refrigerator for several hours or overnight. Set the bowl or basin over a pan of water kept at 82°C (180°F) and leave until the top of the milk is crusted with a nubbly yellowish-cream surface. This will take at least 1½ hours, but it is prudent to allow much longer. Take the bowl from the pan and cool it rapidly in a bowl of iced water, then store in the refrigerator until very cold. Take the crust off with a skimmer, and put it into a basin with a certain amount of the creamy liquid underneath: it is surprising how much the clotted part firms up—it needs the liquid. You can now put the milk back over the heat for a second crust to form and add that in its turn to the first one. The milk left over makes the most delicious rice pudding.

The next recipe is for a raisin and liqueur muscat tart. The original recipe came to me from my friend Marieke Brugman. Marieke and her partner, Sarah Stegley, own and operate the gourmet retreat Howquadale in Victoria's beautiful countryside near Lake Eildon.

Marieke had submitted this recipe for publication in one of our cooking journals and had then gone on holiday and was quite uncontactable. The editor was desperate for photography and rang to ask if I would be prepared to make the tart. So I did and set up the photograph with a big jug of the aforementioned King Island cream. At the end of the session, the tart was carried upstairs to our private apartment. Just as the waitress reached the very top of the elegant, carpeted staircase she was momentarily distracted, turned, and the tart slid from the platter, somersaulted and splattered on the carpet below. Most dramatic. I never did taste that tart.

I now make it as individual tartlets, but the quantities given are for a tart made in a loose-bottomed flan tin of 28 cm (11 in) diameter.

The dessert wines of northern Victoria are perhaps the most classic wines of Australia. The muscats, tokays and ports of the area with their lush flavour, their heady perfume and pronounced raisin character offer a glorious finish to a meal. I have substituted liqueur muscat for the whisky that originally featured in Marieke's recipe and made a few other changes.

## RAISIN and RUTHERGLEN MUSCAT TART

- 1 flan tin of 28 cm (11 in) diameter
- 250 g (8 oz) shortcrust pastry (page 214)
- 150 g (5 oz) raisins
- 1 cup liqueur muscat
- 100 g (3 oz) castor sugar
- 1 teaspoon powdered cinnamon
- ½ teaspoon nutmeg
- ¼ teaspoon ground cloves
- 2 eggs, beaten
- 250 g (8 oz) double cream or sour cream
- juice of 1 lemon

Soak raisins overnight in the muscat. Next day, strain off any remaining liquid.

Line the flan tin with the pastry. Prick the base with a fork. Line the pastry with a doubled sheet of aluminium foil. Bake the shell at 200°C (400°F) for 10 minutes. Remove foil, reduce oven heat to 180°C (350°F) and continue to bake until the shell is cooked and golden.

Combine the filling ingredients and stir in the drained raisins. Pour carefully into the tart shell and cook at 180°C (350°F) until set. This will take about 25 minutes. Serve warm.

The tart can be successfully re-heated in a moderate oven for 5 minutes.

# APPLE and CANDIED QUINCE STRUDEL

We have a very large and vigorous dried fruits industry, and this dish features a speciality of the Barossa Valley, which I have never seen anywhere else. Angus Park produce superb glacé quinces. They are pink-gold in colour and have all the haunting perfume of fresh quinces. Sliced into fingers they offer a sticky but delicious treat with a cup of after-dinner coffee. I like to use them in this strudel.

## — STRUDEL DOUGH —

Like the basic recipe for shortcrust (page 214), this strudel dough recipe comes from my dear friend Damien Pignolet in Sydney. It produces a lovely flaky strudel.

- 250 g (8 oz) plain flour
- pinch salt
- 2 tablespoons vinegar
- 2 egg whites
- ¼ cup vegetable oil
- ¼ cup iced water

Place all ingredients in an electric mixer and beat—with a dough-hook, for preference—on low speed for 10 minutes. The heavy beater will do if your machine has not got a dough-hook.

Transfer the dough to your pastry bench or marble and knead it as for bread for 15 minutes. The dough will develop noticeable blisters. Rest the dough in a bowl covered with a cloth or plastic wrap for as long as possible. The resting should take place at room temperature, away from draughts.

If you wish to make the pastry one day ahead, wrap it tightly in plastic wrap and keep in the refrigerator. Just ensure that the dough has come back to room temperature before you start to work it.

This amount of strudel dough should make a rectangle of 100 × 50 cm (36 × 18 in). With experience it is possible to stretch it even further.

When you wish to assemble your strudel, flour your board and roll the dough lightly until it is very thin. Transfer the dough to a floured, large cloth and, using your knuckles and working from underneath, stretch the dough until it is tissue-thin. Usually one is instructed to work the dough until the pattern of the cloth is visible. A German friend told me that she was instructed to stretch the pastry until a love letter could be read through it.

## — FILLING —

- 400 g (13 oz) golden delicious apples, weighed after peeling and slicing and cut into 1 cm (½ in) pieces
- 400 g (13 oz) candied quince cut into 1 cm (½ in) pieces
- 6 tablespoons castor sugar
- 3 tablespoons lightly toasted flaked almonds
- 60 g (2 oz) melted butter
- ¾ cup fine, fresh breadcrumbs or ground almonds

### TO ASSEMBLE STRUDEL

Mix the apples, quince, sugar and almonds in a bowl. Brush the stretched pastry all over with the melted butter. Scatter over the breadcrumbs, leaving a margin of 3 cm (1 in).

With the short edge facing you, pile the filling in a log shape, leaving the first 12 cm (5 in) free of filling. Tuck the edges in, fold the first 12 cm (5 in) of pastry over the filling. Brush this underside with butter and continue to roll up the strudel, brushing the exposed sections of pastry with the melted butter until the filling is firmly encased with many layers of tissue-thin buttered pastry. Carefully roll the strudel onto a conveniently placed baking sheet, seam down.

Cook at 180°C (350°F) for 1 hour, basting the strudel with butter three or four times during the baking. Fifteen minutes before the end of the cooking time, sprinkle the roll with 1 tablespoon of castor sugar.

Allow to cool to warm before slicing. Cut slanting slices using a sawing motion and a serrated knife. Serve with either cream or a vanilla crème anglaise (page 278). Other glacé fruit may be substituted for the quince in this strudel.

## QUINCE TART with BROWNED BUTTER TOPPING

This tart is made with quinces, which I poach for hours in a low oven to coax out as much glorious colour as possible. The tart also tastes excellent if made with pears, but the colour is not as dramatic.

- 250 g (8 oz) shortcrust, baked as for the raisin tart (page 214)

## — TO POACH QUINCES —

- peels and cores of 3 quinces
- 3 quinces, peeled, cored and quartered and left in a bowl of water with the squeezed juice of a lemon, while the sugar is dissolved
- 1.2 litres (2 pints) water
- 600 g (20 oz) sugar

## — FILLING —

- 2 eggs
- ½ cup sugar
- 1 heaped tablespoon flour
- 125 g (4 oz) unsalted butter

### TO POACH QUINCES

Simmer the sugar and water together until the sugar has dissolved.

Drop in the peels and cores of the quinces and the quartered fruit and poach, covered, in a low oven for at least 4 hours or until the quinces are tender and have taken on a good colour. Allow to cool in their syrup.

### TO ASSEMBLE TART

Beat the eggs and sugar together until thick and pale. Add the flour. Melt the butter and cook until it is a deep gold. This is said to be noisette butter. Add the noisette butter to the egg mix. Drain each quarter of quince on kitchen paper and cut into thick slices. Arrange the slices in the cooked tart shell and pour over the topping.

Cook the tart at 180°C (350°F) for approximately 25 minutes or until the topping has set. It will look golden brown and be a little puffed. The topping will subside as the tart cools. The noisette butter seems to ooze into the crust so that the crust takes on a lovely nutty character.

Australian flora is noticeably lacking in edible varieties, so the macadamia nut is very special. Not only is it an Australian native, it is edible and delicious. The trees produce nuts that are covered in a soft husk. Underneath the husk is found the extremely hard shell. It is difficult to retrieve the meat without shattering it. Perhaps this problem is one of the reasons why Australian cooks have not made more extensive use of this native resource. Many of the macadamias one buys have been produced in Hawaii, although they are grown commercially in Queensland. A macadamia nut cracker has appeared on the market to help with cracking the nut.

Two years ago I held the first of our special dinners, which I called Stephanie's Australiana Banquet. I made this macadamia tart as the sweet course and accompanied it with a sorbet made by infusing 150 blooms of *Grevillea pteridifolia*, a native plant from the north of Australia much prized by tribal Aboriginals as a source of nectar. The flavour of the sorbet was honey-like, but elusive.

## MACADAMIA NUT TART

### — PASTRY —

- 60 g (2 oz) butter
- 100 g (3 oz) plain flour
- 60 g (2 oz) castor sugar

- 1 teaspoon grated orange zest
- 3 tablespoons orange juice

### — THE FILLING —

- 3 eggs
- 60 g (2 oz) sugar
- 180 ml (6 fl oz) light corn syrup
- 30 g (1 oz) melted butter

- ½ teaspoon grated orange zest
- 2 cups macadamia nuts
- 27 cm (11 in) loose-bottomed flan tin

#### To make pastry

Combine all ingredients in a food-processor and process until the pastry comes into a ball. This pastry is extremely fragile, so it is best chilled for an hour, then rolled out between two sheets of greaseproof paper. Lift off the top sheet of paper and up-end the pastry into the tin. Carefully peel off the other sheet of paper and gently press the pastry into the corners of the flan tin. Prick the base of the pastry and line it with foil. Bake at 200°C (400°F) for 8 minutes. It may need a further 2 minutes to be set, but check after 8 as it tends to burn easily.

#### To make the filling

Whisk all ingredients together, except the nuts. Remove the foil from the pastry and scatter the nuts over the pastry. There should be quite a solid covering of nuts. Pour in the filling. Reduce oven temperature to 180°C (350°F) and place the tart low in the oven for 30 minutes, then move to a higher rack for a further 15 minutes. The topping should look brown, bubbling and toffee-like. Allow the tart to cool before cutting. It is best warm or at room temperature. It should be cut with a good, heavy knife. It is easier to cut if the nuts are lightly chopped before sprinkling them in the shell, but I prefer the look of them whole.

## GALETTE BEARNAISE

This rustic and substantial prune tart originates in Bearn, one of the picturesque provinces of the Pyrenees, but I have eaten versions of it far from the Pyrenees. It makes excellent picnic food, being solid enough to transport without difficulty, and it tastes just as good cold as it does warm. It keeps wonderfully for several days.

- 400 g (13 oz) best-quality prunes, pitted
- 500 ml (16 fl oz) cold tea
- 1 egg white
- castor sugar for sprinkling on the tart
- loose-bottomed flan tin 24 cm (9½ in) diameter

### — PASTRY —

- 500 g (1 lb) plain flour
- pinch of salt
- 2 eggs
- 2 teaspoons eau-de-vie or cognac
- 2 teaspoons orange-flower water
- 300 g (10 oz) unsalted butter

#### TO PREPARE PRUNES

Soak prunes overnight in the cold tea. Next day, drain them well and remove the stones if they were not already pitted.

#### TO MAKE PASTRY

Sift flour with the salt onto your pastry bench. Make a well in the flour. Break the eggs into the well, add the liquids and the butter cut into small pieces. Mix lightly and then cut the butter into the flour using a pastry cutter. Using the heel of the hand, smear the flour and butter away from you until nearly combined. Gather the pastry into a ball. Rest for 30 minutes. Roll out thinly, fold the pastry in four, like folding a napkin in four. Divide into 3 pieces. Roll each piece again as thinly as possible.

Line the base and sides of the flan tin with one round of the pastry. Arrange half the prunes over this layer of pastry. Cover the prunes with a layer of pastry (remember that the pastry should be very thin), then arrange the rest of the prunes on this layer of pastry. Cover them with the remaining layer of pastry and seal the edges very well.

Brush the top of the tart with egg white, scatter over some castor sugar and bake the tart in a moderate oven for about 45 minutes at 180°C (350°F). Check that the top is not becoming too brown, and if necessary protect it with a sheet of foil.

One of the most popular pastries in every French cake shop are the barquettes de marron, boat-shaped cakes filled with an almond frangipane mixture and with a rich and delicious domed chestnut layer, usually iced in both chocolate and vanilla. One can buy moulded baking sheets that contain 10 or 12 barquette shapes, and which enable the cook to turn out professional-looking cakes for a special afternoon tea or to accompany an almond milk or chestnut ice-cream. The recipe can be made as a single large tart. The disadvantage of this is that the tart is so rich one should really serve only a minute sliver, which will look mean, whereas an individual little cake looks charming.

## CHESTNUT TARTLETTES

Ensure that the tin of chestnut purée you buy has corn syrup or sugar listed as one of the ingredients. The recipe will not work if you use natural chestnut purée. Use fondant in place of the icing if you like.

• 250 g (8 oz) shortcrust pastry

### — ALMOND LAYER —

• 60 g (2 oz) butter
• 60 g (2 oz) ground almonds
• 60 g (2 oz) castor sugar

• 1 egg
• 1 teaspoon rum
• 1 teaspoon flour

## — CHESTNUT LAYER —

- 250 g (8 oz) sweet chestnut purée
- 90 g (3 oz) unsalted butter
- 1 tablespoon rum

## — ICING —

- icing sugar
- hot water
- vanilla to flavour

Lightly butter the barquette moulds and line them with the pastry rolled as thinly as possible. Mix all the ingredients for the almond layer in the food-processor. Spoon the mixture into the pastry-lined boats, filling each one two-thirds full. Bake at 200°C (400°F) for about 10 minutes. The almond layer will feel lightly springy and will be a golden brown. Allow to cool completely.

Mix the butter and chestnut purée and the rum in the food-processor until the mixture lightens in colour and is also light in texture. Divide the chestnut mix between the tartlettes, moulding each one with a spatula to the traditional domed shape.

Place in the refrigerator to firm the chestnut/butter filling before icing.

Make a glacé icing and pour it over the cold cakes. If you are able to buy cake decorating fondant it softens readily in a basin over hot water. Warm it until it is lukewarm and then pour it over the cake. It coats very well.

For a very fancy finish, you could melt a little dark good-quality chocolate over hot water and then, using a small piping bag with a writing nozzle, pipe a few chocolate lines or twirls on the plain icing.

The next recipe follows on logically from the chestnut tartlettes, as it also is made using a frangipane mix.

# WALNUT and RUM TART

This walnut and rum tart is so easy and so delicious that the recipe has been moved all over town by various cooks who first made it at Stephanie's. There is very little that is original in the world of cookery, but I do find it irksome that some cooks don't, can't or won't do their own research and establish their own specialities.

- 1 loose-bottomed flan tin, 28 cm (11 in) diameter
- 250 g (8 oz) shortcrust pastry
- ½ cup smooth apricot jam
- 12 perfect walnut halves, blanched, peeled and lightly toasted in the oven
- 100 g (3 oz) best-quality chocolate for icing
- 30 g (1 oz) unsalted butter

## — FILLING —

- 250 g (8 oz) castor sugar
- 4 eggs separated
- 250 g (8 oz) walnuts, ground fine in the food-processor
- 100 g (3 oz) unsalted butter
- 1 heaped tablespoon double cream
- ½ cup rum
- a pinch of salt

Line the flan tin with the pastry. Brush the pastry with the warmed, smooth apricot jam.

### To make filling

Beat sugar and egg yolks until thick and white, add walnuts, soft butter, cream and rum. Whisk the egg whites until stiff, but not dry, with a pinch of salt, and fold gently into the creamed mixture. Pour the filling into the tart shell.

Bake at 180°C (350°F) for 30–35 minutes until the filling is golden and feels springy, not liquid, when touched lightly with your hand. Leave to get quite cold before icing.

In the meantime, pour boiling water over the walnut halves, leave for 5 minutes and then peel off the skin from each half. This is undeniably tedious, but makes a great difference to the taste. Dry the nuts in a towel and then place them in the oven to toast lightly. Check after 5 minutes.

Melt the chocolate with the butter in a basin over hot water. Stir till smooth. Pour over the tart, tilting it to enable the chocolate to flow smoothly. Mark each portion with a toasted walnut half.

```
┌─────────────────────────────────────────┐
│  ╔═══════════════════════════════════╗  │
│  ║   COGNAC AMBER TART with          ║  │
│  ║   SLICED ORANGES                  ║  │
│  ╚═══════════════════════════════════╝  │
└─────────────────────────────────────────┘
```

# COGNAC AMBER TART with SLICED ORANGES

Some of the plainest dishes succeed where more elaborate ones fail. Amber puddings occur in many collections of British recipes, but I had never made one until recently. This tart has quite a lot of cognac in it, and I would urge you to make it with the best cognac you can afford. It truthfully reflects the character and nose of the liquor used. We serve it garnished with a heap of golden, candied orange slivers and a bowl of chilled, perfectly filleted orange sections.

It is best eaten soon after baking as the texture is not improved by standing around.

- 6 eggs
- 8 egg yolks
- 8 tablespoons good-quality cognac
- 250 g (8 oz) castor sugar
- 300 g (10 oz) unsalted, melted butter
- 250 g (8 oz) shortcrust pastry
- loose-bottomed flan tin 22 cm (9 in) diameter

Whisk eggs, egg yolks, cognac and sugar together until well combined but not frothy. Stir in the warm, melted butter. Pour filling into pre-baked tart shell and bake at 180°C (350°F) for 25 minutes or until just set. The tart filling will always be softly set, which is part of its charm. The filling will be golden and translucent—like amber, in fact.

Line the flan ring with the pastry. Prick the base with a fork. Line the pastry with a doubled sheet of aluminium foil. Cook 10 minutes at 200°C (400°F) and then lower the oven to 180°C (350°F). Remove the foil and cook for a further 10 minutes until the shell is lightly golden.

## TO CANDY ORANGE ZEST

Take 3 oranges. Cut a slice from both ends of each orange so that they stand firmly. With a sharp knife and following the curve of the fruit, slice off the peel. Turn the pieces of peel flat on your working board, coloured side down, and with a sharp knife slice away the white pith and discard it. Cut slivers of the peel as finely as you are able and put them in a pan of cold water. Bring the orange zest to the boil, strain off the bitter water, cover the zest with more water and repeat twice. Dissolve 1 cup of sugar in 1 cup of water. When the syrup is boiling, drop in the blanched orange zest and cook it gently until the zest is shiny and tender.

Once cooked, the zest can be stored in a screw-top jar in the refrigerator. To use, just lift out the required amount with a fork. The orange-flavoured syrup can be used to flavour other dishes when all the zest has gone.

### To fillet oranges

Return to the three oranges. Check that you have removed all the white pith, exposing the bare flesh of the orange. Using a sharp, small knife, slice into each segment as close to its covering membrane as possible. Free the section by slicing down the other side of the same segment. One always does this over a bowl so that the juice is caught. When the orange has been freed of all its segments, you will have in your hand the skeleton of membranes. Give it a good squeeze over the bowl and then discard the fibre.

Oranges prepared in this manner are totally luxurious to eat.

For reasons that I don't understand, many of the varieties of plum most suited to delicious tarts and jams are rarely found in this country. I remember with pleasure tarts I have eaten in France made from the golden mirabelle plum and similarly the greengage plum. A friend gives me dense, dark and delicious jam made from her damson plums. I suppose the answer has to do with commercial considerations of yield. The varieties are available in nurseries for home planting, but the fruit don't appear at the local markets.

Jane Grigson says, in her book *Fruit*, that the finest eating plums all have yellow or green skins. Maybe. Many of our red and purple-skinned plums are tasteless or very acid, but an exception must be made for the wonderful satsuma or blood plum. It is available right throughout the summer. It is a commonly grown tree, which crops heavily, so that if one has such a tree it becomes essential to find lots of uses for the fruit. We pickle several jars and use them to accompany cold meats and terrines. But my favourite way of enjoying them is to make Mieze's plum cake.

# MIEZE'S PLUM CAKE

- 275 g (9 oz) butter
- 250 g (8 oz) sugar
- 200 g (7 oz) plain flour
- 200 g (7 oz) self-raising flour
- pinch of salt
- 3 eggs
- 100 ml milk
- 1 cup ground almonds or flaked almonds
- 20 ripe blood plums, halved, stone removed
- 1 large springform tin 28 cm (11 in) diameter

## — TOPPING —

- 200 g (8 oz) sugar
- 2 teaspoons cinnamon
- 125 g (4 oz) melted butter
- 4 eggs

Cream the butter and sugar until light and fluffy. Add the flours and salt. Add the lightly beaten eggs and the milk to make a soft dough. The consistency should be such that the mix will drop easily from the spoon. Spoon it into the lightly buttered springform tin. The batter should not fill more than one-quarter of the depth of the tin. It rises a great deal. Cover the batter with the ground almonds and then arrange the halved plums, cut side up on top. Start with a circle at the outside edge and work towards the centre.

### TO MAKE THE TOPPING

Melt the butter and stir in the sugar and cinnamon. Allow to cool 1–2 minutes. Whisk the eggs well and stir into the cooled cinnamon butter mixture. Spoon the topping over and around the plums on the cake.

Bake the cake at 180°C (350°F) for about 50–60 minutes. Test that the cake mixture has cooked through in the middle. This plum cake is quite superb and should be served warm with cream.

The quantities given would easily serve 12 people. You could halve the recipe and use a smaller springform tin. It is important that there not be too thick a layer of cake. The proportions should favour fruit. The glory of the dish is the way that the juice of the plums seeps into the cake.

And, lastly, I cannot resist adding a few words regarding the ubiquitous strawberry tart. Such a delicious dessert, providing the cook has paid proper attention to the details of its construction.

1. The pastry shell must be completely cooked through—that means golden brown, not pasty white.
2. The shell should have been brushed with egg white and returned to the oven for 2 minutes to help seal the crust.
3. The pastry cream must have been thoroughly cooked, and it must have been strained to ensure there is not a suspicion of a lump. The cream may have been lightened with some whipped cream, and possibly flavoured with a spoonful of a chosen liqueur.
4. There must be lots of strawberries, and the strawberries must be sweet and juicy.
5. The glaze should consist of best-quality redcurrant jelly and not anything thickened with arrowroot, cornflour or gelatine.
6. The glaze should be generously applied.
7. Each mouthful should register the delightful contrasts of crisp and soft, sweet and acid.
8. Cream is not needed with this tart.

All the above applies to any of the miraculous creations made possible during our bountiful summer, whether you are using strawberries, raspberries, blackberries, mulberries, blueberries, redcurrants, loganberries or some other berry. The principles are the same, only the character of the glazing jelly may differ.

Many of these tart recipes require 250 g (8 oz) of shortcrust pastry. In most cases this will be far more than is needed for the one shell. I find it a convenient quantity to make, and always find that a small amount of pastry left over can be put to good use. However, you may prefer to make half the quantities.

Unless otherwise specified, I always use this basic shortcrust. You may sweeten it, if you wish, or use another recipe. I have given this recipe in *Stephanie's Menus for Food Lovers*. It is repeated here for convenience.

## DAMIEN'S PATÉ BRISÉE
### (buttery shortcrust)

- 180 g (6 oz) unsalted butter
- 240 g (8 oz) plain flour
- pinch of salt
- 60 ml (2 fl oz) water or mineral water

Remove butter from the refrigerator 30 minutes before making the pastry.

Sieve flour and salt onto a marble pastry slab or work bench. Chop butter into smallish pieces and toss lightly in the flour. Make a well in the centre and pour in the cold water. Using a pastry scraper, work the paste to a very rough heap of buttery lumps of dough.

Using the heel of the hand, quickly smear the pastry away from you across the board. It will lightly combine. Gather the dough together, press quickly into a flat cake, dust with a little flour, wrap in plastic film and refrigerate for 20 minutes. Roll out, dusting with flour as necessary, drape pastry over pin and roll over flan tin. Prick the bottom with a fork and place shell in freezer or refrigerator for at least 20 minutes before baking.

Line with a double thickness of foil, pressed well into the corners. Cook 10 minutes at 200°C (400°F), then remove foil and lower temperature to 180°C (350°F). Cook a further 10 minutes until quite dry, golden and crisp.

If it is to be filled with a liquid, have the filling hot and pour straight into the tart while the crust is still hot. In this way you will have no seepage of liquid into the base.

Remember! Do not fill tart with beans or rice. The pricking of the base will prevent undue rising, and will permit a little bubbling of the surface, which adds to the flaky quality.

Completed shells can live happily in the freezer for days until needed. Do not defrost them. They go straight from freezer to oven at 200°C (400°F).

Always roll the pastry out after a short rest only. It should never be hard. Let it warm up at room temperature if it has been in the refrigerator overnight.

Chill pastry in the freezer for 20 minutes before baking.

# CITRUS FRUITS

◄ F E A S T S   &   S T O R I E S ►

Citrus fruits are among my favourite raw materials. Always available, mostly of good quality and capable of infinite use. Many years ago an aunt took me to Kew Gardens in London promising to show me a rare and wonderful sight. It was a small tree in the conservatory with one or two lemons hanging from it. I hope I hid my scorn from her! Practically every backyard in eastern Australia has its lemon tree, and a glut of the fruit is a fairly normal occurrence.

Lemons are indispensable to squeeze on a freshly opened oyster, or to slice into a jug of iced tea. They provide the necessary acid note in many sauces, they lift and reveal the flavour in a fruit sorbet. Grated and mixed with chopped garlic and parsley the gremolata mingles with and heightens the aroma of an ossobuco. A pin of grated zest adds piquancy to many stuffings, and a curl of peel is always added to the syrup for poaching fruits. A special flavour is achieved in all dishes if you grow the Meyer lemon. It is less acid and thicker-skinned. It makes special marmalade, candied peel and lemon cordial. Lemons seem to be especially delicious in sweets that include quite a lot of cream.

The first *citron pressé* that one discovers in France is always memorable. As is so often the case with travel memories I find it hard to decide whether my affection for the drink is purely for the sharp refreshing jolt it delivers to the system after a long, hot day or whether it is because of its essentially French presentation. It is always served in a tall thick glass with a long parfait spoon, a sugar shaker with a cunning pourer, together with the squat carafe of water extolling the virtues of Byrrh or Suze or some other exotic aperitif.

I drink lots of *citrons pressés* during my happy summers in France, but I would suggest that the English traditional lemon barley water has more finesse and is just as refreshing.

Another traditional English sweet is known in our family as Spanish cream. I found a recipe for it in a British food journal under the name of honeycomb mould. Traditionally made with the zest and juice of lots of lemons, we in the Antipodes often use part lemon and part passionfruit. The seeds are left in to create powerfully flavoured orange stains in the otherwise creamy pudding. Passionfruit are rather like lemons. Once one has a mature specimen growing in the garden the problem becomes how to utilise the bountiful crop. I have a plastic bag of whole, ripe passionfruit in the bottom of the freezer. They probably keep indefinitely—certainly for a year, which is the longest I've stored any—and reconstitute as perfect passionfruit pulp to add to either Spanish cream or lemon delicious pudding or simply to spoon onto everybody's favourite pavlova.

But back to lemons. From time to time we make something for the first time and love it so much that it becomes a kitchen staple. Our first jar of preserved lemons was such an experience. They are the starring ingredient in our version of a Moroccan tagine made with lamb shanks (page 89), and it was in order to make that dish that we first preserved lemons. But it hasn't stopped there. Slices of the soft rind are excellent in a salad of fresh crabmeat. Chopped and added to a chicken and coconut milk curry, they add a refreshing sourness, which is welcome against the rich coconut. And although I have given a recipe for butter-roasted chicken (page 120) using fresh lemon as a flavouring, a really good alternative would be a thick slice of preserved lemon.

There are lots of different recipes for preserving lemons (and limes). I have given the version from *The Good Cook Time-Life* series in the volume on *Lamb*. Claudia Roden has an interesting recipe where the lemons are sliced and salted and then layered with sweet paprika and covered with a light oil.

We make a lovely dessert of layered tissue-thin crêpes, alternately spread with lemon curd and whipped cream. The 'cake' is iced with a thin layer of passionfruit jelly, like the fashionable miroir sponges in France and is served cut into wedges. It is sharp and acid, delectable after a rich main course.

The overwhelming majority of recipes I have chosen for this section are for sweet dishes. This is not coincidence or chance but definite bias. I certainly use lemons whenever I cook or serve fish, but I have preferred to keep all the fish recipes together. Probably citrus desserts are my absolute favourites and I cannot remember a menu that has not included at least one.

## LEMON BARLEY WATER

- 1 cup pearl barley
- 2.5 litres (4 pints) hot water
- ½ cup sugar
- 1–1½ cups lemon juice

Bring barley to the boil with 500 ml (16 fl oz) of hot water. Simmer 5 minutes. Put sugar into the barley mixture and add the balance of the water. Allow to simmer for a further few minutes, then cool. Add the lemon juice to taste and strain. Serve very cold over ice. A bruised mint leaf can be added if you like.

## SPANISH CREAM or HONEYCOMB MOULD

- grated zest of 2 lemons
- 500 ml (16 fl oz) milk
- 6 leaves gelatine
- 3 eggs, separated
- 100 g (3 oz) castor sugar
- 125 ml (4 fl oz) cream
- juice of 2 lemons

Place grated lemon zest in the milk in a heavy pan. Bring just to scalding point. Remove the pan from the heat, cover and infuse for 30 minutes. Soak the gelatine leaves in a bowl of cold water for a few minutes. Heat a few spoonfuls of water in a pan and when just simmering drop in the squeezed gelatine. Swish to ensure that it has totally dissolved.

Whisk the egg yolks and the sugar together to combine but not until frothy. Pour on the lemon-flavoured milk and the cream. Cook the custard until it has thickened, 86°C (180°F). Strain into a bowl. Stir in the gelatine mixture and the lemon juice. Whisk the egg whites until they are stiff but not dry. Fold the whites into the mixture and pour into a fancy basin or into individual jelly moulds. Allow to set.

### Passionfruit variation

Substitute the pulp of 2 passionfruits for the lemon zest. Add the passionfruit after the custard has thickened.

## NORTH AFRICAN PRESERVED LEMONS

- 10 lemons
- 500 g (1 lb) coarse salt
- 1 bay leaf
- 1 cinnamon stick
- extra lemon juice if necessary

Quarter the lemons lengthwise, but leave the quarters attached for the last 1 cm (½ in). Stuff the lemons with salt and reform. Place a 1 cm (½ in) layer of salt in the bottom of a clean, sterilised preserving jar and place in the lemons, crumbling the bay leaf and the cinnamon among them. Scatter over the rest of the salt. Press the lemons down really hard to release their juice. If it doesn't cover them, add some additional lemon juice. Seal the jar.

Leave the lemons for a month before using, and during this time invert the jar from time to time to mix the flavours.

- 10 thin crêpes, approximately 22 cm (9 in) diameter

## — FILLING —

- 2 leaves gelatine
- juice and rind of 3 lemons
- 6 egg yolks
- ½ cup castor sugar

- 100 g (3 oz) soft butter
- 150 ml (5 fl oz) + 600 ml (20 fl oz) cream
- 2 tablespoons boiling water

## — TOPPING —

- 3 leaves gelatine
- ½ cup passionfruit juice

- ½ cup orange juice

### TO MAKE LEMON FILLING

Soak a leaf of gelatine in cold water.

Put juice, rind, egg yolks and sugar into a bowl and whisk well to combine. Pour into an enamelled or cast-iron pan. Add the soft butter. Cook, stirring all the time, until the curd has thickened. Squeeze gelatine and drop into a spoonful of the boiling water. Swish to dissolve. Stir the gelatine into the lemon curd mixture. Scrape into a bowl and allow to cool completely. Cover with a piece of buttered paper to prevent a skin forming. Leave overnight. Next day, place the lemon curd in the bowl of an electric mixer. Mix briefly to soften, add the 150 ml (5 fl oz) cream and whip until light. Refrigerate until it has set slightly before assembling the 'cake'.

Soak, squeeze and dissolve the second leaf of gelatine using the second spoonful of boiling water. Add the gelatine to the 600 ml (20 fl oz) cream and whip it until thick.

### TO ASSEMBLE

Spread one of the pancakes with lemon curd. Settle it on the base of a 22 cm (9 in) diameter springform tin. The sides should be completely detached from the base at this stage. Place a second crêpe over the first. Spread with approximately a quarter of the whipped cream. Continue in this manner until the tenth and final crepe has been placed in position.

Fit the sides of the springform tin into position and close firmly around the cake. Gently even out the cake so that the top crêpe is sitting as horizontal as possible. Refrigerate.

Dissolve the next 3 leaves of gelatine in the same manner as before. Pour the dissolved mixture into the combined orange/passionfruit juice. Allow to cool. When the fruit jelly is just turning syrupy, remove the assembled 'cake' from the refrigerator and pour over the 'icing'. Return it to the refrigerator to set. Cut into wedges to serve. Sometimes I serve some luscious strawberries alongside.

## — BASIC CRÊPE RECIPE —

Ignore this if you make pancakes or crêpes all the time and have your own foolproof mixture.

- ¾ cup sifted plain flour
- ½ teaspoon salt
- 3 eggs
- 4 tablespoons melted butter
- 1 cup milk

Sift the flour and the salt. Place in the food-processor and whirl in the eggs, the melted butter and the milk. Stop the machine and scrape the base of the bowl at least once. The mixture should be like thin cream. Adjust with a little extra milk if necessary. Allow to stand for an hour before using.

## LEMON SOUFFLÉ CRÊPES

Crêpes could also be filled with a light lemon soufflé and baked in a hot oven for around 10 minutes or the lemon soufflé could be cooked in conventional soufflé dishes.

- 6 crêpes

## — SOUFFLÉ MIXTURE —

- 60 g (2 oz) butter
- 125 g (4 oz) sugar
- 100 ml (3 fl oz) lemon juice
- 4 egg yolks
- rind from 2 lemons
- 5 egg whites
- icing sugar
- 6 ovenproof shallow gratin dishes

Pre-heat oven to 220°C (450°F).

Arrange crêpes in the buttered gratin dishes so that one half is lining the dish and the other half is draped over the side ready to be folded lightly over the soufflé mixture. Arrange the dishes on a baking tray ready for the oven.

In a heavy pan, heat the butter, half the sugar and all the lemon juice until the butter and sugar are melted. Remove from the heat and beat in the 4 yolks, one by one. Add the lemon rind. Heat gently, stirring constantly until the mixture thickens. Do not allow it to boil. Remove the mixture from the heat.

Whip the whites until they are foamy. Add the rest of the sugar and beat until the meringue is shiny. Stir a quarter of the egg whites into the lemon mixture to lighten it. Tip the rest of the egg whites onto this mixture and fold together lightly. Spoon generous heaps of the soufflé mixture onto each crêpe. Fold over the other half and transfer the tray at once to the hot oven. Bake about 10 minutes until puffed and brown. Scatter with a little icing sugar before serving.

I like these served with a jug of thin, cold cream.

## COLD LEMON SOUFFLÉ with RASPBERRIES

- 1 soufflé dish, 16 cm (6 in) in diameter
- double band of oiled foil for the collar
- string or a large rubber band
- small oiled jam jar to stand inside soufflé dish
- 6 leaves gelatine

- 300 ml (10 fl oz) cream, whipped
- juice and grated rind of 3 lemons
- 200 g (7 oz) castor sugar
- 5 eggs, separated
- ½ cup whipped cream
- ¼ cup toasted flaked almonds
- 1 punnet raspberries

Tie the band of foil around the soufflé dish or secure it with a rubber band. Place the oiled small jar in the centre of the dish.

Soak the gelatine in a basin of cold water and dissolve it in 1–2 spoonfuls of boiling water. Whip the 300 ml (10 fl oz) cream and refrigerate it until needed. Have ready a large basin of ice cubes.

In another basin and over a pan of boiling water whisk the juice, rind, sugar and egg yolks. Whisk really hard until the mixture triples in volume and becomes pale in colour. Whisk in the dissolved gelatine. Continue to whisk the mixture away from the stove. After a few minutes, place the pan over the ice and whisk continuously until it is quite cold. Remove the basin from over the ice and whisk the egg whites to a firm snow.

Gently fold in first the cream (the heavier ingredient) and then the egg whites. Pour the mixture into the prepared basin around the jam jar. The level of the lemon soufflé should be higher than the basin. Place it in the refrigerator until it is quite set.

### To decorate and serve

Using a knife held against the inside of the foil collar, gently ease the foil away from the soufflé. Spread the ½ cup whipped cream on top, scatter the almonds over the cream and press them onto the exposed edges. Gently ease out the jar. Fill the centre of the soufflé with the raspberries.

The final lemon recipe is for another English treat: syllabub. This is the simplest version of syllabub. It is quite delicious. I serve it either spooned around or with a compote of quinces and dried figs, or with a Middle-eastern salad of dried apricots, almonds and pistachios soaked overnight and then poached gently in syrup. It was also very good at Christmas time spooned generously over the custard layer of our festive trifle instead of plain cream.

## SIMPLE SYLLABUB

- 100 ml (3 fl oz) late-picked white wine or Sauternes
- 2 tablespoons brandy
- juice of 1 lemon
- spiralled rind of 1 lemon
- 2 tablespoons castor sugar
- 750 ml (24 fl oz) cream

Place the first five ingredients in a basin and leave in the refrigerator overnight.

Next day, remove the lemon rind and place the liquid and the cream in the bowl of the electric mixer and whip together until quite firm. If the syllabub is not all consumed the first day, it will probably separate the next day. Try re-whipping it. It will come back together with no harm.

If you prefer the texture, the lemon rind can be grated rather than spiralled and be left in the sweet.

After some rather pointed hints one year I was enthralled by a Christmas present of Genevieve Dormann's lovely book, *Colette—a passion for life*. Colette not only loved to eat, but she anticipated and verbally evoked her culinary pleasure in the most beautiful prose. In the same way one refers to armchair travellers, one can imagine her culinary images satisfying the desires of an armchair gastronome.

There is a splendid photograph of Colette preparing a tartine from a huge cartwheel loaf of country bread and another of her slicing it in the terrifying manner still employed by French countrywomen. The large loaf is tucked under the chin, a little like playing a violin, and a sharp long-bladed knife is used to sever the slice, working from wrist to breast. Colette gives her recipe for orange wine.

> This dates back to a year when the oranges around Hyères were particularly fine and had ripened until they were red. I took 4 litres of dry, yellow Cavalaire wine and added to it 1 litre of good Armagnac, making my friend exclaim: 'What a tragedy! Fancy sacrificing the best brandy to an undrinkable ratafia!?' Amid the protests I cut up and dropped in 4 thinly sliced oranges, a lemon which a moment ago had been hanging from its tree, a vanilla pod silvery as an old man, and 600 g of cane sugar. A large jar was pressed into service, stoppered with a cork and cloth, and it was left to steep for 50 days; all I had to do then was strain and decant it into a bottle.
>
> Is it good? Parisiennes, you arrive home at the end of a bitter winter afternoon, or after one of those deceptive spring days lashed with rain and hail and whipped by piercing sunbeams, your shoulders are shaking, you blow your nose, you feel your forehead, examine your tongue, and you moan, 'I don't know what's the matter with me . . .' Well, I know, you need a little glass of orange wine. (*Prisons et paradis*)

Colette is recommending her orange wine as a warming and comforting drop. My own experience of orange wine, peach wine and quince wine took place in totally different circumstances, but was equally delightful. On one of my holidays in France we stayed in Gréoux-les-bains, a spa town near the spectacular Gorges de Verdun. Sunday is always the day to head for a country restaurant for lunch, and especially when it is Fête des Mères. We were lucky to find a table at the Hostellerie de la Fuste where all the tables in the cobbled courtyard were prettily set with pale pink damask cloths and small vases of field flowers: cornflower, red poppy and pink rock roses. The courtyard was edged by ancient lime trees and the gentle breeze kept a gentle drift of seed pods drifting over everyone and everything. I had always thought that hayfever was a phenomenon of Melbourne, but our waiter suffered terribly. He maintained his presence despite streaming eyes and the occasional sneeze.

The house aperitif was either orange wine or peach wine, both served icy-cold and both poured over a generous amount of crushed ice. Later in the meal we were served a sorbet of quince wine, served straight from the churn, so that it melted instantly on the tongue. The slight graininess of poached quince was still present.

I have been making both orange and peach wine, and we serve it as an aperitif or as a dessert wine, usually very cold over ice. As I write this our first batch of quince wine is maturing, so it is too soon to say if it will be as good as the orange. I have very slightly modified Colette's recipe for orange wine, as we found it too sweet. Also our Tahitian vanilla beans are so luscious that they quite overpowered the citrus flavour in the first batch. We halved the quantity the second time.

## ORANGE WINE
### (after Colette)

- 10 ripe oranges
- 1.2 kg (40 oz) sugar
- 8.5 litres (13½ pints) dry white wine (a good chardonnay or semillon)
- 2.25 litres (3½ pints) brandy
- 1 vanilla pod

Slice the oranges thinly, place in a sterilised container. Combine the sugar, wine and brandy and pour over the fruit together with the vanilla pod. Cover to prevent anything falling in, and leave in a cool place for 3 days until the sugar has dissolved. Stir once a day with a sterilised metal spoon.

Transfer fruit and liquid to sterilised glass preserving jars and store in a cool (not the refrigerator) place for 50 days.

Strain through a nylon jelly bag into sterilised bottles. Cap and store.

## STEPHANIE'S PEACH WINE

I realise this has no right to be in a chapter dealing with citrus fruits, but where else to record it?

- 20 ripe yellow peaches
- 1.2 kg (40 oz) sugar

- 8.5 litres (13½ pints) dry white wine (chardonnay or semillon)
- 2.25 litres (3½ pints) brandy

Wash the unpeeled peaches. Slice from the stone into chunks into a sterilised container. Heat the wine and sugar just to boiling point. Add the brandy. Pour this liquid over the peaches.

Transfer fruit and liquid to sterilised jars and store as before for 50 days. Ladle the clear liquid through a nylon jelly bag into sterilised bottles and seal tightly. This wine is more volatile than the orange version. After opening, the bottle should be consumed without delay (over a few days) or it may start to ferment.

The peaches left will look dreadful: a murky dark-brown. They actually taste very good. At least eat one or two after the bottling session.

It is always interesting when one reads recipes of dishes that have travelled and have recurred with significant local variations. It is very common in the Mediterranean region. I have an Italian friend whose mother used sometimes to prepare a plate of biscuits she called *crostoli* over which she drizzled honey while hot. Later a Greek friend and I made a dough called *diples* with very similar ingredients. And recently I came across a Spanish version, *borrachuelos*. All of these pastries are deep-fried and are served either with honey, sugar or spices. I find them ideal to partner a delicate ice, especially those made from citrus fruits.

Once we made a plaited basket from the *diples* dough and filled it with black grapes, each one dipped into a veil of batter and fried. On another occasion, we made a pyramid of citrus ices, the colours pale and translucent like tissue paper and topped it with a frivolous bow with long streamers made from a strip of *crostoli*.

I recommend using the hand pasta machine to roll these pastries, as they are nicest if quite thin. Roll the dough to the second last thickness. The usual rules for deep-frying apply to these pastries, of course. The oil must be thermostatically controlled to avoid overheating, the oil must be clean, the pan must not be crowded, the food must be well drained.

## CROSTOLI

- 500 g (1 lb) plain flour
- 4 egg yolks
- grated peel of an orange and a lemon
- 1 tablespoon orange-flower water
- a little rum or milk to bind the dough (approximately 1 tablespoon)
- honey

Make the dough in the food-processor, using the on/off action. Do not overwork. Allow the dough to rest in the refrigerator wrapped in plastic. Roll out thinly. Either cut like wide fettuccine or more traditionally cut the strips of dough with a serrated pastry wheel into rectangles 4 × 2 cm (2 × 1 in).

Deep-fry the pastries until golden brown, drain on kitchen paper and sprinkle generously with icing sugar. Alternatively, pile the pastries on a serving platter, and while they are hot, drizzle over some warm honey.

## DIPLES

- 4 eggs
- grated rind of 1 orange
- 5 tablespoons olive oil
- 250 g (8 oz) flour
- 1 teaspoon baking powder
- pinch of salt
- 1 cup honey
- 1 teaspoon powdered cinnamon or ½ cup icing sugar, mixed with 2 teaspoons powdered cardamom

Lightly whisk the eggs with the orange rind and the oil. Sift the flour with the baking powder and salt. Place the flour in the food-processor and, using the on/off control, add the liquid. Process until you have a soft dough. Rest for 30 minutes in the refrigerator before rolling. Use a pasta machine or roll very thinly on a floured board.

Using a pastry wheel, cut whatever shapes you wish and deep-fry in hot clean oil. This dough will expand quite a lot. Drain and serve while warm with warmed honey and cinnamon, or icing sugar mixed with powdered cardamom.

## BORRACHUELOS

- grated zest of 1 orange
- ⅔ cup vegetable oil
- ⅓ cup dry white wine
- ⅓ cup sweet white wine
- 3 tablespoons fresh orange juice
- 2 teaspoons sesame seeds
- 1 teaspoon anise seeds
- 400–425 g (13–14 oz) plain flour
- 1 cup honey
- ¼ cup water
- icing sugar

Combine the orange zest with the oil in a small pan. Heat for 3–5 minutes until the orange rind turns a dark brown. Strain. Keep the oil, discard the zest. Allow the oil to cool to lukewarm.

Combine the oil with the wines, the orange juice, the sesame seeds and the anise seeds.

Place the flour in the food-processor, reserving a few spoonfuls. With the motor running add the liquid mixture. The dough should be quite soft. If it is too soft to handle, add the extra flour. Knead by hand for 1 or 2 minutes until you have a smooth elastic dough. Allow to rest at room temperature for 30 minutes.

Traditionally, this Spanish dough is rolled into small balls and then each ball is flattened and stretched into an oval. But roll and cut the dough anyway you like as long as you keep it thin.

Deep fry until golden brown, drain on paper.

Make a light syrup of the honey and water and dip each pastry into it briefly. Drain on a rack and dredge with icing sugar before serving.

For reasons that no one can explain to me, blood oranges and pink grapefruit are rarely seen in this country. They do exist, I have seen them, but they are very elusive. In the tropical north we have pomelos and limes and even ugli fruit, but I couldn't find commercial quantities of the pink grapefruit.

Blood oranges not only look sensational, they are exceptionally sweet. I have often enjoyed them in Italy freshly squeezed, a delightful variation on the world's best-loved fruit juice. They abound in markets in France during the warm months. I once bought some there, sliced off all the skin and cut them crosswise. I placed them around the edges of a flat glass plate, piled the centre with dark-red strawberries, made a caramel with 1 cup of sugar and ½ cup of water, which I stopped at the dark amber stage by adding ½ cup of the blood-red juice, and poured this exotic sauce over the fruit. It looked better than any dessert I have ever seen: rich and exotic, somehow like Ava Gardner lying on a tigerskin. Where has this image come from?

## ORANGE SAUCE
### to serve with DUCK

The traditional English sauce for many cold meats is Cumberland sauce. A variation that I use sometimes, particularly for a duck salad, is this.

- 1 tablespoon freshly grated horseradish
- 2 teaspoons redcurrant or quince jelly
- juice of 1 orange
- blanched, julienned rind of 1 orange

Mix the horseradish with the jelly and leave it to stand for an hour or so to blend the flavours. Add the orange juice and the blanched rind and spoon over the slices or chunks of duck meat.

If you are interested in making fruit jellies, orange combines particularly well with quinces to make a subtly flavoured preserve.

## ORANGE and QUINCE JELLY

- 15 ripe quinces (that is, yellow and scented, not green)
- 6 large oranges (Seville if you can get them)
- granulated sugar
- nylon jelly bag or butter muslin

Take half the quinces, wash them very well to remove all the fluff, quarter them, remove the cores and chop coarsely. Put into an enamelled saucepan, barely cover with water, and simmer for 1 hour. Strain and discard the quince pulp. Peel the rest of the quinces, peel and slice the oranges, removing all white pith. Chop both roughly and cook gently in the quince juice for 1 hour. Strain again, using a nylon jelly bag, or a doubled piece of muslin and discard the fruit pulp. Measure the remaining liquid and add an equal quantity of sugar. Return it to the saucepan and bring slowly to the boil, stirring once or twice until sugar is dissolved.

Skim off the foam which rises. Test for setting after 10 minutes by placing a little on a cold saucer in the traditional manner. Pour finished jelly into sterilised jars and seal. This quantity will yield 4 pots.

## PICKLED ORANGES

Another garnish for a roast duck salad is pickled oranges. They taste good mixed with paper-thin slices of mild red onion and olives or capers. Serve a bowlful as a surprising sambal for a curry. Or serve the chunks or slices just as they are with pre-dinner drinks as a change from nuts.

- 6 oranges
- 1 teaspoon salt
- 500 g (1 lb) sugar
- ¾ cup white vinegar
- ½ cup water
- 6 cardamom pods
- 6 peppercorns
- 6 whole cloves
- ½ teaspoon powdered cinnamon
- ¼ teaspoon ground allspice

Put oranges and salt in a large saucepan and cover with cold water. Place over a moderate heat and bring to the boil. Simmer for 45 minutes, by which time the oranges should be quite tender. Drain the fruit and allow to cool.

Bring sugar, vinegar, water and all spices to the boil. Simmer together for 5 minutes.

Using a sharp knife, cut oranges either into 5 mm (¼ in) slices or into 2 cm (1 in) cubes. Place in a pan and then strain over the pickling solution. Simmer gently to avoid breaking up the slices or chunks for about 30 minutes until the peel is quite tender and translucent and can easily be pierced with a fine skewer. Cool a little before ladling into sterilised preserving jars. Allow the pickle to mature for one month before serving it.

Before leaving oranges I should remind any reader who has read *Stephanie's Menus for Food Lovers* that one of my favourite recipes, for an orange crème caramel, is described in that volume. Then there are mandarins. Their haunting perfume is very special. We have had rave reports from customers who have eaten our mandarin bavarian cream, which we serve with a small, hot puff pastry filled with carefully cleaned segments of fruit.

A good bavarian cream should have the texture of velvet. It should not be spongy or mousse-like. The amount of gelatine is critical and needs to be considered in regard to size of the mould (small individual bavarois can have one less leaf of gelatine than if the mixture is to be set in one bowl), the length of time the sweet has to set before being served, and the 'body' of the main flavour. A purée of peach will take less gelatine than mandarin juice. For all these reasons I prefer to have individual recipes for my bavarois repertoire rather than one basic formula.

## MANDARIN BAVAROIS

- zest of 2 mandarins (if possible choose fruit with tight skins as they are much easier to grate)
- 150 g (5 oz) castor sugar
- 4 egg yolks
- 350 ml (12 fl oz) milk
- 4 leaves of gelatine
- 60 ml (2 fl oz) mandarin juice, measured after straining
- 350 ml (12 fl oz) softly whipped cream

Mix the grated mandarin zest with one-third of the sugar. Bruise well together with the back of a spoon.

Briefly whisk the rest of the sugar with the egg yolks. Scald the milk with the sugar/zest mixture. Pour onto the eggs and sugar. Stir to combine.

Return to washed-out pan and cook over moderate heat, stirring all the time until the custard has thickened: if you use a thermometer it will thicken at around 80°C (180°F). Strain custard into a bowl.

Soak gelatine in cold water for a few minutes. Squeeze and drop into a pan containing the simmering mandarin juice. Swish to ensure that it has completely dissolved. Pour the gelatine/juice mixture into the custard. Mix to combine. Cool the custard over ice. When completely cold and just starting to thicken at the edges, fold in the softly whipped cream.

Pour into the chosen moulds and allow to set. The texture is best if the bavarois is served on the day it is made.

If the hot puff pastry turnover does not appeal, why not make a mandarin juice and champagne jelly? The shiver and tremble of the jelly provides a marvellous contrast to the smooth velvet of the cream.

When making any sort of champagne jelly, ensure that your sweetened base syrup, be it quince, pear, nectarine or raspberry is quite cold with the dissolved gelatine already included, so that there is as short a delay as possible after stirring in the champagne before the jelly sets, imprisoning the tongue-tingling bubbles.

## MANDARIN JUICE JELLY

- 7 leaves gelatine
- 400 ml (13 fl oz) mandarin juice, strained
- 250 g (8 oz) castor sugar
- 300 ml (10 fl oz) champagne

Soak the gelatine in cold water. Squeeze. Heat a spoonful or two of the mandarin juice with the sugar. Stir until all the sugar has dissolved and the liquid is just simmering. Drop in the gelatine, swish to ensure that it is completely dissolved.

Add the rest of the mandarin juice, stir, and then leave until the mixture is quite cold. Gently pour in the champagne and carefully ladle the jelly into the selected jelly moulds. Refrigerate until set.

One can peel a small mandarin, strip it of all cottony pith, and dip it into a golden caramel. Sit the toffeed mandarin on an oiled plate until you are ready to serve the dessert. Like all toffeed fruit it will last only a few hours in a cool place before the toffee will soften. Tuck a small citrus leaf under it before settling this little jewel alongside the jelly and the bavarois.

I have always had a cumquat tree and every year I find something else to use them for. Always with duck, often with pork, or finely minced with a salad of mixed offal or trotters, or tossed through some plain pasta with lots of pepper, parsley and parmesan cheese, and one year I used them to make a compound butter, which in turn I used to make a cumquat butter sauce for an asparagus custard served with steamed baby zucchini.

And I am convinced that cumquat marmalade is the finest marmalade in the world, especially when spread on home-made wholemeal toast. There are two varieties of cumquat (or kumquat) available in Australia. The more usual (Marumi) variety, and the one usually grown as an ornamental tree, has round fruit, the rind is perfumed and pungent, the flesh puckery-sour. The other variety one sees cumquat nagami has oval-shaped fruits. Once again the rind has the sweet-sharp character, but the fruit of this variety is less acidic.

The latter is the variety used at Berowra Waters Inn by Gay Bilson and Janni Kyritsis in their version of Sussex Pond pudding. In the traditional English pudding a whole lemon is cooked inside a suet crust, and the pudding runs with sharp, buttery juices when cut. Gay has kindly consented to my using her recipe in this book. Berowra Waters Inn is a very special place. Architecturally, visually and emotionally one is unforgettably in Australia.

## BEROWRA WATERS INN
## SUSSEX POND PUDDING

This recipe is sufficient for eight.

### — JANE GRIGSON'S SUET CRUST —

- 500 g (1 lb) self-raising flour
- 250 g (8 oz) grated suet (from the butcher—do not use packaged suet, which has added flour)
- 125 ml (4 fl oz) milk
- 125 ml (4 fl oz) water
- pinch of salt

- 16 oval, seedless cumquats, pricked all over
- 8 teaspoons Seville orange marmalade (preferably homemade)
- 8 walnut-sized knobs of unsalted butter
- 8 heaped teaspoons dark brown sugar

### TO MAKE SUET CRUST

Sift flour with salt. Rub in suet lightly with the fingertips, then tip in milk and water. Combine to form the dough. Knead briefly. Roll out the crust and cut into 16 cm (6 in) circles. Cut a quarter from each circle to form the lid.

### TO LINE MOULDS

Grease each individual pudding mould. Fit the larger piece of pastry in the mould, pressing the two cut edges together. Work the crust well into the mould. The crust should come slightly above the rim.

Place the marmalade, sugar, butter and pricked fruit in each pudding basin. Roll the reserved piece of pastry into a ball and roll to form a lid. Brush the rim of the pudding pastry with water, lay on the lid and firmly pin the edges together.

Completely enclose each mould in buttered aluminium foil, pleating the top to allow for the expansion of the crust and steam the puddings for 1 1/2 hours.

Serve with a hot custard sauce, either a crème anglaise as at Berowra Waters, or a custard made from fruit syrup and egg yolks, such as Eliza Acton's quince custard on page 280.

## CUMQUAT BUTTER

- 500 g (1 lb) unsalted butter at room temperature
- 2 tablespoons spiced cumquats, seeded and finely chopped (see page 159)
- 1 tablespoon spiced cumquat liquor
- 4 tablespoons very well-reduced chicken stock (optional)
- pepper
- 1/2 teaspoon finely chopped garlic
- 2 tablespoons finely chopped parsley

Whiz all ingredients in the food-processor. Press through sieve for a very fine texture if butter is to be whisked in a sauce, such as for the butter sauce, otherwise just mix well. Scrape into a large and doubled piece of foil and form into a roll by smoothing and twisting the ends in opposite directions.

Omit the reduced stock if intending the sauce for vegetables.

## CUMQUAT BUTTER SAUCE

- 3 tablespoons water
- 1 tablespoon cream
- 300 g (10 oz) cumquat butter as in previous recipe, cut into chunks
- few drops cider vinegar

Bring water to simmering point in small pan. Add cream and boil until cream is a little reduced. Start to whisk in the chunks of butter, not adding a chunk until the one before is incorporated. Remove the pan from the heat if the sauce seems to be in danger of oiling. Continue until all the butter is incorporated and the sauce is thick and creamy. Taste for acidity and seasoning. Add a few drops of the vinegar if necessary.

It is not difficult mounting a sauce with butter. A sauce can get quite hot without danger, providing you continually add pieces of cold butter and keep whisking. Be brave! Don't go too slowly!

Try this same sauce on a quickly grilled chicken breast. With an excellent green salad, it is a family favourite.

## EASIEST CUMQUAT MARMALADE

Buy or pick the required amount of fruit. Wash it carefully and cut into quarters. Put into a bowl and barely cover it with cold water. Leave this overnight. In the morning measure it into cups, noting the number. Cook the fruit in this same water until tender, then add the sugar, 1 cup to each previously measured cup of fruit. Boil this briskly till it sets in the usual manner. (From *Through My Kitchen Door* by Mary Burchett.)

I have always loved glacé fruit: apricots, chestnuts, quinces or grapefruit. The glowing fruits look very festive and remind me of Christmas and of the children's story *The Night before Christmas*, 'while visions of sugarplums danced in their heads'. Sugarplums always sounded *really* special

It is very difficult to candy fruits, and I would prefer to let a professional do it for me. Unfortunately, I have not seen any professionally candied cumquats in Australia, so I have had to have a go myself. I have given my recipe in the chapter called Love Bites. For those with lots of patience and a good hydrometer, I recommend the recipe in Mireille Johnston's *The Cuisine of the Sun*. Her recipe takes 30 days. Mine takes 9.

## CITRUS SORBETS

I have mentioned these several times. A properly made orange or mandarin or grapefruit sorbet finishes a meal beautifully. They should never be served rock-hard, but should be softly spoonable. Practically, this means that the sorbet should be served several hours after it has been churned, certainly not the day after. I have discussed the principles of sorbet-making in my earlier book, and don't wish to cover the same ground, but it is important to realise that the lower the sugar density the harder the sorbet will freeze. The higher the sugar density the sweeter it will be, but it will not freeze as solid. So one tries to balance and control these factors by keeping the sugar level palatable and by serving the sorbet before it has a chance to set like an ice-block.

It is a good idea to buy a saccharometer, but perfectly good sorbets can be made without one, relying on your taste-buds.

Put 500 g (1 lb) of sugar in a pan with 500 ml (16 fl oz) of water. Simmer, stirring until all the sugar has dissolved. This will result in a syrup at 32°C if you measure it when cold with a saccharometer. Stock syrup can be made in large quantities and stored indefinitely.

To make citrus ices, add some zest of lemon, orange, grapefruit, mandarin or cumquat to the cold water so that the flavour of the oils in the skin flavour the syrup. This adds finesse and subtlety to the finished sorbet.

Dilute the syrup with strained citrus juice until the mixture measures around 13°C to my taste. Some people prefer their sorbets at 15°C or 16°C. Without a saccharometer, add the juice and decide when to stop purely on taste. Churn and freeze for a few hours.

A delicious variation is the following champagne sorbet.

## CHAMPAGNE and ORANGE JUICE SORBET

- Make stock syrup as above, using a few curls or orange zest.
- 1 cup strained orange juice
- 1 bottle champagne
- 2 teaspoons Grand Marnier

Mix the orange juice, the champagne and Grand Marnier. Add 2 cups of the syrup and taste. You may need a little more syrup. (It will probably measure 14°C on a saccharometer.) When you are happy with the flavour, churn. Serve it in a chilled champagne flute (but not your most precious one) with some fresh segments of orange. Remember alcohol will not freeze, so this sorbet does not need to be very sweet.

Should you find some blood oranges, they make a stunning sorbet. Watermelon looks pretty with the pale pastels of lime, lemon and orange.

Proust's favourite small cake—madeleines—served warm from the oven, sprinkled with icing sugar, are a delectable contrast to a coupe of soft, sharp citrus ices.

# LEMON MADELEINES

- 4 eggs
- 200 g (7 oz) castor sugar
- grated zest of 2 lemons
- 225 g (8 oz) plain flour
- 175 g (6 oz) unsalted butter, melted and cooled
- extra butter, just melted for the moulds
- dusting flour for the moulds

Brush madeleine moulds with the barely melted butter. Dust well with flour. Shake to get rid of the excess. Pre-heat the oven to 180°C (350°F).

Beat the eggs and the sugar with the lemon zest until thick and lemon-coloured. Fold in the flour quickly and lightly. Trickle in the melted butter, fold in quickly but thoroughly. Fill each madeleine shell two-thirds full, Bake for around 10 minutes. Allow tray to cool for a few seconds, and then rap it sharply on the table or bench. The little cakes should fall out, golden brown and well marked on the underside. Cool a little on a rack and dust lightly with icing sugar. Serve warm or as soon as possible.

A properly cooked madeleine should bite crisply and be soft and buttery inside. If the outside is not golden brown and crisp, increase the oven temperature for the next batch.

# ICE-CREAMS

FEASTS & STORIES

I once served a slice of vanilla semi-freddo seamed with espresso-soaked amaretti at one of our special dinners. It was accompanied by the beautifully wrapped amaretti di saronno, unique Italian macaroons, each pair wrapped in twists of pastel tissue. I also like serving mandarin, passionfruit and tamarillo ices in their own shells. A plateful of these 'fruits' looks very charming, and currently we are arranging our selection on a large velvet leaf of peppermint geranium and nestling a small scoop of refreshing peppermint sorbet alongside the more intense fruit flavours.

My special interest in combining textures and flavours has resulted in some delicious iced desserts. An ice or an ice-cream is always accompanied by at least one other preparation for balance, contrast or surprise value.

Classic ice-cream is based on a cooked custard. One can use all milk, half milk and half cream, or for a super-rich mixture (too rich, I feel), some recipes suggest all cream. Made with the scraped seeds of a fresh vanilla bean a home-made vanilla ice-cream is sensational. It is at its most sublime as part of a peach melba. Early in the summer we get small, yellow peaches of intense flavour and juiciness. Raspberries are abundantly available, so there is never any discussion as to what will be served that month.

FEASTS & STORIES

238

Some of the later peaches look luscious, but taste most disappointing. I suggest that when you have found a variety whose taste lives up to its look that you preserve as many as possible.

## VANILLA ICE-CREAM

- 250 ml (8 fl oz) cream
- 125 g (4 oz) castor sugar
- ½ vanilla bean, split
- 5 egg yolks
- 250 ml (8 fl oz) milk

Heat cream with half the sugar and the split vanilla bean.

Stir until sugar is dissolved. Heat to scalding point and then leave to infuse for 15 minutes, covered. Remove the vanilla pod and scrape the seeds into the cream. Wash and dry the pod and bury it in a jar of castor sugar. Whisk the yolks lightly with the rest of the sugar. Add the warm cream. Rinse out the pan and return the custard to the heat and cook until it coats the back of the spoon. Strain into a basin set over ice. Stir. When cold, add milk. Churn.

There is no end to the variations possible based on this standard and delicious ice-cream. One just needs to keep on the qui vive. For instance, when I was making the raisin and Rutherglen muscat tart (see page 201) there was quite a bit of liqueur left after soaking the raisins. I added it to a batch of vanilla ice-cream before churning it and it made a delicious ice-cream, the colour of palest caramel. It was perfect with the hot tart.

## PRESERVED PEACHES in VANILLA SYRUP and BRANDY

Prepare a light poaching syrup in the proportions of 600 ml (20 fl oz) water to 300 g (10 oz) sugar. Add half a split vanilla pod to the syrup. Poach the peaches a few at a time. When cool enough to handle, slip off the skins and place gently in a sterilised preserving jar. When all peaches are poached and skinned, pour over the syrup to fill the jar by two-thirds. Top up the jar with brandy. Clip-seal the jars, invert carefully to mix the brandy and syrup and leave for as long as you can resist. You will be able to serve a wonderfully heady peach melba in the autumn (with fresh raspberries) or in the winter (with frozen raspberries). Serve a few spoonfuls of the syrup around the peach.

A parfait is exceptionally rich and creamy owing to the large number of egg yolks and the high proportion of cream used. It is not churned, but is poured straight into a mould or parfait glass. A parfait mix is used for soufflés glacés, those formal desserts that rise high above their dishes to resemble a cooked soufflé. I have included two recipes for parfaits, one is a classic coffee flavour, the other is slightly unusual, being based on cooked apples rather than the usual sugar syrup.

The coffee parfait is scooped into balls, chocolate-coated and served with a heap of espresso granita granules, a marron glacé and a *thin* slice of chestnut pavé.

## COFFEE PARFAIT

- 300 g (10 oz) sugar
- 1 cup (250 ml) water
- 12 egg yolks
- 900 ml (30 fl oz) whipped cream

- 4 tablespoons instant coffee dissolved in 3 tablespoons boiling water; OR 200 g (9 oz) finely ground strong coffee; OR 4 tablespoons Trabilt coffee extract

Dissolve the sugar in the water. Bring to the boil stirring only until all the sugar has dissolved. Boil vigorously until the syrup measures 110°C (225°F) on a candy thermometer.

Have the lightly beaten yolks ready in an electric mixer. Allow the bubbling of the syrup to settle for a few seconds and then, with the machine running, slowly pour the syrup onto the beaten egg yolks. Continue to beat until the mixture is quite cold. Fold the whipped cream into the mixture and flavour with the coffee.

If you wish to make balls of the ice-cream, tip it into a large bowl and freeze until firm. Scoop the balls with an ice-cream scoop and place them on a cake rack over a tray. Return to the freezer while you prepare the chocolate coating. Alternatively pour the parfait into any preferred mould.

# — CHOCOLATE COATING FOR ICE-CREAM —

- 300 g (10 oz) best-quality dark chocolate
- 200 g (7 oz) unsalted butter

Melt chocolate and butter together in a double-boiler. Stir gently to ensure that the mixture is smooth. Strain into a jug and when nearly cold remove the tray of ice-cream balls from the freezer and pour over the chocolate. Do not dab at the balls—pour generously. The run-off can be scraped up, re-melted and re-strained for a second pour if you haven't enough.

Quickly replace the ice-cream balls in the freezer to set the chocolate.

## ESPRESSO GRANITA

- 1 litre (32 fl oz) strong espresso-style coffee (using at least 1 cup of coffee)
- 100 ml (3 fl oz) Kahlua
- 4 tablespoons coffee extract or

4 tablespoons instant coffee dissolved in water
- 200 ml (7 fl oz) sugar syrup (200 ml water to 200 g sugar, simmered 5 minutes)

Combine all the above ingredients. The mixture should taste really strong and oily at this stage, like Turkish coffee without the mud. Stir, taste and adjust for strength and sweetness. Freeze in a shallow tray.

To serve, scrape flakes from the surface with a strong metal spatula. Alternatively, agitate the mixture from time to time as it freezes so that it freezes into a slushy tray of granules. The ice will start to melt as soon as it hits the plate, so ensure that the plates or parfait glasses are very cold.

## CHESTNUT PAVÉ

- 400 g (13 oz) best-quality dark chocolate
- 60 g (2 oz) unsalted butter
- ½ cup castor sugar
- 430 g (14 oz) natural chestnut purée (i.e. unsweetened)
- 1½ tablespoons cornflour
- ⅓ cup cognac or rum
- 3 eggs + 1 egg yolk
- ⅓ cup cream

Melt chocolate, butter and sugar in a double boiler. Stir till smooth and cool slightly. The rest of the pavé is made in the food-processor. Blend the chestnut purée until very smooth. Blend in chocolate mixture. Blend in cornflour and cognac. Blend eggs and egg yolk. Blend in cream.

Prepare a cast-iron log mould by lightly oiling it with sweet almond oil or a tasteless salad oil. Line it with a long doubled foil strip long enough to extend over each end and serve as a help when unmoulding. Pour in the mixture. Bake at 180°C (350°F) for 40 minutes. The pavé will not test clean with a skewer and may still look a little wobbly. However it is cooked. Transfer immediately to a refrigerator and allow to cool completely (even overnight) before unmoulding.

Prepare the chocolate coating as for the coffee parfait balls. Unmould the pavé onto a cake rack as before and coat generously with the chocolate. Place briefly in the freezer to quickly set the coating, and then wrap the log until needed. Because it is very rich, cut a very thin slice. The dessert could be arranged on a slick of cold, thin cream or coffee crème anglaise.

The following recipe for apple parfait is a useful one. Substitute peaches or apricots for the apples—or any other ripe fruit. With the apple parfait I serve apple fritters dipped into a light saffron batter, deep-fried and sprinkled with a mixture of powdered ginger and castor sugar in the same proportion as for cinnamon toast.

If made with peaches, the parfait would be delicious poured into a glass and topped with one of the peaches preserved in brandy.

## APPLE PARFAIT

- 6 golden delicious apples
- 300 ml (10 fl oz) white wine
- 125 g (4 oz) + 90 g (3 oz) castor sugar
- ½ cinnamon stick
- Calvados to taste
- 5 egg yolks
- 300 ml (10 fl oz) cream, whipped

Peel, core and slice the apples. Heat wine, 125 g (4 oz) sugar and cinnamon and dissolve the sugar. Add the apples and cook uncovered until soft. Remove the cinnamon stick. Purée and then rub through a sieve. Flavour the purée with Calvados when cold.

Whisk the egg yolks and 90 g (3 oz) sugar until thick and creamy. Stir in the apple purée. Fold in the whipped cream. Pour into selected mould and freeze.

One hardly needs a recipe for apple fritters. I use the white wine batter on page 57 or the simple egg white batter included in my first book *Stephanie's Menus for Food Lovers*. In both cases dissolve a pinch of saffron in a little hot water and add with the other liquids.

A semi-freddo is a simplified version of the parfait and is amazingly versatile. It can include moistened cake or biscuit crumbs, liqueured or candied fruit, fruit purées, nuts or liqueurs. At Christmas time I add a jar of best-quality fruit mince and a little of the special Christmas brandy and offer it with the Christmas pudding.

Here are a few favourites.

## AMARETTI LOG

- 4 egg yolks
- 2 drops vanilla extract
- 175 g (6 oz) sugar
- 60 ml (2 fl oz) milk
- 500 ml (16 fl oz) cream, whipped
- 80 ml (3 fl oz) Amaretto di Saronna liqueur
- 6 double amaretti macaroons soaked in 100 ml (3 fl oz) of strong espresso-style coffee

The first 5 ingredients comprise the basic mixture.

Beat the egg yolks and vanilla really well in an electric mixer until they are thick and lemon-coloured. Put the sugar and milk in a non-stick saucepan and simmer, stirring until the sugar is dissolved. Boil for 2 minutes and pour onto the yolks. Beat well. Allow to cool.

Fold in the cream whipped with the liqueur and the soaked biscuits. Pour into a cast-iron log mould lined with a doubled strip of either foil or parchment paper cut long enough so that the ends extend and will be a help when you unmould the log.

If you wish to present the log as I have shown in the picture, pour half the semi-freddo into the mould, then crumble the biscuits over, then pour in the rest of the mixture.

Serve with liqueured cherries or the peaches in brandy.

# PRUNE and MUSCAT
# FROZEN TRIFLE

- 24 pitted prunes
- 500 ml (16 fl oz) muscat (OR tokay or port)
- 500 ml (16 fl oz) red wine
- 100 g (3 oz) castor sugar
- 1 orange, sliced thickly
- 1 lemon, sliced thickly
- 4 egg yolks
- 175 g (6 oz) sugar
- 60 ml (2 fl oz) milk
- 500 ml (16 fl oz) cream
- 2 drops vanilla extract

## — CAKE —

- 3 eggs
- 75 g (2½ oz) castor sugar
- 60 g (2 oz) plain flour
- 1 tablespoon Dutch cocoa
- 2 tablespoons melted, cooled unsalted butter

## — CHOCOLATE COATING —

- 300 g (10 oz) best-quality dark chocolate
- 200 g (7 oz) unsalted butter

### To prepare prunes

Start soaking the prunes 4 days before wishing to serve this dessert. Soak the prunes in the muscat and red wine overnight. Next day put the prunes and wine into a pan. Add the sugar, orange and lemon. Bring to the boil and simmer for 15 minutes. Steep the prunes in this liquid for at least 3 days. Any prunes not used will make a simple dessert on their own in little glasses with some of their liquor. (They would also be delicious and appropriate as an accompaniment to the amaretti log.)

After 3 days, remove 12 of the prunes and allow them to drain really well.

### To make cake

This is a classic genoese sponge.

Place eggs and sugar in a basin over hot water and whisk until light and warm to the touch. Transfer the mixture to an electric mixer and continue to beat until thick and mousse-like. Sieve flour and cocoa and fold lightly but thoroughly into the mixture. Trickle the cooled butter down the sides of the basin and fold it in thoroughly. Pour the cake into a greased and floured swiss roll tin. You are aiming at a thin layer of cake.

Bake at 180°C (350°F) for about 10 minutes, until the cake feels springy to the touch. Let the cake cool on a rack for a few minutes still in its tin and then invert onto a clean cloth and leave until completely cold.

Prepare a cast-iron log mould by cutting a doubled strip of foil or parchment as described in the last recipe.

### TO MAKE ICE-CREAMS

Follow the instructions for the amaretti log up until the folding in of the biscuits. Divide the ice-cream into two slightly unequal parts. Purée the reserved and well-drained prunes in a blender. Whisk the prune purée into the smaller quantity. Pour prune ice-cream mixture into the mould to come a little less than half way. Cover with a piece of plastic wrap and smooth with your hand or a spatula to even the surface. Place in the freezer for 2 hours. Remove the log from the freezer, peel off the plastic and pour in a layer of the vanilla ice-cream to come just below the top. You may have extra prune ice-cream. Freeze it in a small bowl for another day. Place a piece of plastic wrap over the vanilla layer and even the surface. Freeze for 2 hours.

Cut a piece of cake to fit exactly the top of the mould. Freeze the rest of the cake, or make a miniature frozen trifle using the excess prune ice-cream.

Soak the cake with the prune liquor. Remove the log from the freezer, remove the plastic and press the moistened cake into position. Cover the whole log with plastic and freeze overnight.

### TO COAT THE TRIFLE WITH CHOCOLATE

Prepare and cool the chocolate topping as in the recipe for the coffee ice-cream balls. Remove the log from the freezer. Run a knife along the sides of the mould and tug gently at the ends. Invert the ice-cream onto a cake rack suspended over a tray to catch the drips. Pour a generous layer of chocolate over the log—once again, no dabbing. Return to the freezer to set. After 20 minutes or so, the log can be entirely wrapped in plastic ready to be sliced.

Serve the dessert surrounded by several spoonfuls of the reserved liquor and 2 soaked prunes.

## STRAWBERRY TORTONI

Iced confections known as tortoni are also moulded in terrine moulds. Although the semi-freddo does not make a very hard ice-cream, it does keep very well in the freezer. Tortoni are best eaten the day they are made or the next day. They should also be allowed to soften a little before being served. Having said this, they are so easy and so delicious that you will make one often.

- 1 cup roughly chopped strawberry pulp
- ½ cup toasted flaked almonds
- 6 crushed amaretti biscuits
- 60 ml (2 fl oz) fraise de bourgogne or 60 ml (2 fl oz) brandy

- 2 egg whites
- ½ cup icing sugar
- pinch of cream of tartar
- 500 ml (16 fl oz) cream

Mix the strawberry pulp, the almonds, the crushed biscuits and the liqueur in a bowl. Allow to stand for 10 minutes. Whip egg whites till stiff, but not dry. Add the icing sugar and a tiny pin cream of tartar and beat until shiny. Whip the cream. Tip the fruit mixture onto the cream. Tip the egg-white meringue onto the cream and fruit and fold together lightly but thoroughly.

Pour into a foil-lined mould and freeze. When frozen, the log can be turned out and spread with whipped cream or, even more deliciously, a layer of strawberry fool (below). Refreeze to set the fool.

Obviously this very simple recipe is perfect for all fresh berry fruit. I have made it with cherries preserved in eau-de-vie, using the preserving liquid and walnuts.

## STRAWBERRY FOOL

- 1 punnet of ripe strawberries
- sugar to taste

- 300 ml (10 fl oz) cream, whipped

Crush the strawberries with a fork or run them very briefly through the food-processor. Sweeten to taste and fold into the whipped cream.

Tortoni can also be moulded in springform pans. In this case have extra biscuit crumbs or flaked almonds to press onto the sides after the tin has been removed.

## PEACH TORTONI

This recipe illustrates a method that could be used with pears poached in red wine, stewed rhubarb or any desired fruit.

- 3 large ripe peaches
- 2 tablespoons lemon juice (OR poaching liquid, if using poached fruit)

- 350 ml (11 fl oz) cream
- 3 egg whites
- pinch cream of tartar
- 1/3 cup castor sugar

Dip the peaches into boiling water, peel. Cut the fruit into chunks and purée in a food-processor with the lemon juice.

Whip cream stiffly. Beat egg whites with the cream of tartar until they hold soft peaks. Add the sugar a little at a time until you have a shiny meringue.

Fold the cream into the peach purée. Fold in the meringue. Pour into desired mould and freeze. Allow the peach tortoni to soften in the refrigerator before serving.

The next recipe is for a nougat ice-cream, which we make with candied angelica and the Barossa Valley's speciality: candied quinces. I serve it cut into slices and, as it is quite sweet, with a passionfruit and orange juice syrup.

At our Great Duck Dinner we lined Easter egg moulds with lightly tinted white chocolate, filled the eggs with this nougat ice-cream, and added a small scoop of orange ice as the yolk. The eggs were presented on a nest of baked Greek kataifi pastry shreds and they looked exquisite.

# QUINCE and ANGELICA NOUGAT ICE-CREAM

## — PRALINE —

- 90 g (3 oz) whole blanched almonds, toasted till pale brown
- 125 g (4 oz) castor sugar

## — ICE-CREAM —

- 100 g (3 oz) castor sugar
- 60 g (2 oz) liquid glucose
- 150 g (5 oz) honey
- 8 egg whites
- 800 ml (28 fl oz) cream
- 180 g (6 oz) candied quince
- 90 g (3 oz) candied angelica

## — PASSIONFRUIT AND ORANGE SYRUP —

- ½ cup castor sugar
- ¼ cup water
- ½ cup strained orange juice
- ½ cup strained passionfruit juice

### To make praline

Melt sugar in a heavy-based saucepan. Have near by a cup of cold water and a small brush to wash the sides of the pan. When the sugar has turned a golden colour, add the toasted almonds. Pour the praline onto an oiled tray. When it is cold, break into pieces and pulverise in the food-processor or with a meat mallet. (You could double the praline quantity as it is so useful.) Store any extra in a screw-top jar.

### To make ice-cream

Place sugar, glucose and honey into a pan. Simmer and stir once or twice until the sugar is dissolved. Boil until the mixture registers 116°C (240°F) on a candy thermometer. When the honey syrup is nearly ready, beat the egg whites until they hold stiff peaks. When the syrup has reached the correct temperature, pour it onto the egg whites with the mixer running. Continue to beat until the mixture is quite cold.

Whip the cream softly. Fold it into the cooled nougat. Fold in the chopped quince, the chopped angelica and the praline. Pour into prepared log mould foil-lined as described for the amaretti log. Neaten the top with a spatula. Cover with plastic and freeze.

Serve cut into generous slices with the syrup around.

## To make syrup

Make a deep golden caramel with the sugar and the water. Wash down any crystals that form with the brush and cold water. Stop the caramel cooking any further by carefully pouring on the orange juice. Stir gently until the caramel is dissolved. Add the passionfruit juice and refrigerate until needed.

I have made over and over again the orange and cardamom ice-cream recipe given by Jane Grigson in her *Fruit* book. She, in turn, credits the recipe to Josceline Dimbleby, who serves it apparently with an orange-blossom and peeled-walnut syrup. I usually serve it with either carefully peeled segments of orange in an orange juice and caramel syrup, or with a halved orange sprinkled with brown sugar and briefly grilled. In both cases I serve a slice of cake as well: sometimes the well-known Middle-eastern cake made by cooking oranges, peel and all, and combining them with ground almonds, or a simple steamed sponge pudding soaked in a caramel or orange syrup. On one occasion when I planned to serve the ice-cream, I had lots of orange-blossom on the tree, so I frosted the delicate flowers with egg white and sugar. When I ate one of these sugared morsels I was astounded at how pungent and aromatic it was. I had always assumed that orange-flower water had been concentrated or otherwise tampered with. But the dainty petals had just that same intensity. I should have infused some of the blossoms for my own home-made orange-blossom syrup. Next time.

As Jane Grigson comments, the use of concentrated orange juice in the recipe is not a mistake. The result is far superior to the flavour obtained by using the same quantity of fresh juice.

- 175 g (6 oz) castor sugar
- ½ cup water
- 4 eggs
- 125 ml (4 fl oz) concentrated orange juice
- 5 cardamom pods, seeds removed and crushed
- 300 ml (10 fl oz) cream

Bring sugar and water to the boil. Stir until sugar is dissolved. Lightly beat eggs in an electric mixer. Pour on the boiling syrup, beating well until the volume has doubled. Beat in the orange juice and crushed cardamom seeds. When well blended, stir in the cream and churn. Freeze.

This ice-cream is lovely partnered with an orange-juice sorbet.

## PERSIMMON ICE-CREAM

I have an infant persimmon tree in the garden. I planted it after visiting a friend in the Adelaide Hills and seeing for the first time a laden persimmon tree. Those glorious fruits were so beautiful. So far my tree has not had any fruit at all, but I was contacted one year by a lady whose tree was laden.

Persimmons have to be really soft to be edible. Before this they are horribly astringent. If you have a tree or have bought some that all ripen at once, this ice-cream is very good. Scooped-out persimmon pulp, bagged and labelled, can be stored in the freezer ready for this or any other recipe.

- 6 persimmons
- 200 ml (7 fl oz) heavy sugar syrup (200 ml water to 200 g sugar, simmered 5 minutes)
- few drops lemon juice
- 300 ml (10 fl oz) cream

Carefully cut a lid off each persimmon with a sharp knife, as if beheading a breakfast egg. Scoop out the pulp with a teaspoon. Place the skins in the freezer to become rigid containers for the ice-cream. Press the pulp through a sieve. Add the smooth pulp to the syrup and add lemon juice to taste. Add the cream and churn.

Refill the frozen shells and replace the lids. Wrap each filled fruit in plastic and freeze several hours. The texture of this ice-cream is fine the next day.

Either serve the ice-creams just as they are, or slice them lengthwise and serve with a platter of other fruit-filled ices or ice-creams as in the picture.

While holidaying in Port Douglas, far-north Queensland (FNQ to the locals), I visited the Sunday produce market. It is held under the shade of immense mango trees and was great fun. As the fruit plopped down, it was totally ignored and squashed underfoot. At the Carmen Miranda tropical ice-cream and fruit juice stall I bought a soursop ice-cream. My companion had a jackfruit ice-cream. Passionfruit seemed a bit ordinary, but the ice-cold watermelon juice looked inviting. It was already 28°C at 10 a.m. Another beautiful day in this paradise of north Queensland. The fruits were exciting: star apples, five-corner fruit, strawberry pawpaw, custard apples and many, many more I could not identify. Later I met Deirdre and Bruno Scomazzon, leaders in the development of the rare fruits industry, which has great potential for this part of the country. They agreed to send me some of these exotic fruits to bring a little tropical lushness into the cooler climate down south.

So I devised a dessert that we call banana ice-cream in a coconut cone with fruits from the north. The cone was to evoke the wafer cones in which all ice-cream used to be sold. Ours were especially delicious. The fruits were served sliced or segmented or whole, depending on the variety. Over a period of three months we saw some amazing fruits. The chocolate-pudding fruit (black sapote or Diaspyros digyna), for example. It is a member of the Ebenaceae family, and has velvet soft flesh of exactly the colour and texture of a chocolate pudding. We had fresh lychees and rambutans and red bananas. We had rollinias, very special custard apples with creamy perfect flesh, a mammee americana with exquisite peach-pear flavours, and Malay apples with their pretty rose-pink skin. It was most exciting.

Another friend from the north, Mogens Bay Esbensen, ran a restaurant, the Nautilus, and he turned many of these superb fruits into ice-creams. I was delighted to find recipes for several of them in his published book, Thai Cuisine. I have included two here for those who may have a supply of tropical fruit.

## BANANA ICE-CREAM in a COCONUT CONE, served with FRUITS from the NORTH

- 350 g (11 oz) ripe bananas
- juice of ½ lemon
- 100 ml (3 fl oz) sugar syrup (simmer 100 g–3 oz–sugar with 100 ml water for 5 minutes)

- white rum to taste
- 300 ml (10 fl oz) cream

Peel and break up the bananas and process until smooth with the lemon juice. Add the sugar syrup and the rum. Add the cream. Taste for rum. Churn. Do not churn this ice-cream too much; it should stay creamy, not granular.

### — COCONUT CONE —

Have the oven ready and the trays lined with baking parchment before starting these biscuits. The batter shouldn't wait around too long. Have 6 champagne flutes at the ready.

- 75 g (2½ oz) desiccated coconut
- 125 g (4 oz) castor sugar
- 1 teaspoon plain flour

- 1 teaspoon baking powder
- 75 g (2½ oz) butter
- 2 egg whites

Combine coconut, sugar, flour and baking powder. Mix well. Melt butter and add to the mixture. Stir in the egg whites. Spoon onto baking parchment and spread into circles with the back of a spoon: about 14 cm (5½ in) in diameter.

Cook at 200°C (400°F) for about 7 minutes. The biscuits will first spread a little, then puff and still be pale, and then they will subside and become golden brown. Cook one first to observe all these stages. When cooked, wait for a few seconds and then lift the biscuit with a palette knife into the champagne flute and curl it around to form the shape of a cone. When all the biscuits are cooked, they may be stored in an air-tight container.

Spoon the banana ice-cream into the cone, lie it on a plate and surround with a selection of tropical fruit. Don't forget, at least one passionfruit!

## ICE-CREAM NOI NA: CUSTARD APPLE ICE-CREAM
### (from *Thai Cuisine*, by Mogens Bay Esbensen)

- 3 cups custard apple pulp
- 200 g (7 oz) castor sugar
- 2 whole eggs
- 2 tablespoons lime juice
- 2 cups whipping cream

Slice open custard apples, scoop flesh into a sieve and push through, removing pips. Extract 3 cups of pulp in a bowl, adding castor sugar. Beat the eggs with a fork, add to pulp with lime juice. Whip cream lightly and fold into mixture. Churn in an ice-cream machine and place in freezer to set. Serve soft and creamy, not ice hard.

## MANGO PARFAIT
### (from *Thai Cuisine*)

Mogens specifies using a copper bowl. The ice-cream can be made using a stainless steel bowl quite satisfactorily.

- 4–5 mangoes, peeled and puréed to make 2 cups
- 150 g (5 oz) castor sugar
- 5 egg yolks
- juice of 1 lemon
- 2 teaspoons kirsch
- 1½ cups cream

Pass the mango purée through a sieve. Place in a saucepan with sugar and cook over a low heat for 10–15 minutes until the mixture becomes transparent.

Beat egg yolks in a copper bowl over a double boiler. Add mango mixture and continue to whisk until thickened. Place copper bowl immediately over crushed ice to stop any further cooking. Add lemon juice and kirsch. Leave to chill. Whip cream lightly and fold into the mango mixture. Churn and pour into mould and freeze overnight.

## — MANGO SAUCE —

- 2 ripe mangoes, peeled and puréed
- 60 g (2 oz) castor sugar
- 2 teaspoons kirsch

Place all ingredients in food-processor and blend.

Either of these two tropical taste sensations could replace the banana ice-cream in the coconut cone.

The lamington is considered to be an Australian invention. Two books that investigate the history and traditions associated with Australian cooking are Michael Symons's *One Continuous Picnic*, and Richard Beckett's *Convicted Tastes: Food in Australia*. Both volumes agree that while claims to originality in other areas are spurious (pavlova is claimed equally by New Zealand; and after all Peach Melba was invented by Escoffier at The Savoy in London), the lamington is ours. It is a cake made of a genoese sponge, cut into squares, sometimes dipped into thinned jam and then into chocolate icing, sometimes split, filled with raspberry jam, re-formed, and then dipped into chocolate icing, and then rolled in desiccated coconut.

Richard Beckett observes, 'so-called sophisticated Australians think that the Country Women's Association lamingtons are funny. In the United States they'd be a national treasure, and the roast leg of lamb would be enshrined.' There is a suggestion, although no proof is offered, that the cakes were named after Baron Lamington, who was Governor of Queensland from 1895 to 1901. Michael Symons offers the following: 'A nice embellishment to the theory is that the word refers to a "lamina" of gold, apricot jam filling to provide moisture to left-over cake.'

In 1987 Australian women were still baking lamingtons to raise money for the local basketball team and the like, and there was still a lamingtons category in the home produce section of the Royal Agricultural Show.

I cannot let this national treasure be ignored. We now make our own lamingtons and serve them alongside a *trompe-l'oeil* lamington, in reality a square of coconut ice-cream, chocolate-coated and rolled in coconut. Alongside is a third square, this one of coconut ice, a childish taste I cannot resist. I have noticed that the customers cannot resist it either.

## LAMINGTONS

### — GENOESE SPONGE CAKE —

- 5 eggs
- 150 g (5 oz) sugar
- 150 g (5 oz) sifted plain flour
- 60 ml (2 fl oz) cooled, melted butter
- 200 g (7 oz) smooth raspberry or apricot jam

### — CHOCOLATE ICING —

- 500 g (1 lb) icing sugar
- 4 tablespoons Dutch cocoa
- ½ cup boiling water
- 1 tablespoon butter
- few drops vanilla
- 2 cups desiccated coconut
- lamington tin 28 × 20 cm (11 × 8 in)

#### To make cake

Place eggs and sugar in a basin over hot water and whisk until light and warm to the touch. Transfer the mixture to an electric mixer and continue to beat until thick and mousse-like. Sieve the flour over the egg/sugar mixture in the bowl and fold it in thoroughly but lightly. Trickle the cooled butter down the sides of the bowl and fold it in thoroughly. Pour the cake into the greased and floured tin. Bake at 180°C (350°F) for about 15 minutes until the cake feels springy to the touch. Allow to cool for a few minutes in the tin and then invert onto a clean cloth and leave until completely cold.

Chill before coating with melted jam or icing. Cut cake into squares. Prepare a basin of warm melted jam, a basin of warm chocolate icing, and a tray of coconut. Spear the cake on a carving fork, dip into the warmed jam, into the chocolate icing and then into the coconut. Allow to rest for an hour or so before eating.

#### To make icing

Sift icing sugar and cocoa. Mix till smooth with boiling water, butter and the vanilla.

## COCONUT ICE-CREAM

- 1½ cups desiccated coconut
- 350 ml (12 fl oz) + 175 ml (6 fl oz) cream
- ½ cup boiling water
- 125 g (4 oz) castor sugar
- 60 ml (2 fl oz) milk
- 4 egg yolks

Place coconut and 350 ml (12 fl oz) cream in a pan and slowly bring to the boil. Remove from heat, cover the pan and infuse for 10 minutes. Process in a food-processor, adding the boiling water. Either pass the contents through a sieve lined with a doubled piece of muslin, or do as we do and pass the liquid through a clean juice extractor. In either case keep the squeezed coconut. You should have obtained 300–325 ml (10–11 fl oz) of liquid.

Boil the sugar with the milk until the sugar is dissolved. Pour the mixture onto the yolks, beating well. Add the coconut-flavoured liquid and the remaining cream. Allow to become quite cold before churning.

Scrape the ice-cream into a bowl and stir in ½ cup of the squeezed coconut. Pour into a suitable mould to freeze. This quantity should fit a log tin, so that you could cut 6 squares from the ice-cream if you wished to make coconut ice-cream lamingtons. When frozen firm, cut squares from the ice-cream, place them on a cake rack, coat with chocolate as in the other recipes, and immediately scatter over some coconut before the chocolate has set. The underside of the ice-cream, that is the side attached to the cake rack, will obviously not be coated. You may find it easier to spear the cube of ice-cream with a fork and dip it in the warm chocolate and then into the coconut.

## COCONUT ICE

This coconut ice-cream could be used instead of the banana ice-cream in the coconut cone. If you live in the north or somewhere with access to 'jelly' coconuts, a scoop of coconut jelly with this ice-cream would be very special. 'Jelly' coconuts are immature nuts. The flesh is soft, translucent and very sweet and delicious. Like most coconut preparations, it is very rich, so small servings are essential.

- 125 g (4 oz) copha
- 250 g (8 oz) desiccated coconut (or, better, squeezed coconut after making milk, or after infusing with cream as above)
- 500 g (1 lb) pure icing sugar
- 2 drops vanilla extract
- 2 egg whites (if using dry coconut, you may need a few more drops of egg white)
- a few drops pink colouring

Melt copha till it is just warm to touch.

Mix the coconut, sieved icing sugar, vanilla, copha and egg whites in a bowl. Divide in half. Tint one half a pale pink. Quickly press the plain half into a square tin and smooth evenly with a piece of plastic and something flat, such as a wrapped block of hard butter or whatever. Remove the plastic and top with the pink half. Press evenly.

You do need to be quick, and it looks best when cut into squares if the layers are even.

There are times when a dish is so popular that it is difficult to get it off the menu. Word spreads and the dish is constantly asked for. This has been the case with our Chocolate, chocolate and more chocolate. Although a chocolate extravaganza, the tastes and textures balance, and it is not overwhelming. To satisfy myself and prevent boredom in the kitchen, I continually change one component of the dessert.

The original version linked together our chocolate and cinnamon sorbet with a chocolate cream log (very similar in texture to the chestnut pavé) and a fudgy chocolate mousse. The recipes for all of these three are in my first book, Stephanie's Menus for Food Lovers. The second version omitted the mousse and substituted a pot of mocha custard, served with a pool of Kahlua on the top. This recipe is also in the first book. Next I served the chestnut pavé instead of the chocolate cream log. Then we made a white chocolate cream and substituted it for the mocha custard. And then, on our current menu, I managed to change the name to Coffee, tea and chocolate, and we are serving a slice of Elizabeth David's chocolate and almond cake (from Stephanie's Menus for Food Lovers), the white chocolate cream, a heap of espresso granita, and a jasmine tea ice-cream sitting on a leaf of peppermint geranium. A chocolate tuile in the shape of a heart is stuck into the ice-cream and a few coffee chocolate beans are scattered in the coffee crème anglaise. The servings are small and the diners love it and scrape their platters clean.

## WHITE CHOCOLATE CREAM

- 150 g (5 oz) best-quality white chocolate, NOT compound
- 60 ml (2 fl oz) cold milk
- 2 leaves of gelatine
- 2 tablespoons cold water
- 2 tablespoons brandy
- 200 ml (7 fl oz) thickened cream
- 2 egg whites

Melt the chocolate and milk in a bain-marie. Blend mixture in a blender until quite smooth. Soak the gelatine in cold water for 2–3 minutes, squeeze, then drop into the simmering water. Swish to dissolve and add the brandy. Add this mixture to the melted chocolate. Stir in the lightly whipped cream. Cool over ice, stirring occasionally, until the mixture becomes syrupy.

Beat egg whites until soft peaks form, and fold gently into the mixture. Spoon into moulds and refrigerate until set. To unmould. Run a knife around the edges of each mould, dip very briefly into hot water and unmould. The cream is best made 12 hours in advance.

## JASMINE TEA ICE-CREAM

- 500 ml (16 fl oz) milk
- 150 g (5 oz) sugar
- 30 g (1 oz) Chinese jasmine tea (not Twinings)
- 5 egg yolks
- a drop or two of green colouring (optional)
- muslin

Heat milk and sugar, stirring to dissolve. Divide the tea into two and tie each heap in a muslin square. Infuse the first teabag in the hot milk. Allow to infuse for about 5 minutes until the milk has a delicate jasmine flavour. Discard the tea-bag before there is any taste of tannin. Re-heat the milk a little, and repeat with the second bag to strengthen the flavour. Discard the second bag.

Re-heat milk to scalding point. Pour over the well-beaten egg yolks, whisking well. The mixture will thicken almost instantly. Cool over ice, stirring from time to time. Strain and add the desired number of drops of apple-green colouring. Churn.

This ice-cream is very refreshing, as it has a most elusive perfume and is not overly sweet.

You may leave out the green colouring, or make some from a few leaves of blanched spinach, wrung tightly in a piece of muslin. The ice-cream churns naturally to a slightly dirty grey-green.

## CHOCOLATE HEARTS

- 100 g (3 oz) castor sugar
- 110 g (3½ oz) plain flour
- 1 tablespoon Dutch cocoa
- 150 g (5 oz) best-quality dark chocolate
- 125 g (4 oz) unsalted butter, softened
- 3 egg whites

Combine the sugar, flour and cocoa. Sift well. Melt the chocolate in a double boiler, cool. In a food-processor combine the dry ingredients with the cooled chocolate, the soft butter and the egg whites.

Line baking trays with parchment. Make a template of a heart or any other shape, using stiff cardboard. Place the template on the baking tray and, with a clean pastry brush, brush the mixture onto the parchment. Lift off the template.

Bake at 160°C–180°C (320°F–350°F), depending on your oven, for about 4 minutes until crisp. Allow to cool for 1 minute, and then slide the biscuits onto a rack to cool completely.

If you wish to bake these as tuiles, you must have curved tuile racks or bottles or glasses at the ready. In this case do not bake more than 2–3 tuiles at one time as they need to be lifted quickly from the trays and draped immediately over or into the moulds to cool in their curved shape.

I love cassata ice-cream with its hidden treasure of candied peel and nuts. I prefer to make it myself, as some of the commercially available varieties lean towards red and green artificial cherries and heavy dashes of lemon essence. In Italian Cooking in the Grand Tradition, authors Jo Bettoja and Anna Maria Cornetto say that cassata was so adored in Sicily that in 1575 the Catholic Church forbade the nuns to make it during Holy Week, because it distracted them from religious ceremonies. Their recipe for an Easter cassata is a lavish and baroque dessert, which in Italy would be decorated with pistachio-flavoured marzipan, candied fruit, and silver chocolate balls. The dessert is refrigerated, but not frozen. It is constructed rather like a charlotte with the mould lined with a light lemon cake. When I make this, I sprinkle the cake with a lemon syrup and pour more over the finished dessert.

I have also included a recipe for a frozen cassata. Good Italian deli-catessens, such as our marvellous Lygon Food Store, sell candied citron, which gives a nicely authentic touch to the filling.

## SICILIAN CASSATA

- ½ recipe torta al limone (lemon cake)
- 675 g (22 oz) ricotta cheese
- 1½ cups castor sugar
- 6 tablespoons light rum
- ⅓ cup toasted pinenuts
- 90 g (3 oz) candied orange peel, cut into small dice
- 90 g (3 oz) chocolate chopped into small dice
- lemon syrup (see page 261)
- additional grated chocolate for garnish
- sweet almond oil to oil the charlotte mould

Make the lemon cake the day before, so that it will be easy to slice the next day. Run the ricotta in a food-processor to make it quite smooth. Add the sugar and mix well. Add the rum and fold in the nuts, peel and chocolate.

Lightly oil a charlotte mould or a log mould and line with cooking parchment. Line the mould with slices of the lemon cake to fit. Paint with lemon syrup. Pour the ricotta mixture into the mould. Cut away any excess cake. Cover the top with slices of cake, sprinkle with the remaining syrup and cover the whole mould with aluminium foil. Refrigerate for at least 4 hours before serving.

Unmould onto a serving platter and spoon over a few spoons of the lemon syrup. Decorate with grated chocolate and serve with whipped cream.

Add silver balls or whatever else you fancy!

- ¾ cup sugar
- ¼ cup lemon juice
- 3 tablespoons orange juice
- ¼ cup orange liqueur

Simmer together until sugar is dissolved, boil till syrupy. Cool before using.

## TORTA AL LIMONE

- 1½ cups plain flour
- 1½ teaspoons baking powder
- pinch of salt
- 1 tablespoon fresh lemon juice
- 3 tablespoons milk
- 125 g (4 oz) unsalted butter, softened
- ¾ cup sugar
- 3 eggs

Pre-heat oven to 160°C (350°F). Butter a 23 × 13 × 8 cm (9 × 5 × 3 in) loaf pan and line it with paper. Sift together the flour, baking powder and salt. Mix together the lemon juice and milk and set aside. Cream the butter and sugar well. Add the eggs, beating thoroughly after each one. Add one-third of the flour, beat lightly. Add half the milk mixture. Add another third of the flour, the rest of the milk and the remaining flour. Combine very lightly. Bake approximately 1 hour, until a skewer comes out clean. Remove from the pan and cool completely before cutting.

A variation on the lemon cake would be to make a classic genoese spongecake which results in a more delicate lining. It also needs to be made the day before if to be used for the Sicilian cassata.

## BASIC GENOESE SPONGECAKE

Many cooks insist on making this cake by hand, whisking their eggs and sugar over hot water with a balloon whisk. Have an experimental afternoon and make the cake both ways and then decide for yourself.

- 5 eggs
- 150 g (5 oz) castor sugar
- 150 g (5 oz) plain flour
- 60 ml (2 fl oz) cooled, melted butter

Prepare a 20 cm (8 in) sandwich tin by brushing it with a little of the butter and lining the base with a circle of parchment paper.

Half-fill the bowl of your electric mixer with hot water. Place the eggs (still in their shells) in the water to warm them for a few minutes. Remove the eggs and dry the bowl thoroughly. Break the eggs into the warm bowl, add the sugar and beat for at least 5 minutes until the mixture is white and mousse-like. It will have quadrupled in volume. Delicately sift the flour over the foam and fold in lightly, quickly and thoroughly. Drizzle the melted butter down the edges of the mixture. Mix in quickly.

Pour into the prepared tin and bake at 180°C (350°F) for about 12 minutes until the cake feels springy to the touch. Cool for a minute or two before turning out. Peel off the paper and allow to cool completely on a clean towel. It is too delicate to cool on a cake rack as the wires will damage the cake.

## STEPHANIE'S FROZEN CASSATA

I have included my grandmother's recipe for a traditional Christmas pudding in the next section. For those who cannot face a hot pudding (Christmas in Australia is during the summer), why not make a version of this frozen cassata, substituting fruitcakes for the cake crumbs, and moistening the cake with rum or brandy instead of the citrus syrup?

- I cup sultanas, soaked overnight in ¾ cup grappa or tokay or brandy or something else strong and spiritous
- 2½ cups cream
- I vanilla bean, split lengthwise
- I tablespoon grated lemon zest
- 9 egg yolks
- I cup sugar
- I cup cake crumbs (such as from the lemon cake above)
- 2 tablespoons syrup from candied peel or lemon syrup, as for Sicilian cassata
- I tablespoon candied angelica, chopped
- 500 g (I lb) ricotta
- I cup double cream (45 per cent butterfat)
- I tablespoon candied orange peel, chopped
- I tablespoon candied lemon peel or candied citron, chopped
- 2 tablespoons toasted flaked almonds or peeled, unsalted
- pistachio nuts
- mould of I.8 litre capacity

In a saucepan combine the 2½ cups cream (not the double cream), the vanilla bean and the lemon zest. Simmer together for 1 minute and then remove from the heat.

Beat the egg yolks with the sugar until light. Whisk in the hot cream. Pour the mixture into the rinsed-out pan and cook until thickened: 80°C (180°F) on a thermometer. Strain the custard into a bowl over ice and stir several times as it cools.

In a small bowl sprinkle the cake crumbs with a little of the syrup, add the chopped angelica to the cake crumbs.

In a food-processor blend the ricotta until quite smooth. Blend in the heavy cream and any liqueur still left after soaking the sultanas. Fold this mixture into the cooled custard. Churn until nearly firm. Scrape the ice-cream into a bowl and stir in the chopped orange and lemon peels and/or the candied citron, the nuts and the drained sultanas.

Select a suitable mould and line it with a doubled strap of foil or parchment to assist the unmoulding. I use a pudding basin, as I like to cut the cassata in wedges, but a cast-iron log mould would be fine.

Press half of the mixture into the mould. Cover with the soaked cake crumb/angelica mixture, top with the rest of the ice-cream. Press down firmly to avoid any air-holes. Cover with foil or parchment and freeze. Allow the cassata to soften a little before serving it.

It goes very well with one or two prunes soaked as for the frozen trifle, or with one of the peaches you have preserved in brandy.

## MINIATURE FRUITCAKES

The fruitcakes are made using the mincemeat normally used to fill Christmas pies.

- 1 egg
- 60 g (2 oz) sugar
- few drops vanilla
- 60 g (2 oz) cool, melted unsalted butter
- 125 g (4 oz) plain flour
- pinch salt
- ½ teaspoon powdered cinnamon
- 125 ml (4 fl oz) cultured buttermilk
- ½ teaspoon carbonate of soda
- 400 g (13 oz) best-quality fruit mincemeat, preferably home-made
- 50 g (2 oz) chopped walnuts

Blend the first 4 ingredients in a food-processor. Sift the flour with the salt and cinnamon. Mix the buttermilk with the carbonate of soda. Alternately add the flour mixture and the buttermilk mixture to the food-processor with the motor running. Stir in the fruit and nuts.

Bake in very well-buttered tins or small paper cake-cases for 15 minutes at 180°C (350°F). Allow to cool before crumbling and sprinkling with the rum or brandy if they are to be used for a Christmas cassata, or dust them with icing sugar and serve with the coffee on Christmas night.

This recipe will make about 20 small cakes.

# OTHER PUDDINGS

Each year the season for local berry fruits seem to extend a little longer. One has the illusion that summer time has also been stretched, with cherries appearing in November, always in time for the Melbourne Cup, and the second crop of raspberries still bountiful at the end of April, the middle of autumn in Australia. By Christmas time the fruit shops are a joy to behold. There are bins of golden apricots (but beware the very first apricots, which can be hard and sour), trays of yellow and white peaches, yellow and white nectarines and plums of every colour, from the pointed blue-violet angelina plums, the orange-scarlet Wilson plum with its sweet yellow meat, through to the glorious satsuma or blood plum. Local strawberries are in the markets and the first blueberries. If it has been a good season, there will be punnets of jewel-like redcurrants for summer pudding.

All fruit tastes superior eaten properly ripe from the tree. Once I lived in an old house in an inner suburb, which had a very old and very large Moor Park apricot tree. Its crop was embarrassingly large, but of superb quality. I made lots of apricot chutney and jars of jam, and I also made for the first time the simple and charming recipe that appears in several books for halved apricots pressed onto day-old bread. Elizabeth David includes the recipe in her *Summer Cooking*. My children particularly enjoy this. Sometimes I make it with leftover brioche instead of bread. The hollows where the stones were are filled with castor sugar and the slices are baked until the bread is crisp, the fruit soft and the sugar turned nearly to caramel.

The next recipe is for a classic upside-down cake. The fruit can be changed at will. Jane Grigson gives a recipe for an unusual one using pawpaw and lime zest.

## APRICOT UPSIDE-DOWN CAKE

- 20 cm (8 in) cake tin liberally buttered with 60 g (2 oz) butter

### — CARAMEL —

- 100 g (3 oz) sugar
- 3 tablespoons water

### — FRUIT —

- 750 g (1½ lb) ripe apricots (or plums or apples) halved

### — CAKE TOPPING —
(From Jane Grigson's *Fruit* book)

- 175 g (6 oz) butter
- 150 g (5 oz) castor sugar
- 175 g (6 oz) self-raising flour
- ½ level teaspoon baking powder
- 1 heaped tablespoon unblanched almonds, ground
- 3 eggs, beaten

Make a caramel with the sugar and water. Stir only till the sugar has dissolved, washing down any grains that stick to the sides of the pan with a brush dipped in cold water. When the caramel is a deep golden brown, pour it carefully over the base and sides of the pan.

Line the buttered tin with the cooled golden caramel. Halve and stone the apricots and place in an even layer in the tin, rounded sides onto the caramel. Cut the rest of the apricots in half and place them on top of the first layer so that the pan is well filled with fruit. The apricots will subside as they cook.

Cream butter and sugar. Combine flour, baking powder and almonds. Fold into the creamed mixture, alternating with the eggs. The sponge should be fairly soft. Drop spoonfuls over the fruit as carefully as possible, trying not to disturb it. Smooth the cake. Bake in a moderate oven 180°C (350°F) for 45–50 minutes until the cake tests cooked.

Allow to cool for a minute or two in the pan and then place a plate over and invert as for the tart. Check that all fruit has been dislodged. When spooning on the cake, remember that the balance should be leaning towards fruit. If you have too much cake mixture, bake a small plain one and soak it with a little lemon or orange syrup. It will be delicious the next day.

If I had to choose my favourite fruit, it would be a toss-up between a perfect white peach and a perfect white nectarine. They should be so ripe that the only way to eat them is bent over the kitchen sink or outside in the garden. As I do not own a nectarine or peach tree, I patronise a greengrocer who lets me choose the fruit myself. Sliced ripe peaches sprinkled with sugar with perhaps a little champagne poured over is a special summer treat. I have already mentioned the perfection of a peach Melba: dramatic and glowing when made with a yellow peach, subtle and romantic when made with white peaches. Our peach tart is a triumph. Its special charm is that the puff pastry is hot and crisp, but the tart cooks so fast that the peeled and halved peaches stay practically raw and are warm only. I have given the recipe for a pear tart baked on puff pastry in *Stephanie's Menus for Food Lovers*. Usually we poach the pears before placing them on the cut-out pastry shape. If you had superbly juicy fruit, the pear tart could be made the same way as the peach. Recently the repertoire has been extended again. Pineapple tart has arrived.

## PUFF PASTRY FRUIT TARTS
### as at STEPHANIE'S

Make a template of either a pear with stem (see *Stephanie's Menus for Food Lovers*), or of a peach with stem with rather exaggerated curves, as the two peach halves are placed side by side like two cheeks, or of a pineapple with its characteristic plume of leaves. The actual cardboard shape will be cut 1 cm (½ in) larger than is needed for the final tart, as the pastry will shrink after cutting.

You will need 250 g (8 oz) of puff pastry for 6 peach or pineapple shapes. Cut the pastry 5 mm (1/4 in) thick and allow to rest for at least 30 minutes before using.

## PEACH

Dip perfectly ripe fruit into boiling water for 1–2 minutes, and then slip off the skin.

## PINEAPPLE

Peel and remove the eyes of a beautiful pineapple. Slice the fruit 1 cm (½ in) thick, remove the cores and cut the slices into chunks. Toss them with some finely chopped candied ginger.

## TO ASSEMBLE AND BAKE TARTS

Pre-heat the oven to 220°C (430°F).

Remove the puff pastry from the refrigerator. Brush the entire surface with an egg wash made by whisking lightly 1 whole egg, a pin of salt and a little water. Do not allow the egg wash to drip over the edges, as it will prevent the puff rising properly. Position the peach halves, or pile on a heap of pineapple. Scatter a small amount of icing sugar on the pineapple. The highest points of the pile will scorch a little and will resemble the bumps and shadings of a pineapple skin.

Bake for 15–20 minutes until the pastry is quite crisp and golden. Serve with a caramel sauce made from the puréed fruit.

## — PEACH OR PINEAPPLE CARAMEL SAUCE —

Poach a quantity of the fruit in a poaching syrup—1 litre (32 fl oz) water to 500 g (1 lb) sugar. Make a golden caramel with 1 cup sugar to ½ cup water. Stop the caramel cooking by adding a little extra cold water. Stir until it is smooth. Purée the drained poached fruit—pass through a sieve if you want an absolutely smooth sauce. In a blender combine the fruit purée with the caramel.

The sauce will be thicker or thinner depending on the amount of fruit poaching syrup included in the fruit purée. A few drops of lemon may be used to sharpen the sauce and to highlight its flavour.

Your peach sauce will gain extra character if you poach the peaches in Muscat de Beaumes-de-Venise. This beautiful wine has a raisin quality and a golden colour with a hint of pink. I like it with many fruit desserts as I appreciate its aroma and its comparative dryness against many more august dessert wines. Interestingly, the only time I was offered this wine in France, it was offered as an aperitif, and I was looked at quite askance when I admitted to enjoying it with dessert.

## POACHED PEACHES in MUSCAT DE BEAUMES-DE-VENISE

- 6 ripe peaches
- 3 cups sugar
- 4½ cups water
- ½ split vanilla bean
- 1 bottle Muscat de Beaumes-de-Venise

Stir the sugar, water and vanilla bean until the sugar is dissolved. Simmer for 2–3 minutes. Add the wine.

Poach the peaches in the syrup, held at poaching temperature. Poaching temperature is between 50–75°C (120–170°F). The surface of the liquid should barely move. When tender, remove each peach with a slotted spoon, peel and place either in a beautiful glass bowl or in a sterilised preserving jar. In either case, pour over the syrup, boiled to concentrate the flavour a little. Cool the syrup before pouring it on the fruit. After all, they do not need further cooking.

## POACHED PEACHES with FIG SAUCE

Poach peaches as in above recipe. Peel about 12 fresh, ripe figs. Purée in a food-processor. Pass the purée through a sieve and simmer the purée with either 3 tablespoons of castor sugar or ¼ cup of the syrup made with Muscat de Beaumes-de-Venise. Cook the purée for 7–10 minutes, stirring from time to time. Remove from the heat, cool and add about 1 cup of lightly whipped cream. Pour this sauce over 1 or 2 poached peaches.

With a simple dessert such as this, a plain, good-quality cake often seems to be the best accompaniment. This recipe was given to me by Julie, one of our waitresses, who is also an enthusiastic cook, and a talented artist. Julie created the drawings for this book.

## JULIE'S POPPYSEED CAKE

- 300 g (10 oz) sifted plain flour
- pinch of salt
- 2 teaspoons baking powder
- ½ cup poppy seeds
- 1½ cups castor sugar
- ½ cup butter
- 1 cup milk
- few drops vanilla extract
- 4 egg whites
- icing sugar

Pre-heat oven to 180°C (350°F).

Mix flour, salt, baking powder and poppy seeds. Cream 1¼ cups of the sugar with the butter. Stir in the milk and vanilla extract. Add the flour mixture. (To this point the cake can be made in a food-processor.) Place mixture into a large bowl. In a separate bowl or an electric mixer, beat the egg whites until soft peaks form. Beat in the rest of the sugar.

Fold the egg white mixture into the batter. Turn into a greased 22 cm (9 in) springform tin or a tube pan.

Bake about 45 minutes. Cool on a rack, invert from tin and, when cold, dust with icing sugar.

Mr Stafford Whiteaker, the author of a lovely book, The Compleat Strawberry, comments that in fashionable restaurants in London strawberries are offered throughout the year. Many of them have been transported before the sun has sugared their juice and deepened their colour. 'They are,' he says, 'hard, unsweet and desperately sad.' I have eaten quite a few desperately sad strawberries in my time. But our local strawberries have been wonderful this year. Small or large, pointed or regular, round or bumpy, crimson or scarlet, I have enjoyed them all. I also agree with Mr Whiteaker that it is hard to find a way of eating strawberries that surpasses plain strawberries. Certainly with cream, real, country cream, or with soft white cheese, but I am not at all interested in recipes that suggest cooking the fruit. For days of self-indulgence there is always strawberry shortcake!

# STRAWBERRY SHORTCAKE

The quantities given will make 2 × 18 cm (7 in) rounds, that is 10–12 generous wedges. Handle the dough gently, like a scone dough.

For a super-luscious filling, the sliced strawberries can be mixed with 1-2 tablespoons of sweetened raspberry purée. The shortcakes can be formed into small rounds and baked individually. This is easier to assemble as the larger round may crumble a little when cut.

A superb but rare variation is to make the shortcake and fill it with tree-ripened mulberries.

- 500 g (1 lb) self-raising flour
- tiny pinch salt
- 125 g (4 oz) sugar
- 175 g (6 oz) soft, unsalted butter
- 4 egg yolks
- 100 ml (3 fl oz) milk

- soft butter for spreading
- sliced strawberries, sweetened to taste
- 1–2 tablespoons raspberry purée (optional)

Mix the flour, salt and sugar in a large basin. Rub the butter into flour till it resembles breadcrumbs. Mix the yolks lightly, stir into the milk. Make a well in the dry ingredients and add the liquid. Work together lightly and quickly until you have a soft dough. Form into two rounds about 3–4 cm (1–1½ in) thick.

Bake in a pre-heated oven at 180°C (350°F) for 15 minutes or until golden. Cool a little.

Split the shortcakes and while still warm spread with additional soft butter. Pile on a generous amount of sliced strawberries, tossed with some sugar, lightly place on the shortcake lid, dust with icing sugar, cut into wedges and pass the cream bowl.

Stafford Whiteaker writes that one of Marie Antoinette's ladies-in-waiting is said to have bathed in the juice of strawberries and raspberries and afterwards she was gently washed with sponges soaked in milk and perfumes, her skin glowing sensually pink from the fruit.

Unlike strawberries, raspberries are delicious cooked! Both raspberry and blackberry crumble bring rave reports from the dining-room. They are sublime, and so very simple that I am surprised that the pudding is not made often during our astonishingly long raspberry season. I speak, of course, for the southern states. Some of my colleagues from Sydney complain that we have the best raspberries and for much longer. Certainly they are the most perishable of fruit, and one furry raspberry in a punnet will quickly affect the taste of the rest.

A gratin of raspberries seems to appear on nearly every restaurant menu during the summer. Here is our version.

## GRATIN of RASPBERRIES

### — PASTRY CREAM —

- 250 ml (8 fl oz) milk
- 4 egg yolks
- 60 g (2 oz) castor sugar
- 2 tablespoons cornflour
- few drops vanilla extract
- 60 g (2 oz) soft unsalted butter
- 300 ml (10 fl oz) cream, softly whipped

- 2 tablespoons raspberry eau-de-vie or raspberry liqueur or brandy
- 500 g (1 lb) raspberries
- 100 g (3 oz) flaked almonds, toasted
- icing sugar

#### TO PREPARE THE PASTRY CREAM

Scald the milk. Whisk the egg yolks and the sugar together until well mixed, but not fluffy. Add the cornflour. Gradually add the hot milk, mixing well. Add the drops of vanilla. Return the mixture to the rinsed-out pan and cook, stirring all the time, until the mixture has thickened smoothly. It will be quite thick and will need vigorous stirring. Strain into a bowl and leave to cool. Rub a tiny piece of the butter over the surface of the cream and press a piece of plastic down onto it.

When nearly cold, work in 1 tablespoon of cream to lighten the mixture. Fold in the rest of the cream and the liqueur.

Butter 6 ovenproof shallow gratin dishes. Half-fill each one with the cream. Cover with a thick layer of the raspberries. Scatter over the flaked almonds. Top with the rest of the lightened pastry cream, smoothing it so that the raspberries are hidden.

Pre-heat a grill to very hot. Shake a good layer of icing sugar over each gratin dish and place under the grill for 3–4 minutes until the top is golden and bubbling. Serve at once.

## BERRY CRUMBLE,
### but not STRAWBERRY

- 500 g (1 lb) blackberries, loganberries, mulberries, youngberries, boysenberries, raspberries
- ½ cup castor sugar or to taste

### — CRUMBLE MIXTURE —

- 180 g (6 oz) flour
- 1 teaspoon powdered ginger
- 1 teaspoon baking powder
- 125 g (4 oz) brown sugar
- 90 g (3 oz) + 60 g (2 oz) butter

Choose shallow pie dishes or gratin dishes. Divide the fruit among the dishes and strew with the castor sugar.

Mix the flour with the ginger and baking powder and brown sugar. Rub in the 90 g (3 oz) butter until the mixture is very roughly combined. Spread a good layer over the berries. Flake the 60 g (2 oz) butter over the crumbles.

Bake in a medium oven 180°C (350°F) until the topping is golden and smells toasted, and the crimson juice is bubbling at the edges. Serve with the very best cream. The fruit is very hot under its bumpy, insulating crust.

## BLACKBERRY CRANACHAN

In southern Australia blackberries are a noxious weed and are vigorously discouraged from country properties. Any abandoned byway or piece of land will soon sport the creeping tendrils, which strangle anything in their rampant path. None the less, in autumn it is still possible to find luxuriant blackberries that have escaped the spray. The reward, after battling with the tangling and scratching brambles might be this Scottish pudding, a cranachan, or crannachan as Jane Grigson spells it.

- 250 g (8 oz) blackberries
- 60 g (2 oz) castor sugar
- 2 tablespoons malt whisky
- 100 g (3 oz) rolled oats

- ½ cup sour cream, softly whipped
- 1 cup cream, softly whipped
- few drops vanilla extract

Combine blackberries, castor sugar and whisky and allow to marinate for 1–2 hours. Toast oats on a buttered tray for 10–15 minutes at 180°C (350°F) until golden brown. Cool. Fold the softly whipped sour cream into the whipped cream. Add the vanilla extract.

Assemble the dessert in tall parfait glasses or in a traditional glass or crystal bowl as one does with a wine trifle. A layer of berries and liquid, a layer of oats, a layer of cream and repeat. The crunch of the oats contrasts beautifully with the berries and the tang of the cream mixture.

Rock melon or canteloupe, halved and served with a scoop of vanilla ice-cream, must be a good candidate for the archetypal southern Australian dessert. It is loved by just about everyone. We have beautiful melons in abundance, and it is with a certain sense of superiority that I read European food writers waxing lyrical about the rare phenomenon of a perfectly ripe and perfumed melon. They are a commonplace in our fruit shops for at least 4–5 months of the year. The Australian tendency to deride what we have that is excellent or unique has been sufficiently well documented without any further comment from me. I have already quoted Richard Beckett on the subject.

Throughout the summer one can partner fine raw ham with luscious melon. Along the beaches, enterprising kiosks will sell a chunk of melon with ice-cream. I also like to make a fresh melon tart. No need for a recipe. It requires a pre-baked shortcrust shell, a quantity of pastry cream, lightened exactly as for the raspberry gratin on page 272, and thin slices of melon overlapped. A freshly assembled tart such as this should not sit around too long. The fruit will ooze juice. Make it and eat it!

```
┌─────────────────────────────────────────┐
│         FRITTERS of MELON with            │
│          PERSIMMON SAUCE                  │
└─────────────────────────────────────────┘
```

A more elaborate dessert is this combination of deep-fried melon fritters, with a sauce of fresh persimmon.

- ½ quantity of beer batter as given on page 57
- oil for deep frying
- melon chunks
- sifted plain flour
- icing sugar

— SAUCE —

- 6 perfectly ripe persimmons (they will feel quite squashy)
- ½ cup poaching syrup
- few drops lemon juice

### TO MAKE SAUCE

Cut the persimmons in half and scoop all the pulp into a blender or food-processor. Add the syrup, blend and add the lemon juice to taste. Place a pool of sauce on each plate.

### TO MAKE FRITTERS AND SERVE

Heat oil to 190°C (375°F). Pat the melon chunks dry with a piece of kitchen paper, sift a little plain flour over them. Impale each chunk on a bamboo or other skewer, twirl in the batter. Allow excess to drip off and deep-fry until golden brown. Don't drop the skewers into the oil. You may use your fingers for dipping the fruit in the batter coating, if you prefer.

Drain briefly on crumpled paper and then place the fritters in the centre of the persimmon sauce. Dust lightly with icing sugar. Because the oil is very hot, the batter will be crisp and golden, but the melon chunk will still be firm and barely warm. Texture again!

Not only do we have canteloupe melon and ice-cream, but we have the pavlova. Michael Symons's fascinating book, One Continuous Picnic, has the best, clearest and fairest account of the creation of this truly splendid dessert. The abbreviated story is as follows (but do read the original!). As Michael Symons says, the story of the pavlova illustrates how history and cookery intermingle. 'Its arrival is a tale of boom versus bust, the luxury life versus back-breaking poverty, and Australia versus New Zealand. It involves two converging stories: that of a grand hotel and that of a small settler who turned into a cook.'

Herbert Sachse was born on the goldfields of Western Australia in 1898. As a young married man he attempted to go on the land, and when the collapse of the Western Australian and world economy came in 1926, he walked off his land and, like many in the depression years, entered the catering industry, first as a shearers' cook and later, in 1934, at the newly invigorated Esplanade Hotel in Perth.

The licensee, Mrs Elizabeth Paxton, approached the chef to create something special for the very popular afternoon teas. Bert Sachse experimented for a month, and in his own words (he was interviewed in 1973), 'I had always regretted that the meringue cake was invariably too hard and crusty, so I set out to create something that could have a crunchy top and would cut like marshmallow.'

Michael Symons continues that according to Paxton family tradition the cake was named at a meeting at which the licensee, Elizabeth, or the manager, Harry Nairn, remarked, 'It is as light as Pavlova.'

When the New Zealand claims were investigated, Michael Symons found that there was indeed a meringue cake well in evidence in cookery books of 1927 and 1934, and a prize-winning recipe appeared in a women's magazine in 1935. Bert Sachse apparently read such magazines for ideas, so that Symons concludes that New Zealanders discovered the delights of the large meringue with the 'marshmallow centre', but that it is reasonable to assume that someone in Perth attached the name of the ballerina.

---

## HERBERT SACHSE'S ORIGINAL RECIPE for PAVLOVA

- 6 egg whites
- pinch of cream of tartar
- few drops vanilla extract
- 1 heaped cup castor sugar
- 1 teaspoon cornflour
- 2 teaspoons vinegar
- arrowroot

— TOPPING —

- cream
- 3–4 passionfruits

Put the egg whites, cream of tartar and vanilla into a bowl and beat well until the mixture becomes firm and snowy. Mix sugar and cornflour together, and fold into the egg white mixture, taking the spoon to the bottom of the mixing bowl each time. As soon as the sugar and cornflour are incorporated with the egg white mixture, add the vinegar and combine well.

Line the bottom and sides of a standard fairly deep cake tin with brown paper, and sprinkle 1 tablespoon of both arrowroot and sugar over the paper, reserving a little for sprinkling over the top. Pile the mixture (which should be fairly stiff) into the middle of the cake tin, and sprinkle the remainder of the arrowroot and sugar mixture over the top.

Turn the gas oven on full heat for 15 minutes before putting the pavlova in, then turn it down as low as possible. Place the cake tin on the half-way shelf. If the pavlova shows a faint tinge of brown after 15 minutes in the oven, the temperature is correct, and the cake should be fully cooked after 1 1/2 hours. If the cake starts to go too brown, turn the oven off completely, re-light after 15 minutes and keep an eye on the pavlova.

Remove from the oven and turn upside-down onto a serving plate. Whip the cream and ice the pavlova with this. Scoop out the passionfruit pulp and place it on top of the cream. (Reprinted from Richard Beckett, *Convicted Tastes: Food in Australia*.)

## Modern notes

Use baking parchment rather than brown paper. Pile the pavlova mixture directly onto an oven tray rather than a cake tin. Some cooks like to use a springform tin. The pavlova is successful *only* when the outside is crisp and brittle with a faintly cream colour and the middle is white fluff. Fill the 'pav' (as it is affectionately known by everyone) at least an hour before serving to allow time for it to soften. Be generous with the cream and never sweeten it. Passionfruits are essential, strawberries are tolerated.

Passionfruits also star in this variation of the classic bavarian cream based on a stirred custard, a crème anglaise.

## PASSIONFRUIT BAVARIAN CREAM
### in a CARAMEL-LINED MOULD

### — CARAMEL FOR MOULD —

- 1 cup sugar
- ½ cup water

### — CRÈME ANGLAISE —

- 375 ml (12 fl oz) milk
- strained juice of 6 passionfruits, about 100 ml (3 fl oz)
- 5 leaves of gelatine (if to be made in a bowl, 4 leaves if to be set individually)
- 5 egg yolks
- 200 g (7 oz) sugar
- 400 ml (13 fl oz) cream, softly whipped

### To make the caramel

Dissolve the sugar in the water, stirring until it has completely dissolved. Brush down any grains of sugar sticking to the pan with a pastry brush dipped in cold water. Cook briskly until the mixture turns to a deep-gold caramel. Remove the pan from the heat, dip the base into cold water to stop further cooking and pour the caramel into the selected mould or moulds. Twirl to coat the sides.

### To make the custard

Before commencing the custard, have ready a large basin with ice cubes and cold water in it and a second basin resting in the ice and water. Suspend a fine strainer over the basin.

Scald the milk. Add the passionfruit juice. Soak the gelatine leaves in cold water. Lightly beat the egg yolks and sugar. Pour on the scalded, flavoured milk. Mix lightly. Rinse out the pan. Return the mixture to the pan and cook, stirring all the time until the custard thickens and coats the wooden spoon: 83°C (178°F) standard on a thermometer.

When thickened, pour at once through the strainer into the basin. Squeeze the gelatine leaves and swish them into a small portion of the hot custard. When completely dissolved, pour through the strainer into the rest of the custard. Stir well to mix.

Cool the custard, stirring frequently. When it is quite cold, and is starting to thicken, remove from the ice and fold in the softly whipped cream. Pour the bavarois into the moulds without further delay and refrigerate until set. Try to leave the bavarois at room temperature for 20 minutes or so before serving, for a more delicate texture.

The classic bavarois would omit the passionfruit juice and include a split vanilla bean. I also make a cinnamon bavarois. Two whole sticks of cinnamon are infused in the milk, and the cinnamon is left in the custard until it is quite cold. The cinnamon bavarois is very successful with a compote of poached quinces.

Each autumn I find myself irresistibly drawn to a quince dish of some kind. I let it be known in a newspaper article that I loved quinces and I received a delightful letter from a reader detailing her favourite quince recipes. She recommended steaming quinces in order to make quince fool (sweeten to taste and fold cream into the puréed fruit), or baking them filled with raisins and brown sugar as one does with apples. Her most novel suggestion was a method for drying out quince paste, known as cotignac (France), membrilo (Spain), cotognata (Italy) and quince cheese in English. After cooking the purée with an equal quantity of sugar and a small spoonful of water until it came away from the sides of the pan and allowing it to cool in a shallow tin, my resourceful correspondent put the tin under the rear window of her car. She said: 'In the course of normal use for a couple of weeks, [the car] will be standing in the sun sufficiently to firm up and dry out the paste.'

Eliza Acton has two interesting quince recipes. One she calls a quince blancmange, where the juice of quinces is sweetened to taste, a little gelatine is added, and when cold it is folded into thick cream. Curiously, I have this in my file of tried and true recipes called quince cream. I serve it with an orange and quince juice jelly as described on page 229.

Eliza Acton's second recipe is for a stirred custard cooked in a bain-marie, using quince juice in the place of milk or cream. She suggests serving poached quince halves with the hollow made by the removal of the pips filled with this fragrant custard. We cook this over direct heat, with care, as for other stirred custards.

My mother, Mary Burchett, published a small cookery book in 1960, *Through My Kitchen Door*, long since out of print. I still use it frequently, and I find her chapter introductions very charming. She commences her chapter 'Was it fourteen or fifteen?' by saying:

> Though I have now reached the age when I should put away childish things, I still have very warm memories of one of Christopher Robin's playfellows—Pooh, the bear of very little brain, whose thoughts were always returning lovingly to his store of honey-pots. Remember how he was never sure if he had 14 or 15?

The recipe this leads to is quinces baked in honey, and we serve it with Eliza Acton's stirred quince juice custard, made with egg yolks.

## ELIZA ACTON'S QUINCE CUSTARD

- 600 ml (20 fl oz) quince syrup (from poaching quinces)
- 12 egg yolks

Whisk the egg yolks well. Bring the quince syrup to simmering point. Pour onto the yolks. Mix well. Return to the rinsed-out saucepan and cook gently, stirring all the time, until the custard thickens. Pour into a bowl and stir while the custard cools. Serve with the following baked quinces or offer with a bowl of poached quinces. This custard is very sweet. We sometimes add 1 cup of milk to the cooked custard.

## QUINCES BAKED in HONEY

- 3 quinces
- 4 tablespoons light honey
- 2 tablespoons butter
- 1/4 cup water

Wash the quinces very well to remove all greyish down from them. Halve the quinces, remove the seeds and core with a spoon, making a neat hollow. Do not peel. Butter a baking dish that will hold the quince halves neatly without too much extra space. Place the quince halves in the dish, hollows uppermost. In each hollow place 3 teaspoons of honey and divide the butter between them. Pour the water gently around the sides, cover with foil and bake in a slow oven 150°C (310°F) for at least 3 hours (probably 4) until the quinces are soft and a rich red. After 1½ hours, turn the quinces over.

Serve hot or warm, with the hollows filled with a little of the quince custard and the honey juices poured around them.

While writing the recipe for the quinces baked in honey, I was reminded of Savoy-style pears. I have seen this dish dressed up with caramel and butterscotch sauces, but it is essentially a country dish of convincing simplicity. Hard winter pears, good butter, a plump vanilla bean and the most luscious cream one can get. It is a dish absolutely *made* for a slow combustion stove, for the longer the pears take to cook the better it will be.

## PEARS BAKED as in SAVOY

Choose the dish carefully. The halved pears should fit well in the dish with not a lot of extra space.

Butter the dish well. Peel, halve and core the pears. Scatter over them about 1 tablespoon of castor sugar per pear half. Dot with some extra pieces of butter. Split and break a vanilla bean into several pieces and place in the dish. Pour in 2 tablespoons of water and cover the dish tightly with a sheet of aluminium foil. Cook in a very low oven 160°C (320°F) as long as possible.

When pears are tender and smell superb, remove the tray from the oven and spoon in some super-rich cream. Increase the oven heat to hot and return the uncovered tray to the oven for 10 minutes until the cream has reduced a little and made a small amount of rich, magnificent sauce.

## DAVID'S PEAR and ALMOND PUDDING

I was interested to try to make a pear and almond pudding after reading a recipe in a magazine. As so often happens, the recipe was grossly inaccurate. It was leaden, with too much flour and far too sweet. The cooking times were impossibly long, and yet we persevered, as the combinations of flavours and textures were appealing. We have now perfected the pudding, and it has been very popular. It is served with plain crème anglaise, through which we ripple a little plum purée.

- 3 poached pears, drained and puréed to make 250 ml (8 fl oz) pear purée
- 90 g (3 oz) butter
- ⅓ cup castor sugar

- 90 g (3 oz) marzipan
- 2 eggs
- ½ cup self-raising flour
- 2 extra egg whites

In a food-processor combine the butter and sugar. Cream well. Add the marzipan. Add the pear purée and combine very well. Add the whole eggs, one by one. Should the mixture separate, quickly add 1 tablespoon of the flour. Transfer the mixture to a mixing bowl and stir in the sifted flour. Beat the whites to soft peaks and fold into the batter.

Pour the mixture into a well-buttered pudding basin or into 6 individual pudding moulds and bake in a bain-marie at 180°C (350°F). Individual puddings will take about 20 minutes. The large pudding will take about 45 minutes.

The puddings will be dry in the centre when tested with a skewer and will have risen a little in their mould. Serve as soon as possible as they tend to sink a little and lose their lightness.

Another favourite hot pudding is this gingerbread and chocolate pudding. One must begin by making some gingerbread. Often I do this the other way around. I make gingerbread to eat for afternoon tea or to cut in squares to accompany an ice-cream and freeze the rest of the cake. When I need to make the pudding, the gingerbread is ready and waiting. The recipe I have given for gingerbread will make quite a large cake. The ingredients can be halved.

# GINGERBREAD

This is very easy to make entirely in the food-processor. You will need to divide it into two, as the capacity of the mixing bowl will not take the full mixture.

- 400 g (13 oz) flour
- 2 teaspoons carbonate of soda
- 2 teaspoons ground ginger
- 2 teaspoons cinnamon
- 1 cup treacle or golden syrup

- 1 cup boiling water
- 200 g (7 oz) soft unsalted butter
- 250 g (8 oz) light brown sugar
- 2 eggs

Sift the flour, soda, ginger and cinnamon. Stir the treacle/golden syrup into the cup of boiling water.

Cream the butter and sugar very well. Beat in the eggs. Add the flour and flavourings and the treacle/water mixture alternately, one-third of the total quantity at a time. Mix well after each addition.

Grease a 22 cm (9 in) square cake tin and line the bottom with cooking parchment. Pour the batter into the tin and bake at 180°C (350°F) for 25–30 minutes, until cooked. Cool on a rack for a few minutes and then turn out of the tin. Cool completely before cutting. Any portion not needed can be wrapped in plastic and frozen.

# GINGERBREAD PUDDING

- 60 g (2 oz) soft unsalted butter
- 3 egg yolks
- 30 g (1 oz) chocolate, melted and cooled
- 1 tablespoon Grand Marnier or brandy

- 90 g (3 oz) gingerbread crumbled and soaked in 60 ml (2 fl oz) milk and 1 teaspoon Grand Marnier or brandy
- 30 g (1 oz) ground almonds
- 3 egg whites
- 30 g (1 oz) castor sugar

Cream the butter until light and fluffy in the food-processor. Add egg yolks, soft chocolate and the 1 tablespoon of Grand Marnier or brandy. Add the soaked gingerbread and the ground almonds. Turn the mixture into a large mixing bowl. (The gingerbread will have absorbed all the milk and the 1 teaspoon of brandy or Grand Marnier.)

Whip the egg whites until soft peaks form, beat in the castor sugar. Fold the egg white mixture lightly into the cake mixture. Butter a pudding basin or 6 individual moulds. Fill to the ¾ level with the mixture. Cover with aluminium foil and hold in place with string.

Bake in a bain-marie at 180°C (350°F) for about 25 minutes in individual moulds or approximately 50 minutes in a large basin.

Accompany with either a Grand Marnier-flavoured creme anglaise or a chocolate sauce. Serve the puddings as soon as possible as they will sink and become heavy if serving is delayed.

## — SIMPLE CHOCOLATE SAUCE —

In a double-boiler or a basin over hot water combine 200 g (7 oz) best-quality dark chocolate, 125 ml (4 fl oz) of cream, 30 g (1 oz) of unsalted butter with 2 tablespoons of Grand Marnier or brandy. Heat gently and then stir until smooth.

## EMILY BELL'S CHRISTMAS PUDDING

For the very last recipe in this section I wanted to include my grand-mother's Christmas pudding. Every year I read versions that are often someone or other's grandmother's, and as I have always found our pudding marvellous I thought that others might also.

- 180 g (6 oz) plain flour
- 180 g (6 oz) fresh, white breadcrumbs
- 360 g (12 oz) best-quality seedless raisins
- 360 g (12 oz) currants
- 180 g (6 oz) sultanas
- 125 g (4 oz) best-quality candied peel (preferably home-made)
- 360 g (12 oz) finely grated suet (from the butcher, not packet, as packet suet is mixed with flour and will upset the proportions)
- 180 g (6 oz) dark brown sugar

- grated rind of 1 lemon
- ½ nutmeg grated
- ¼ teaspoon salt
- 2 tablespoons lemon juice
- ½ teaspoon powdered cinnamon
- 4 eggs
- 100 ml (3 fl oz) brandy
- 600 ml (20 fl oz) milk (approximately)

Mix all the ingredients in a large basin. The mixture should be fairly wet. Increase the milk, if necessary. Insist that everyone in the family has a stir. Leave overnight. Next day, eat a little. Is the spice flavour right? Pack into buttered basins (2), cover with greaseproof paper and then foil. Tie securely under the rim with a doubled length of string.

Stand on a rack or upturned cake tin inside a large pan and add boiling water to come two-thirds up the basin. Boil for 6 hours. Keep topping up the boiling water (have a large saucepan near to the pudding pot full of boiling water). Cool and store in a cool place or the refrigerator until Christmas Day. The puddings will take at least 1 full hour's boiling to be really hot.

Serve flamed with warmed brandy if you like. Warm the brandy in a small pan, have the pudding turned out onto a large dish, ignite the brandy and pour it all over the pudding

# LOVE BITES

**F E A S T S  &  S T O R I E S**

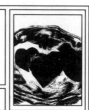

This collection of love bites, as the name suggests, are small, delicious nibbles, to be eaten in a single bite. They are served with coffee, and my preference is for things that are obviously home-made.

I have selected those that have been most enthused over. The first section deals with chocolate love bites. I do not try to rival the chocolatier—I cannot—but I can make a selection of small dainties that have all been lovingly chosen and carefully prepared.

## CHOCOLATE HEDGEHOG

This slice is familiar to those born in the 1940s and perhaps the 1950s. My mother used to make it in a Swiss roll tin, and each of the children would secretly cut a small slice as it rested in the refrigerator, convinced that Mum would not notice just one small slice. By the time the four of us had had a go, one-quarter of it was gone. She always noticed!

- 375 g (12 oz) wheatmeal digestive biscuits
- ¾ cup walnut pieces
- 125 g (4 oz) unsalted butter
- 4 tablespoons Dutch cocoa
- ¾ cup castor sugar
- 2 eggs

- 125 g (4 oz) best-quality dark chocolate
- 60 g (2 oz) butter
- 1 tablespoon rum

Break the biscuits into small pieces and place in a bowl with the walnuts. (Do not pulverise the biscuits into crumbs.) Place the butter, cocoa and sugar in a pan and cook until the sugar has dissolved and the butter is melted. Stir and allow to cool a little. Whisk the eggs lightly. Stir into the cooled mixture in the pan and then pour it all over the biscuits and walnuts. Mix very well. Press the hedgehog into a lightly buttered tin in a layer 2.5 cm (1 in) deep. Chill while you make the icing.

### To make icing

Combine in a double-boiler the chocolate, rum and butter. Stir till melted. Pour onto the hedgehog slice and tilt the tin to achieve a smooth, even layer. Return to the refrigerator. Cut into fingers or small squares when set.

## FLORENTINES

Do not make these in very hot weather. The biscuit part will soften in the refrigerator, and if kept at room temperature the chocolate will melt and leave terrible stains on silk shirts.

- 3 tablespoons melted butter
- 60 g (2 oz) castor sugar
- 60 g (2 oz) finely chopped blanched almonds
- 1 tablespoon flaked almonds
- 3 tablespoons finely chopped candied peel
- 2 tablespoons finely chopped candied angelica
- 1 tablespoon cream
- 100 g (3 oz) best-quality dark chocolate

Place melted butter in a pan, stir in the sugar and bring slowly to the boil. Add the fruits and nuts, stir and then add in the cream.

Place cooking parchment on 2 baking trays and place tiny blobs of mixture on them. Each should be no larger than an Australian 10-cent coin. Place each biscuit well apart from the next.

Bake at 160°C (320°F) for approximately 7–10 minutes. The biscuits must be deep gold and *evenly* coloured when cooked. When the tray is removed from the oven, neaten the edges of each biscuit quickly with a small plain pastry cutter or a flat spatula. After a minute or so, lift each biscuit with a spatula and cool completely on a rack.

Soften the chocolate and paint onto one side of each florentine. Draw the traditional wavy lines with a fork. Place in a cool place, not the refrigerator, until the chocolate has set.

## CHOCOLATE SALAMI

This is delicious and does look remarkably like a salami when sliced. It also keeps very well, so the mixture will make 2 rolls, each yielding about 40 slices.

- 300 g (10 oz) castor sugar
- 400 ml (13 fl oz) cold water
- 600 g (20 oz) walnut pieces, chopped into small pieces, but not ground
- 150 g (5 oz) Dutch cocoa powder
- icing sugar

Mix cold water and sugar, stir and heat until the sugar has dissolved. Increase heat and boil for 3 minutes to form a thin syrup. Add the walnuts and the cocoa powder. Cook until it forms a thick cohesive mass, stirring all the time. Sprinkle the work bench generously with icing sugar. Turn the mixture out onto it. Roll into a long sausage shape. Wrap in foil and store in the coolroom until it has hardened. Slice thinly, like a salami.

## RUM CLUSTERS

- 125 g (4 oz) sultanas
- rum
- 300 g (10 oz) slivered almonds, well-toasted
- 90 g (3 oz) chopped candied orange or grapefruit peel
- 125 g (4 oz) (approximately) best-quality dark or milk chocolate

Soak the sultanas overnight in the rum. Strain them and add the almonds and peel to the sultanas. Mix well. Add sufficient melted chocolate to bind the mixture. Pile in small clusters on a tray lined with baking parchment and leave in a cool place to set. Serve in little paper cases.

Many variations are possible with this sort of chocolate. Try drained preserved ginger or stoned, chopped, fresh dates, or crushed macaroons.

## HAZELNUT CHOCOLATES

- 300 g (10 oz) best-quality dark or milk chocolate
- 375 g (12 oz) Nutella or other chocolate hazelnut spread
- 150 ml (5 fl oz) cream
- 2 tablespoons hazelnut liqueur or spirits, such as Cointreau or brandy
- roasted hazelnuts, skins rubbed off in a tea-towel

Melt the chocolate in a double boiler. Add the hazelnut paste. Stir to combine. Heat the cream. Add to the chocolate mix. Whisk well. Add liqueur. Cool the mixture until it is piping consistency. Whisk 1–2 minutes to lighten the mixture. Using a star nozzle, pipe wavy shapes onto cooking parchment. Top each chocolate with a roasted, skinned hazelnut. Place in a cool place to set.

## WHITE CHOCOLATE TRUFFLES

It is particularly important to buy best-quality white chocolate, as the cheaper varieties taste like soap.

- 200 g (7 oz) white chocolate
- 6 tablespoons cream
- 4 tablespoons Cointreau
- 2 tablespoons grated orange zest
- 100 g (3 oz) crushed amaretti macaroons or sponge cake crumbs
- or gingerbread crumbs (see page 283 for gingerbread recipe)
- 200 g (7 oz) best-quality dark chocolate

Break the white chocolate into a basin and melt over warm water. Stir in the cream, Cointreau and orange zest, and then gradually mix in the cake crumbs or biscuit crumbs. Cover with plastic film and refrigerate until firm. ►

Taking a teaspoonful at a time, roll the mixture into balls. Place the balls on a tray lined with cooking parchment. Freeze the balls. Melt the dark chocolate gently over hot water, protected from steam. Dip each truffle into the chocolate and then place on some more parchment. Serve in paper cases.

The next three love bites contain no nuts. In the restaurant business one encounters many allergies and an allergy to nuts is one of the most common. I try always to have one biscuit or chocolate without nuts.

## PASSIONFRUIT SHORTBREADS

- 180 g (6 oz) butter
- 1 teaspoon finely grated lemon
- 100 g (3 oz) icing sugar
- 3 passionfruits, pulp extracted
- 100 g (3 oz) cornflour
- 180 g (6 oz) self-raising flour

— ICING —

- 2 cups icing sugar
- 100 g (3 oz) butter
- pulp of 4 passionfruits

Cream the butter, lemon zest and icing sugar until light and fluffy. Mix the pulp of the 3 passionfruits into the mixture. Sift the cornflour and flour together and blend well into the mixture.

Pipe rounds or fingers onto greased trays, or trays lined with kitchen parchment, and bake in a hot oven at 220°C (430°F) until golden brown. Cool before icing. The biscuits store well and taste best if freshly iced. Ice only the number you need and keep the rest in an airtight biscuit tin.

### To ice

Melt the butter. Place the icing sugar in a small bowl. Add the passionfruit pulp to the melted butter and stir into the icing sugar. Beat hard for a minute or two over hot water until the icing is really glossy. Dip each biscuit briefly in the icing, or else drip the icing on the top of each biscuit with a small spoon.

# RUM BABAS

To make these miniature babas you must have the appropriate tins. I bought mine at MORA in Paris, the famous cooks' store in Rue Montmartre, which is a treasure-house for moulds and a thousand-and-one other things. I have both very small cyclindrical moulds, no bigger than a thimble, for miniature rum babas and small flat moulds, with a hole in the centre for miniature currant savarins. Very small brioche moulds make attractive babas or savarins. If you have none of these, you will simply have to make full-size babas or savarins and eat them for afternoon tea! The quantities given will yield 50 or so small cakes and 8–10 individual ones. Unsoaked cakes freeze perfectly and can be thawed and soaked in one operation in a low oven.

- 3 tablespoons milk
- I teaspoon dried yeast
- 150 g (5 oz) sifted plain flour
- I teaspoon castor sugar
- pinch of salt
- 3 tablespoon currants, soaked in rum

- 2 eggs
- 90 g (3 oz) very soft butter
- extra melted butter to grease the tins
- 100 g (3 oz) warmed, smooth apricot jam
- whipped cream

## — RUM SYRUP —

- I cup sugar
- 500 ml (16 fl oz) water

- rum to taste

Warm the milk for a moment or two. Sprinkle over the yeast. Sift the flour into a basin with the sugar and the salt. Add the drained currants, if using. Lightly whisk the eggs. Stir the dissolved yeast into the milk and add the eggs. Mix together and pour into the well. Mix and beat until smooth. Add the very soft butter and beat again, either with a wooden spoon or with a dough-hook. Cover with a clean cloth and leave until doubled (2–3 hours). Gently knock back the dough.

Grease the tins selected with a little melted butter. Fill two-thirds full. Leave to rise for 10 minutes or so. Pre-heat oven to 220°C (430°F). Bake small cakes for 4–5 minutes and the larger ones about 15 minutes.

While the cakes are baking, prepare the syrup. Dissolve the sugar in the water, simmer together for 5 minutes and add rum to taste.

I have found that the best results are obtained by soaking warm babas in hot syrup. Soak them for at least 15–20 minutes, turning them once and spooning syrup over them.

Settle the smallest ones in paper cases and brush the tops with warmed apricot jam. Pipe cream into the depression in the centre of the cake and place a small grape or a slice of strawberry in the cream.

## CANDIED CUMQUATS

These little love bites are truly a labour of love, as are the candied cumquats.

Choose perfect fruit with stems intact and no bruises.

1. Put washed cumquats in a brine of 1 tablespoon salt to 1.2 litres (2 pints) water. Put into fresh brine each day for 4 days.
2. Strain and prick the fruit well. Make a syrup using 750 g (1½ lb) sugar to 1.2 litres (2 pints) water. Simmer to dissolve the sugar. Remove from the heat. Add the strained cumquats. Leave for 12 hours or overnight.
3. Next day lift out the fruit. Add a further 500 g (1 lb) sugar to the syrup. Simmer to dissolve the sugar. When dissolved, remove from the heat and return the cumquats to the syrup. Leave overnight.
4. Repeat step 3 over the next 3 days; that is, add an extra 500 g (1 lb) castor sugar each day. Then drain the fruit.
5. Bake very slowly in the lowest possible oven for 4 hours. Roll in castor sugar and serve in paper cases.

In no way will these delicious morsels resemble the true *fruits confits* of Nice. You have only to read Mireille Johnston's recipe in her book, *The Cuisine of the Sun*.

The rest of this section will be taken up with recipes that include nuts in some form or other. I recently helped organise a symposium of gastronomy with several others. Apart from organisational duties, many of the symposiasts were asked and agreed to provide various edibles. My friend Lois made these delectable biscuits for morning coffee, one of the nicest most of us had ever eaten.

## LOIS'S ALMOND and ORANGE BISCUITS

Although I have used almonds, Lois says that they are just as good using brazils or pecans or hazelnuts or walnuts.

- 375 g (12 oz) finely ground nuts
- 1 tablespoon flour
- 100 g (3 oz) castor sugar
- 1 teaspoon finely grated orange zest

- 1 egg
- 1 tablespoon orange juice
- icing sugar for dredging

### — SYRUP —

- ⅓ cup castor sugar
- ¾ cup water

- Grand Marnier to taste

Combine nuts, flour, sugar and orange zest in a mixing bowl. Lightly beat the egg with the orange juice. Add to the nut
  mixture. Knead lightly. Divide dough into two. Roll each half into a long cylinder and cut into little cylinders about 1 cm (½ in) long. Bake at 180°C (350°F) for 15 minutes, until the biscuits are golden brown. Cool briefly on a rack.

While they are baking, make the syrup. Stir until the sugar is dissolved, simmer for 10 minutes. Add the Grand Marnier to taste. Cool a little. Place the still-warm biscuits in the still-warm syrup and leave there until well soaked, 5–10 minutes. Drain and roll thickly in icing sugar.

## TORRONE: ITALIAN-STYLE NOUGAT

It is essential to have an accurate sugar thermometer to make good nougat. If not, you are likely to have a nougat that sticks to the teeth, or else is too hard and impossible to bite.

- 2 cups castor sugar
- ½ cup mild honey
- 1 cup liquid glucose
- ¼ teaspoon salt
- ¼ cup water

- 2 egg whites
- 125 g (4 oz) butter
- few drops vanilla extract
- 125 g (4 oz) toasted almonds
- chopped candied angelica (optional)

Place the first five ingredients in a heavy pan, bring to the boil and cook until it registers 122°C (252°F) on a sugar thermometer.

While the honey syrup is cooking, prepare a 22 cm (9 in) square tin and line it with rice paper (obtainable from an Asian supply shop or a cake decorating shop).

As the honey syrup is just about at the required temperature, commence beating the egg whites until they are very stiff. Pour a quarter of the honey syrup over the egg whites with the motor running. Return the honey syrup to the heat and continue cooking until it now registers 157°C (315°F). Pour it in a thin steady stream onto the egg whites with the motor still running. Add the roughly chopped butter and the vanilla and continue to beat for a further 5 minutes.

By hand, stir in the almonds and candied fruit (if using) and pour the nougat into the prepared tin. Press hard and very quickly to flatten the surface. Refrigerate until firm. Cut into pieces to serve.

Nougat can be flavoured with orange-flower water and a honey can be chosen for its special flavour. Australia produces a leatherwood honey in Tasmania that is very pungent and very famous. For an Australian banquet we served squares of nougat made with this honey.

## PANFORTE

This recipe for Italian panforte was given to us by Josephine Pignolet of Claude's restaurant in Sydney. It is wonderfully spicy. Serve it cut into thin slivers to display the shape of the nuts and figs.

- 400 g (13 oz) whole unblanched almonds
- 350 g (11 oz) chopped candied fruit
- 60 g (2 oz) dried figs
- 100 g (3 oz) plain flour
- 1 tablespoon Dutch cocoa

- 1 teaspoon cinnamon
- ½ teaspoon cloves
- ½ teaspoon white pepper
- ½ teaspoon nutmeg
- ½ teaspoon coriander

— SYRUP —

- 1 tablespoon water
- 110 g (3½ oz) honey

- 160 g (5½ oz) sugar

Combine all the ingredients, fruit, nuts and spices in a large bowl with the cocoa and flour. Melt the honey, water and sugar until the sugar is completely melted. Simmer together for 1 minute and then pour the syrup onto the dry ingredients. Mix very well. It will be very difficult to combine. A few extra drops of water may be added, but only a few drops.

Line a 22 cm (9 in) square tin with edible rice paper and press the mixture firmly into the tin. Bake at 160°C (320°F) for 30 minutes. The panforte is cooked when the edges are firm but the middle is still a little soft.

Allow to cool before cutting.

## WALNUT BRITTLE

This curious recipe has obvious Chinese connections. Honey walnuts are sometimes served as one of the appetisers before a formal Chinese banquet. We serve them at the end of a Western-style meal. Does it matter, I wonder?

- 250 g (8 oz) best quality walnut halves
- ¾ cup light honey
- 1 tablespoon lemon juice
- 1 tablespoon light soy sauce
- castor sugar
- light oil for frying

Soak the walnuts in the honey, lemon juice and soy sauce. Drain. Roll the nuts in castor sugar. Heat light oil in a wok, deep enough to cover the walnuts. When the oil is smoking, add the walnuts and fry until they are golden brown. Drain on kitchen paper. Be careful! They are very hot.

## SPICY FINGERS

Do not omit the lemon icing—it gives the biscuits their special character.

- 2 eggs
- 200 g (7 oz) castor sugar
- few drops vanilla extract
- 1 teaspoon ground cinnamon
- 60 g (2 oz) mixed candied peel, chopped fine
- 180 g (6 oz) almond meal, preferably brown almond meal, made from unblanched almonds
- 120 g (4 oz) ground hazelnut meal
- ½ teaspoon baking powder

### — ICING —

- 1 cup icing sugar
- ½ teaspoon grated lemon zest
- juice of a lemon

Beat the eggs, sugar and vanilla until pale and thick. Fold in the spices, peel and nuts and baking powder. Using a plain piping nozzle, pipe the mixture in fingers onto baking parchment-lined trays. Bake at 120°C (250°F) for 30 minutes.

While the spicy fingers are baking, make the icing. Mix the icing sugar with drops of lemon juice and the zest until you have a thin mixture. Dribble icing over the biscuits as soon as they come from the oven.

## STEPHANIE'S ANGELICA TARTLETS

For the very last recipe I have one of the very best. These tiny toffeed tartlets are irresistible. Various cooks are often seen eating two or three for breakfast as they come on duty. It is very important that the filling is quite runny when put into the shells, and it is practically impossible not to burn your fingers as fragments of toffee always stick to the skin as the tartlets are removed from their tins.

- shortcrust pastry, enough to thinly line as many small tartlet tins as you need

## — FILLING —

- 3 sticks candied angelica
- 1 tablespoon slivered almonds
- ½ cup mixed dried fruits (currants, sultanas, apricots, apples)
- 150 g (5 oz) unsalted butter
- ½ cup castor sugar
- 2½ tablespoons light honey
- 2 tablespoons kirsch
- 2 tablespoons cream

Place the angelica, the almonds and the dried fruits in the food processor and process briefly using the on/off action. The fruit, etc., should be quite finely chopped, but certainly not puréed.

In a saucepan melt the butter and combine with the sugar, honey, kirsch and cream. Cook until the sugar is dissolved. Add the chopped nuts and fruits, stir very well. The mixture should be sloppy, not stiff. If it is too stiff, add a little more honey and butter, or lift out a portion of the fruit with a slotted spoon.

Pre-heat the oven to 220°C (430°F). Prick the base of the tart shells and blind-bake them for around 6–8 minutes until they are pale-gold. With a cloth, firmly press down the base of any tartlet case that wants to puff up at this stage.

Place enough filling in each little tart to practically fill it. Return to the oven and bake until the filling has caramelised. It will first form big pale bubbles. This is insufficiently cooked. The filling must be a dark gold, and the rims of each tartlet will look burnished.

Even though you are going to burn your fingers, run a small knife around the edge of each tart and lift onto a rack to cool. If you leave them in their tins, the caramel will fuse to the metal and they will never come out.

# BREADS

When I am so hungry that my knees shake, what I crave is a large thick slice of chewy, solid bread. Bread of substance, of rye or unbleached flour, with olives and rosemary possibly, bread that one can tear from a large loaf, often floury and preferably one day old.

Poilâne bread from Lionel Poilâne's bakeries in Paris was a revelation to me when I first tasted it. Its look and flavour recalled scenes from old black-and-white films of French rural households during World War II, where the family of Resistance workers gathered around a table with a tumbler of wine and one of these giant loaves. In her marvellous book *The Food Lover's Guide to Paris*, Patricia Wells comments that the Poilâne loaf has set the contemporary standard for bread, the loaf against which almost all others are judged. She also says that the bread has been rarely imitated and never successfully. Each giant round loaf is made with pungent sour-dough starter, all-French flour and fragrant sea salt. Each is formed by hand, rising in rustic, yet practical, fabric-lined wicker baskets. The loaves are baked in wood-fired ovens.

I once had working for me a young cook who was an ardent francophile. He had talked his way into the kitchens of several of Paris's most renowned restaurants, determined to wrest away their secrets and to reach the top fast. He managed to talk his way eventually into the Poilâne bakehouse and worked there, while firming up his resolve to create his own business, which would be equally successful.

Back in Australia and during his time at Stephanie's he showed amazing determination. He found an old, abandoned bakery with a traditional brick-fired oven, and fairly soon he set himself up to imitate Poilâne. Potts Bakery was probably the first to make and market natural levain bread. It also was formed in cheesecloth-lined wicker baskets (made for Michael Potts by a local craftsman) and maybe it was not as good as Poilâne, but it was good bread by any other standard.

The bakery has since been sold. It is hugely successful, has expanded its range, but to my mind the bread, while still a quality product, no longer resembles Poilâne bread. We have several other quality bakers producing loaves that taste like 'real' bread. The Natural Tucker bakehouse in an inner Melbourne suburb uses no yeast in its breads and produces superb chewy loaves. Its range includes a black rye that is memorable with herrings or, as I had it recently, with borscht on a cold winter's day.

Patricia Wells has included in her book a recipe for the Poilâne loaf, which takes a week to make. For those seriously interested in bread-making, it is worth while. My first loaf would not have given Lionel Poilane anything to worry about, but I certainly enjoyed eating it.

Yeastless breads are, of course, not restricted to the French. Mark Dymiotis wrote an excellent account in the Epicure section of the Melbourne Age of how he makes the family's weekly loaves using nothing but freshly ground wholemeal flour, leaven, water and sea salt. I have abbreviated the recipe.

---

## GREEK COUNTRY BREAD
### from MARK DYMIOTIS

### TO MAKE STARTER

Put one part (e.g. a Greek coffee cup) of freshly ground wholemeal flour and one part of clean water in a clean earthen or glass container (avoid plastic or metal containers). Mix well until all flour is dissolved, cover with a clean cloth and leave until the mixture starts developing bubbles. This will take from 2–5 days. When it occurs, add twice as much flour and water as the original quantity, mix well and wait until it starts bubbling again. This will take less time than before. Now your starter is ready. For better maturity, you can repeat the process once or twice, but every time you do so, double the quantity of flour and water.

Use the starter immediately after it starts bubbling, because it will become too sour if left for too long.

### To make bread

Use 1 part of leaven to 10 parts of flour. If using salt, dissolve it in the water (I use 1 tablespoon salt to 1 kilogram of flour). Add lukewarm water and mix and knead well. The more you knead, the more elastic the gluten will become, and so the dough will rise better. Do not overdo it, however, because the dough may lose its elasticity. You can make the dough soft or hard: usually it is kept soft.

As soon as you finish kneading, sprinkle the dough with flour, cover it with a clean cloth and place in a warm place.

When the dough becomes double the original size (it will take 3–7 hours, depending on the room temperature), shape it into loaves and place them in bread containers. Cover them with a clean cloth and put in a warm place until they are double in size. It will take 1–3 hours, depending on the temperature. If the rising takes too long the bread will develop a sour taste.

When the dough cracks or becomes double in size, place the loaves in a hot oven, approximately 200°C (400°F). Do not open the oven door for at least 20 minutes. The cooking will take at least 1 hour. Knock the bottom of the loaf, and if it produces a hollow sound the bread is ready. The baking temperature for leaven bread is lower than for yeast bread, but it takes longer to bake . . . When the loaves are ready, take them out of the containers and cover them with a clean cloth until cool . . . They will be ready to eat in 12 hours.

Keep a handful of the final dough, which will be your starter next time. It will keep better if you add more salt, knead it lightly and place it on a plate on which you have sprinkled salt. In a few days it will become very hard. When you need it, put it in water until it is completely dissolved, add more water and flour, mix well for a soft or runny dough, wait until it matures (double in size or starts to crack, in 2–5 hours) and this is your starter for the main dough.

The more moist the dough, and the longer it takes to rise, the sourer the bread will become . . . Northern Europeans like their bread sour, while Greeks prefer it with as little sourness as possible.

After reading this recipe it becomes clear why bread-making in rural communities is left to the baker, or why, in the home, baking is done once a week.

For those who don't have the time or the patience to make this superb bread, it is still possible to produce country-tasting loaves using yeast. In my earlier book I have given a very simple recipe for a crusty loaf, which uses a slightly soured starter dough. After each mix, a portion of the dough is set aside to ripen further as the starter for the next loaf.

Here is another recipe, which produces a bread that has a very definite sour flavour.

## SOUR RYE BREAD with CARAWAY SEEDS

The ¼ cup of water and pinch of sugar are not needed to dissolve yeast if, like me, you use Fermipan yeast, which is combined directly with the flour.

### — RYE SOURDOUGH STARTER —

- 1 tablespoon dry yeast
- 3 cups tepid water
- 3½ cups rye flour
- 1 small onion, peeled and halved

In a ceramic or glass bowl, dissolve the yeast in 2 cups of the lukewarm water, and with a fork beat in 2 cups of the rye flour until smooth. Add the onion, cover with a cloth and allow to stand at room temperature for 24 hours. Remove the onion. Beat in 1 cup of water and the remaining 1½ cups rye flour. Cover again with the cloth and allow to stand for a further 24 hours. The starter should now smell pleasantly sour and be bubbly.

Use at once or refrigerate, covered, for 24 hours. If you must hold the starter longer, the night before it is needed add ½ cup tepid water and ¾ cup rye flour and let it stand at room temperature overnight. ▶

## — SOUR RYE BREAD —

- 3 teaspoons dry yeast
- ¼ cup warm water
- pinch of sugar
- 1 tablespoon salt
- 1 cup tepid water
- 2 cups starter dough, stirred down
  before measuring

- 3 tablespoons caraway seeds
- 1 cup rye flour
- 3½ cups unbleached bakers' flour
- flour for sprinkling on baking sheet

If you are using conventional dried yeast, combine the yeast, warm water and sugar and let stand until foamy, about 10 minutes. If using Fermipan yeast, designed to be mixed directly with the dry ingredients, mix the yeast with the rye flour.

Dissolve the salt in the cup of tepid water and stir into the starter. Beat in the caraway seeds and the yeast mixture (if using conventional dried yeast). Beat in the rye flour (containing the yeast if using Fermipan yeast), a little at a time, and then the unbleached bakers' flour, reserving ½ a cup to add if necessary.

Knead the dough, using a mixer with a dough-hook for preference, until it is elastic and smooth. Place in a bowl and allow to double. It will take at least 1 hour.

Knock down and shape the loaves. I make 2 loaves and roll them into cigar-shapes on a flour-dusted baking sheet. Allow to rise again, slash the top diagonally with a sharp knife to allow for expansion of the dough, scatter some flour over the loaves, and then place, seam-side down in a pre-heated oven at 220°C (430°F).

Bake for 15 minutes at this temperature, and then reduce the temperature to 180°C (350°). The loaves may take another 30 minutes. Rap the bottom to see if they sound hollow before removing and cooling on a rack.

## MADELEINE'S
## OLIVE OIL and FENNEL BREAD

Madeleine Kamman uses cumin seed as a souring agent in her recipe for leaven.

We have used her recipe for olive oil and fennel bread, given in her book In Madeleine's Kitchen, over and over again. Allowed to mature for a day and cut into thick slices and oven-dried a little, it is the ideal bread to place in the bottom of a soup bowl when you are to serve a soupy stew of fish or shellfish. Formed into thinner breadsticks, sliced thin and baked till pale gold after brushing with olive oil, it makes lovely croutons to accompany my mussel soup or a vegetable braise of fennel.

## — LEAVEN —

- 2 teaspoons dried yeast
- 300 g (10 oz) unbleached bakers' flour
- $\frac{1}{3}$ teaspoon ground cumin
- lukewarm water

## — BREAD —

- leaven
- 1½ tablespoons fennel seeds
- 3 teaspoons salt
- 600 g (20 oz) unbleached bakers' flour
- lukewarm water
- ½ cup olive oil

Mix the yeast, flour, cumin and water into a semi-liquid batter. Let it stand, covered, for 2 days.

Combine leaven, fennel seeds, salt and the rest of the flour, adding as much water as necessary to make a smooth dough that is a little sticky. Knead for 10 minutes by hand, less in an electric mixer. Place in a bowl greased with some of the olive oil. Allow to double in bulk.

Pre-heat oven to 220°C (430°F). Punch the dough down, gradually working the olive oil into the dough. Shape and slash the loaf with a sharp knife or a razor blade. Allow to rise again until it has not quite doubled in size. Bake until crisp and golden, about 20–30 minutes, spraying it with water three times during the first 10 minutes of baking.

Madeleine Kamman is very concerned in her writing to explain the 'whys' as well as the 'how tos'. She gives a very clear exposition of why one should slash or 'dock' a crust before baking a loaf. As the loaf rises, the crust starts to dehydrate. The heat of the oven causes the crust to continue to harden through dehydration and as the internal dough expands, the slashes expands, thus keeping the crust from breaking open under the internal pressure of steam and dilating carbon dioxide. It follows that loaves that have not been slashed are far more likely to break or split along one of the sides.

Spraying of the loaf rehydrates the surface and permits better expansion of the bread.

For a complete contrast of method and product I want to share with you the recipe for the magnificent Italian-style olive bread that we make every day in the restaurant to serve with soft cheeses. This olive bread is based on a recipe of Giuliano Bugialli, although the bread itself is an Italian classic and is widely available. We have altered the recipe until we now believe that ours is perfect! Like many of the Italian flat breads and pizza doughs, it uses a lot of yeast.

The olive bread should be handled lightly at all times.

## OLIVE BREAD

### — STARTER SPONGE —

- ¼ cup unbleached bakers' flour
- ¼ cup lukewarm water
- 1½ tablespoons dried yeast

### — BREAD —

- 150 g (5 oz) pitted olives, halved
- 500 g (1 lb) unbleached bakers' flour
- 2 teaspoons rosemary needles, chopped very fine
- 2 teaspoons salt
- 4 tablespoons olive oil
- 300 ml (10 fl oz) water
- Maldon sea salt
- extra olive oil for hands

Mix the ingredients for the starter sponge and let it rise for 1½ hours, until it has doubled in size.

Place the starter dough in a large basin and add the olives, flour, rosemary, salt and the olive oil. Add the water and mix by hand to a very soft dough. You will need to rub your hands with olive oil in order to mix the dough. Leave it to double, about 30 mintues. Do not knock the dough back, but tip it gently onto an oiled bench or marble slab. Pat out to a thickness of 2 cm (1 in) and cut into rounds for individual serves or into larger rounds for slicing. Once again all this should be done with oiled hands. Transfer the breads to an oiled baking sheet, paint lightly with more olive oil and scatter a few grains of Maldon sea salt on each loaf.

Pre-heat oven to 220°C (430°F). Allow olive breads to puff for about 15–20 minutes and then bake. Bake for 20 minutes until golden and crusty. Do not open the oven during this time. When cooked, individual olive breads feel as light as table tennis balls!

Cool on a rack. This bread is at its most delectable served still slightly warm. It can be successfully re-warmed for 1–2 minutes in a hot oven.

Flat breads similar to the olive bread are found all over Italy. They have various names, foccacia, schiacciata or even pizza! Often, these breads are eaten as they are; often, they have delicious toppings, pizza, for example; and sometimes they are split and used to hold a sandwich filling. They make very superior sandwiches. Flat breads are also quite common in the south of France. In fact, one June I purchased a green olive fougasse from a market stall in Orange, having wavered between it and others flavoured with anchovies or roquefort. We set off to picnic, passing fields blood-red with poppies and roadsides a riot of camomile, buttercups and starry blue flowers. Next year I shall take a guide to European wildflowers. It is frustrating to walk past nodding spikes of dark-blue and wonder or not be sure if the dainty lace-like flower is in fact yarrow? At our picnic spot we crushed underfoot sun-crisped thyme in full flower, lavender and rosemary. Birds sang, there was the gentlest of breezes, and if it sounds impossibly idyllic, I can't help it—that's Provence!

## PIZZA DOUGH

- 1 tablespoon dry yeast
- pinch of sugar (to activate yeast, if not using Fermipan yeast)
- ¾ cup warm water
- 1 teaspoon salt
- 2 tablespoons olive oil
- 375 g (12 oz) unbleached bakers' flour

If using conventional dried yeast, dissolve the yeast in a small bowl with the sugar and the warm water. This will take about 5 minutes. Then proceed to mix the yeast mixture and the oil into the flour and salt.

If using Fermipan yeast, mix the yeast and salt into the flour and proceed to mix in the olive oil and the water. Knead until the dough is smooth and elastic, about 10 minutes by hand. You may need a little extra water. The dough should be soft but not sticky. Place the dough into an oiled bowl, turn to coat with the oil. Cover and allow to rise to double, about 1½ hours.

Pre-heat the oven to 220°C (430°F).

Remove dough and knead briefly. Using a little extra olive oil, oil a pizza pan or flat bread tray. Roll the dough to about half the desired size and then with oiled fingertips press and stretch the dough to fill the tray. The dough should never be more than 5 mm (¼ in) thick. Brush with oil and a few grains of salt and allow to rise for 15 minutes. Bake for 20–30 minutes, until golden brown, or top with any preferred filling and bake until the topping is cooked and the dough underneath is golden and crisp.

## SCHIACCIATA with CHEESE TOPPING

The word *schiacciata* refers to the indentations left after the dough is pushed and squashed in the pan. This recipe and the recipe for pizza dough come from *Cooking from an Italian Garden* by Paola Scaravelli and Jon Cohen.

- 1 quantity of basic pizza dough as in the previous recipe
- 2 tablespoons olive oil
- ½ cup pecorino, grated
- ⅓ cup black olives, pitted and chopped
- 1 large onion (red if possible), thinly sliced
- pinch of salt and lots of pepper

Prepare the dough as in the preceding recipe. Press and prod and push into the pizza pan or flat baking tin. Leave all the indentations in the dough. Spread 1 tablespoon of olive oil over the dough and spread with your hand. Bake 15 minutes. Remove from the oven, spread the rest of the ingredients over the surface, drizzle the top with the remaining olive oil and bake for a further 10–15 minutes. Cool a little before serving.

You will have noticed that the recipes are getting simpler and certainly faster in the execution. On a short holiday in Tasmania we were invited to lunch and were served a delicious bread. Our hostess passed on my compliments to her friend Sabrina Pirie, who responded by sending me the recipe. Although we have slightly simplified the instructions, it is still known in the kitchen as Sabrina's bread. It is the crustiest and airiest breadstick that I have eaten outside of the best in France.

Originally in this recipe, and in many others, one is instructed to place a brick in the oven, usually soaked in water or resting in a pan of water. The aim of this is to increase the humidity inside the oven and to prevent too-rapid evaporation of the crust. It is thought to approximate to conditions inside a brick-lined, wood-fired oven. We use a large convection oven exclusively for our bread, and we have done some controlled experiments with and without bricks, and in our situation at least we are convinced that it makes no difference. Here then is Sabrina's bread, minus bricks.

## SABRINA'S BREADSTICKS

- 500 g (1 lb) unbleached bakers' flour
- 1 teaspoon dried yeast
- 2 teaspoons salt
- 300 ml (10 fl oz) lukewarm water
- semolina for scattering on baking trays

If using conventional yeast, place the yeast in a bowl with a small amount of water, dissolve and leave for a few minutes, and then add to the mixer with the flour and water.

If using Fermipan yeast, mix the yeast with the flour and salt. Place in the bowl of an electric mixer fitted with a dough-hook and incorporate the water. Beat well for at least 5 minutes (10 minutes by hand). Place in bowl and allow to rise for 3–5 hours.

After the first rise, gently ease the dough out of the bowl onto a work bench or marble. Fold it in four, return to the bowl, allow to rise the second time for 1½ hours. Remove from the bowl gently as before and divide into 2 or 3 portions. Keep the dough covered with a clean dry cloth while working with each piece.

Roll each piece of dough into a breadstick shape and place seam down on a floured tea-towel. Leave covered for 45 minutes. Pre-heat oven to 250°C (480°F). Sprinkle baking trays with fine semolina, roll the breadsticks from the cloth, right-side up on the baking tray. Slash each loaf with a razor blade.

Cook the breadsticks for about 25–30 minutes, spraying the oven sides and the bread after the first few minutes and then after each 10 minutes.

We now serve small individual olive breads to accompany cheese. We used to make walnut loaves and no doubt will again someday. Here is a recipe for a fruit bread that is delicious served with fine English farmhouse cheddar in the same way as one enjoys this cheese with slightly sweet digestive biscuits. Cut the bread quite thinly.

## FRUIT BREAD for ENGLISH FARMHOUSE CHEESES

- 250 g (8 oz) dried pears
- 100 g (3 oz) dried figs
- 60 g (2 oz) pitted prunes
- 125 g (4 oz) seedless raisins
- ⅔ cup hot water
- ⅓ cup kirsch or brandy
- 1 teaspoon grated lemon zest
- ¼ cup honey
- 2 teaspoons dried yeast
- 1 teaspoon sugar (if using conventional dried yeast)

- 300 ml (10 fl oz) warm water
- 1 teaspoon salt
- 2 teaspoons ground cinnamon
- 1 egg
- 600–750 g (20–25 oz) unbleached bakers' flour
- ½ cup almonds, toasted (optional)
- ½ cup walnuts (optional)

### — GLAZE —

- reserved syrup
- 1 egg

Cut the pears, figs and prunes into 1 cm (½ in) pieces. Place cut-up fruit in a large bowl with the raisins. Mix together the hot water, kirsch, lemon zest and honey and pour over the fruit. Toss well. Store in the refrigerator overnight.

Dissolve yeast with the sugar and add to the warm water with the salt (if using conventional yeast). If using Fermipan yeast, mix yeast, salt and cinnamon with the flour.

Mix egg lightly, add to water. Stir in the flour until you have a fairly soft dough. Mix with the dough-hook until dough is smooth and elastic, adding a little extra flour if the dough seems sticky. Place in a greased bowl and allow to rise until doubled, approximately 1 hour.

Drain the fruit, add the nuts, if using. Punch down the dough, flatten it to a rectangular shape, scatter over the fruit and nuts and knead well. Shape into two cylindrical loaves, or bake in greased bread tins. Allow to rise until almost double, brush with the reserved syrup mixed with an extra egg.

Pre-heat oven to 200°C (400°F). Bake the bread at this temperature for 15 minutes, brush again with the glaze, lower temperature to 180°C (350°F) if the top appears to be browning too fast, and continue to bake for a further 25–30 minutes, until the bread tests hollow. If cooking the bread in tins, turn it out and return to the oven for an extra 5 minutes to brown the sides.

Allow to cool completely before slicing. The bread is excellent the day after it is baked.

# BASIC STOCKS

--- FEASTS & STORIES ---

## DEMI-GLACE

Throughout the book I have mentioned stocks, and frequently I have specified a particular type of stock. Demi-glace is an indispensable resource in a good restaurant kitchen. However, it is difficult to create at home without quite a bit of planning. Basically, it is a well-made stock, which is reduced in order to concentrate its flavour. The need to reduce the stock by at least eight times means that to achieve 1 litre (32 fl oz) you must begin with at least 8 litres (13 pints) of strained, fat-free stock. It should be stressed at once that, because of its concentration, small amounts only are needed. It is always combined with something—either a lump of butter or butter blended with herbs or bone marrow, or with a separately made reduction of red or white wine and shallots, or shallots, mustard and cognac—used to enrich and strengthen pan glazings or braising juices or any number of other more specific additions. In a domestic situation one would never need to use more than 200 ml (7 fl oz) or a scant cup for any meal for six people.

Having said that, I would immediately want to stress another point. Demi-glace is the one thing above all else that deserves prime space in your freezer. If you are serious about your cooking, and you have managed to organise pots of sufficient size, and good meaty bones and knuckles, make as much as you can. Not a drop should ever be wasted.

The following is the method we use, with two differences. As we make really enormous quantities, which commence in a 50-litre (10 gallon) stainless steel boiler, and we reduce it by at least 15 times, we do not roast the bones. The concentration by reduction gives us all the colour we need. The other difference is that after we draw off the first stock and commence its reduction, we make a remouillage in the initial stockpot. That is we refill it with clean water and add fresh vegetables. This second stock is not as good as the first, but is quite satisfactory for such tasks as initial poaching of tripe before it is stuffed, or to use in place of water to make a richer beefsteak and kidney pie, or indeed to incorporate into many different dinners for the staff. (We all eat together at six o'clock before the service.)

I have avoided being specific about quantities. Remember! Start as large as you can. Simmer overnight if you can trust your simmer plate to keep the liquid just murmuring. If not, simmer for at least 6 hours, preferably 8 to 10 hours. Skim well before adding the vegetables.

Cool the final reduction as rapidly as possible. When cold, divide into cupfuls, pour into containers, leaving a little room for expansion. Label, date and freeze.

To thaw. Either place the container on a plate in the kitchen overnight or, if it is needed urgently, place directly in a pan with a little water and heat gently until the iceblock melts. Give it a good boil and a final skim of any impurities.

You will be unable to lift the pot once it has its liquid and bones in it. Therefore, it must be in position on the stove before you add the liquid, and you will have to decant or rather ladle the stock into your next receptacle to commence the reduction as the hot stockpot will similarly be far too heavy for you to try and pour the liquid through a strainer.

## — BONES —

- cracked, sawn veal shin bones
- cracked, sawn beef shin bones (save the bones after you have extracted marrow on another occasion)
- any other veal bones (If your butcher has none, sigh and purchase 3 veal knuckles. Have them sawn into pieces. Believe it or not, butchers often find bones a nuisance, and they have people come to remove them in large

quantities. If you are planning to build stock-making into your life, have a weekly or fortnightly order for bones.) You will need enough bones to come half-way up your stockpot when rammed down hard.

## — MEAT SCRAPS —

- any pieces of skin, gristle, sinew, etc., saved from trimming meat for a stew or braise; skinny ends of oxtail

## — GELATINE —

- a veal knuckle, as above, or 3 or 4 fresh pig's trotters, or a piece of pork rind, or chicken feet, washed thoroughly

## — VEGETABLES —

- onions, unpeeled but quartered; carrots, washed and sliced; celery, washed and sliced (not too much); leeks, washed and sliced; mushroom trimmings; parsley stalks; onion peelings, collected during the day or the day before

## — AROMATICS —

- whole head of garlic, sliced in half crosswise (optional or use less); bay leaf; fresh thyme

## — EXTRAS —

- several spoonfuls of tomato paste: a few juicy tomatoes; white wine to deglaze roasting pan

Roast bones, turning to prevent any from catching. Tip into stockpot. De-glaze the roasting dish with a little wine or vinegar. Tip into the pot. Place the pot on the stove. Add cold water to cover the bones. Bring slowly to the boil. Skim off all scum. When boiling point is reached, skim again, add two cups of cold water. This will cause more scum to be released. Skim this. Wait for boiling point again. Adjust heat to a medium simmer. Tip in all vegetables and aromatics. Push down firmly. There should be sufficient vegetables and aromatics to fill the pot to three-quarters full when added to the bones. Add extra water to fill stockpot to just below the rim. When stock re-boils, skim and adjust heat to lowest possible simmer.

After 6 hours minimum and preferably 8 to 10 hours, ladle off the stock through a strainer into a clean pan already in position on the stove top alongside the stockpot. After you have ladled all the stock you can easily retrieve, bucket out the larger bits of debris until the pot is light enough for you to lift.

Have a strainer placed over a bucket. Tip the stockpot to retrieve the rest of the stock. Add to the reduction pan. At this point you have created a good veal stock. It can be used without any reduction to braise dishes, to make a velouté sauce, to replace water in any stew or soup, to cook a pilaff of rice and hundreds of other uses. To adequately form the base for an unthickened sauce, you must now reduce the veal stock to demi-glace. (The purist will hasten to point out that by mounting a sauce based on demi-glace with butter, one is actually thickening the sauce a little—this is correct.)

Bring the strained stock to the boil, then skim. Adjust the heat to achieve a strong simmer, but not so strong that the stock will boil over. Skim from time to time, and leave until reduced by seven-eighths, that is, if you had 4 litres (6 pints) of strained stock you will stop the process when you have 500 ml (16 fl oz) of demi-glace. Strain this final sauce through a fine strainer. Cool it quickly and then store it.

The actual attention needed is minimal, but the time taken is considerable, and there should be lots of ingredients. A fine demi-glace is a very costly sauce.

## BASIC POULTRY STOCK

- 1 chicken carcass
- giblets, heart, if included
- chicken neck and feet, if included
- 1 bay leaf, sprig thyme, sprig parsley
- 1 onion
- 1 carrot
- 1 leek
- 1 stick celery
- 6 mushrooms
- 1 tomato, seeded
- 1 spring omon
- 1 slice lemon

Put bones and seasonings into a pot and cover with cold water. Bring to boil slowly, skimming off scum and fat. Add vegetables. Simmer for 4 hours. Strain. Let stand and skim off any fat that rises to the top. Reduce by rapid boiling to strength required, depending on final use.

If you have a few bacon rinds or a scrap of veal or a fresh pig's trotter, by all means add it to the pot before adding the water.

# GOLDEN POULTRY STOCK

- 1 chicken carcass
- giblets, heart, if included
- chicken neck and feet, if included
- 1 onion
- 1 carrot
- 1 leek

- 1 stick celery
- 6 mushrooms
- 1 tomato, seeded
- 1 spring onion
- 1 slice lemon
- 1 bay leaf, sprig thyme, sprig parsley

Roast chicken carcass, neck, feet, wing-tips, etc. until well browned. Chop and fry vegetables in a little oil until well coloured. Put bones, vegetables and seasonings into a pot and cover with cold water. Bring to boil slowly, skimming off scum and fat. Simmer for 4 hours. Strain. Let stand and skim off any fat that rises to the top. Reduce by rapid boiling to strength required depending on final use.

If you have a few bacon rinds or a scrap of veal or a fresh pig's trotter, by all means add it to the pot before adding the water. The roasting of the carcass adds colour to the stock. If you wanted a very light stock—for example, to make a vegetable soup or a pale velouté sauce—there would be no need to roast the bones.

# BIBLIOGRAPHY

Alexander, S., *Stephanie's Menus for Food Lovers*, Methuen Haynes: Sydney, 1985.

Beckett, R., *Convicted Tastes: food in Australia*, Allen & Unwin: Sydney, 1984.

Bettoja, Jo, and Cornetto, Anna Maria, *Italian Cooking in the Grand Tradition*, Dial Press: New York, 1982

Bugialli, Giuliano, *Food of Italy*, Stewart, Jason & Chang: New York, 1984.

Burchett, Mary, *Through My Kitchen Door*, Georgian House: Melbourne, 1960.

Cost, Bruce, *Ginger: east to west*, Aris: Berkeley, Calif., 1984.

*Darwin Gardener's Gourmet Guide*, Darwin Garden Club: Darwin, 1978.

David, Elizabeth, *Summer Cooking*, Penguin, Harmondsworth, rev. ed. 1965.

—, *Mediterranean Food*, Penguin: Harmondsworth, 2nd rev. ed. 1965.

—, *French Provincial Cooking*, Penguin: Harmondsworth, rev. ed. 1970

—, *Spices, Salt and Aromatics in the English Kitchen*, Penguin: Harmondsworth, rev. ed. 1973.

der Haroutunian, Arto, *North African Cookery*, Century: London, 1985.

Dormann, G., *Colette—a Passion for Life*, Thames & Hudson: London, 1985.

Esbensen, Mogens Bay, *Thai Cuisine*, Nelson: Melbourne, 1986.

Grigson, Jane, *Fruit*, Penguin: Harmondsworth, rev. ed., 1983.

—,*The Observer Guide to British Cookery*, Michael Joseph: London, 1984.

Guérard, Michel, *Cuisine gourmande*, Macmillan: London, 1978.

Hazan, M., *The Classic Italian Cookbook*, Macmillan: London, rev. ed., 1987.

Hemphill, Rosemary, *The Penguin Book of Herbs and Spices*, Penguin: Harmondsworth, 1959.

Johnston, Mireille, *The Cuisine of the Sun*, Vintage: New York, 1979.

Kamman, Madeleine, *In Madeleine's Kitchen*, Atheneum: New York, 1984.

Kennedy, Diana, *Mexican Regional Cookery*, Harper & Row: New York, 1984.

Klein, Maggie Blyth, *The Feast of the Olive*, Aris: Berkeley, Calif., 1983.

Kuo, Irene, *The Key to Chinese Cooking*, Nelson: Melbourne, 1978.

Larkcom, Joy, *The Salad Garden*, Doubleday: Sydney, 1984.

Madlena, J. C., *The Sea Vegetable Cookbook*, Clarkson N. Potter: New York, 1977.

Meehan, Betty, *Shell Bed to Shell Midden*, Australian Institute of Aboriginal Studies: Canberra, 1982.

Moore, Clement, *The Night Before Christmas*, Award: London, 1980.

Olney, R. (ed.), *Lamb*, Techniques and Recipes Series, Time-Life: New York, 1981.

Ray, Elizabeth (ed.), *The Best of Eliza Acton*, Penguin: Harmondsworth, 1974.

Roden, Claudia, *A Book of Middle Eastern Food*, Penguin: Harmondsworth, 1970.

Root, Waverley, *The Food of Italy*, Vintage: New York, 1977.

Scaravelli, P., and Cohen J., *Cooking from an Italian Garden*, Harvest: New York, 1985.

Solomon, Charmaine, *The Complete Asian Cookbook*, Lansdowne: Sydney, 1976.

Symons, Michael, *One Continuous Picnic*, Duck Press: Adelaide, 1982.

Thomas, Gail, *A Gourmet Harvest*, Five Mile Press: Hawthorn, Vic., 1986.

Wells, Patricia, *Food Lover's Guide to Paris*, Methuen: London, 1984.

*Welsh Recipes: a collection of the traditional dishes of Wales*, John Jones: Cardiff.

Whiteaker, Stafford, *The Compleat Strawberry*, Century: London, 1985.

Wolfert, Paula, *Cooking of South-West France*, rev. ed., Dorling Kindersley, 1987.

# INDEX

prune and muscat frozen trifle, 244-5
puddings
    apricot upside-down cake, 266-7
    berry crumble, 273
    blackberry cranachan, 273-4
    chocolate, 257
    Christmas pudding, Emily Bell's, 284-5
    cinnamon bavarois, 279
    Eliza Acton's quince custard, 280
    gingerbread pudding, 283-4
    gratin of raspberries, 272-3
    Julie's poppyseed cake, 270
    mandarin, 230-1
    passionfruit bavarian cream in a
        caramel-lined mould, 278-9
    pavlova, 275-7
    pear and almond pudding, David's,
        281-2
    pears baked as in Savoy, 281
    poached peaches in muscat de
        Beaumes-de-Venise, 269
    poached peaches with fig sauce, 269
    prune and muscat frozen trifle, 244-5
    quince custard, 280
    quinces baked in honey, 280-1
    simple syllabub, 222-3
    Spanish cream or honeycomb mould,
        216, 217-8
    Stephanie's favourite lemon curd layer
        'cake', 216, 219-20
    strawberry shortcake, 271
    Sussex Pond, 232-3
    *see also*, fritters, ice-creams, tarts
puff pastry fruit tarts as at Stephanie's,
    267-8
pumpkin
    perfumed, 59
    ways to use, 54
puree of Jerusalem artichokes, 80, 81

quail
    eggs, hard-boiled, in spicy coconut
        sauce, 124
    grilled Italian-style, with accompani-
        ments, 126-8
    spiced Indian, with accompaniments,
        122-5

quinces
    and angelica nougat ice-cream, 248-9
    apple and candied quince strudel,
        202-3
    baked in honey, 280-1
    custard, Eliza Acton's, 280
    paste, 279
    tart with browned butter topping,
        203-4
    uses for, 279-80

radicchio, to grill, 73
raisin and Rutherglen muscat tart, 201
raspberries, gratin of, 272-3
raw artichoke salad, 192-3
red pepper mousse, 69
red wine butter sauce, 42-3
reductions, 5, 71-2
rice, to cook, 131
Ristorante Ciccarelli (near Verona), 97
Ristorante il Molino (Spello), 54
roast chicken for Holly and Lisa, 120-1
roasted eggplant with parsley and
    anchovy, 64-5
roasted magpie goose, 150
roasted salmon, larded with anchovies
    and sage, with anchovy butter, 40-1
roasted spice mixture, 63
rum babas, 291-2
rum clusters, 288-9

Sabrina's breadsticks, 307
salade niçoise—Stephanie's version, 195,
    196
salade tahitienne, 48
salads
    baby beetroot and coriander, 197
    carrot, 22-3
    condiments for, 178-80
    in bread bowl, 196
    niçoise—Stephanie's version, 195
    orange-basil, with pinenuts, 193-4
    pan bagnat, 194
    panzanella, 194
    potato, with pesto, 85
    raw artichoke, 192-3